T0157165

Rightly Dividing
The Word of Truth

A Fortified and Comprehensive Guide to Effective Prayer

MSE. Dzirasa

authorHOUSE®

AuthorHouse™
1663 Liberty Drive
Bloomington, IN 47403
www.authorhouse.com
Phone: 1-800-839-8640

Published by AuthorHouse 12/19/2011

ISBN: 978-1-4670-6754-6 (sc)
ISBN: 978-1-4670-6753-9 (hc)
ISBN: 978-1-4670-6745-4 (e)

Library of Congress Control Number: 2011919145

FORWARD:

Is prayer a difficult task for you even when you know it is the only way out of your demise? What steps must you take in order to pray effectively? How do you attract God's attention by the mode of your prayer? How do you decipher God's answer to your prayer from your own willful, anticipated, and desired answer? How can a negative answer to a prayer, that was expected to be affirmative, be nonetheless laden with blessing?

Your answers to these and other faith testing questions regarding your prayer life, gradually unfolds spiritually and methodically, within the anointed pages of this book together with personal testimonies, to equip you with all the necessary divine techniques, and essential prayer tools needed to exude the lacking essence that will rightly awaken your Christian palate, to taste and see the goodness of God, through this divinely innovated source of the scriptural instruction of His word of truth, by way of fervent prayer.

Experience God's paramount majesty and unfailing ability to deliver on a deadline, in this blessed book, written by one who though not a celebrated Minister and author, has nonetheless been authorized by God, to celebrate with you, the magnificence of His faithfulness, and the ultimate spiritual fulfillment, derived from His holy word.

MSE. Dzirasa.

Exclusively Dedicated to the Cherished and Ever Loving memory of

Reverend Stephen Allen Dzirasa
Priest, Patriarch, Philanthropist, Patriot and Politician
(Fofo lolotor dzidzor le Apetor Yesu Christo pe nutifafa me loo.)
Rest in perfect peace Papa.

"For now art thou offered into glory. Yea; the time of thy departure did come and thou art gone to thy rest. Yet doth the Father above, and we whom thou didst leave behind affirm that of a truth, while thou livest, thou didst fight the good fight, thou didst finish the course, and thou didst keep the faith until thine very last breath. Therefore art thou sainted in heaven and art accorded sweet repose in Abraham's bosom. Yea tis accorded unto thee by grace; For tis written that the saints in heaven, once mortals on earth, did fall to sin, turning in humility and repentance to the Father's love and as such are become partakers of His righteous mercies, to rise again victorious and incorruptible, at the sound of the last trump" Amen.
(Verse originally composed by Author with scriptural adaptation from 2:Tim 4: 7)

"...if we believe that Jesus died and rose again, even so God will bring with Him those who sleep in Jesus. Therefore comfort one another with these words." (1Thessalonians 4: 13 to 14, and 18 NKJ)

Exodus, 20:12 KJV.
   "Honor thy father and thy mother, that thy days may be long upon the land which, the Lord thy God giveth thee." (this is the only Commandment with a promise.)

"Praise ye the Lord, blessed is the man that feareth the Lord, that delighteth greatly in his commandments. His seed shall be mighty upon the earth. Wealth and riches shall be in his house: and his righteousness endureth forever. He has dispersed, he has given to the poor; his righteousness endureth forever; His horn shall be exalted with honor." Psalm 112:1,2,3 & 9 KJV.

Author's Note.

What is prayer? it is, " The spiritual outpouring of the contents of the needy or hurting heart and mind of an individual, by way of an earnest request or wish, fueled and driven by faith and expectation, directed towards a higher power, or an icon of worship."(ADA) This is what prayer means to me, in actuality. Is it a difficult thing; prayer? Yes, if you do not know how, and if you do not possess the appropriate tools, which are readily available in the Word of God. Your prayer tool can be accessed and researched, free of charge, requiring only utmost dedication on your path, and the ardent desire to learn of the father. The word of God makes it clear in Philippians 4: 6 & 7. "Be careful for nothing; but in everything, by prayer and supplication with thanksgiving let your request be made known unto God. And the peace of God which passeth all understanding, shall keep your hearts and minds through Jesus Christ." KJV.

INTRODUCTION

Dear reader in Christ. As you wade through the pages of this book by listening to and absorbing my personal as well as spiritual experiences in print, you will gradually realize as you excavate the vast extent of God's providence, his limitless grace, propelled by your very own faith, that comes not from your carnal abilities, but spiritually projected as His loving gift to you with no strings attached. You will discover that, His grace is enough to go around sustaining all including you, especially when the going gets tough; for God is ever-present even when you are too beaten up by adversities to open your mouth in prayer. Together, we will touch on a lot of issues that render our prayers and requests amiss, and stagnant.

We will also discuss levels and methods of prayer, in variant degrees, scopes and gradients. Together, we will learn how to separate God's Divine answer to your prayer from, your own obsessive intuition and long desired result. We will learn how to handle tasking spiritual battles, by means of 'strategic scriptural techniques' (SST) utilizing divine tactics. You will find solutions and answers to questions that have baffled your mind as a child of God, struggling to make it in a world where you have at a time, or oftentimes doubted the love and existence of God, not for reasons of unbelief alone, but because you do not possess or have not had the appropriate experience, and exposure to his word, by acquiring knowledge of it as the indispensable prayer tool that it inspirationally really is. Thus, if you desire this essential prayer tool, then your informatory source is right here in the pages of this book through which, you will surely acquire a rightly divided scriptural resource path to guide you as you depend on His holy word, and a sure way to enjoying a higher rate of 'spiritual acceleration' (SA.) on the road to success and ultimate victory.

I will furnish you with the right 'spiritual survival kit' (SSK) in this prayer guide, filled with scriptural information for reader's like you, grounded in Christ or those seeking Him, from all walks of life. This book, by way of effective prayer, totally overshadows the suffering and the guilt of living with social failures and conventionally unaccepted flaws such as those of: Childlessness, divorce, unwed parenthood, attempted self-destruction and thoughts of the same, substance abuse and other social plights that plague people from all walks of life and Christians alike; a veritable fact of life that I'm afraid, is sneered upon in many a Christian church today, instead of being attended to physically and spiritually. Unfortunately, these issues have baffled and troubled the minds of their victims, some of whom despite their strong spiritual status as grounded Christians, are gradually crumbling underneath the pain, rejection, condemnation and degradation, surprisingly within the body of Christ, for the sheer lack of proper social support through avenues like counseling and spiritual therapy, which can only be derived from the complete knowledge and balanced scriptural utilization of the word of God, within which lies in trust, its incomparable divine function as, the most essential tool for effective prayer.

Thus, as a child of God you must always remember that in Christ, there is no condemnation, because of his sure promises that stand firm through all generations. You are therefore required as a child of God, to keep an open mind as we journey into the undulating divinity and authentic experience of His therapeutic word of truth; An experience of such magnitude that I wager, will in turn inject stability into your sometimes wavering spirit and doubting mind. It is therefore imperative that, you carnally release yourself entirely from all inhibitions of the flesh, in order to appropriately make way for the nutritional absorption of these divinely induced tools of prayer we are to tackle, as you partake of His scriptural feast, by taking this plunge of faith into the river of righteousness, while abandoning every care and frustration. Let us together, as one in Christ, drink deep as we draw renewed strength in faith, understanding and love in God's word, as it relates to your trials. Not only will you feel lighter in the spirit, but also find out how the word of God cuts across all aspects of human life and practical Christian living, in a way that philosophies of men never can, by single handedly overriding negative vices of all categories, into complete and utter annihilation, while totally elevating you its recipient, to the highest and purest self fulfilling therapeutic height. This divine status of well-being will be achieved steadily and surely as the word of truth meticulously pierces through the malignant growth of uncertainties and fears that continually invade your thoughts, by rendering them benign while at the same time, freeing your mind and spirit into a world of health and contentment created in the knowledge of His word.

Dear reader, you may possess a strong sense of accomplishment in the things of God as a Christian of sound footing, or perhaps one who for years, have been a consistent student and adherent of God's word, or may perhaps be newly thirsting for divine wisdom as a convert. Whatever your level of spiritual maturity, or ministerial status in the body of Christ, you must be willing to make room for spiritual growth in the Lord, somewhere in your life, to attain extra footing when pressing on to higher spiritual heights. Yes, you may not think much of the inspiration projected from a mere Christian with no status like me, but I can assure you that, when it comes to the things of God, no one is too grand to be awakened to new revelations and teachings pertaining to His divine kingship. Thus, you too can be blessed in your life or ministry, if you will only allow yourself into God's spiritual laboratory, where you might find an antidote to cure that secret infirmity or weakness that you have been secretly tending all your life as a shepherd of God's church who is busy pastoring others, while your needs are untended. This is also for you the newly saved to grasp and digest, but not without the implicit realization of the full potency of the truth of God's word, which is available for all and sundry, if you will only take on the yielding status as the breathless recipient of His word, by learning to apply them to the wounds inflicted by lack of judgment and the treachery of the prince of the darkness of this world. You see, the word of God is always there as a credible surety for; "The earth is the Lord's and the fullness thereof. The world and they that dwell therein." (see: Psalm 24:1KJV) God our Father knows that, though we are born again and spirit filled, we nonetheless have to live in this world and contend with its pressures, temptations and adversities.

Yet, He expects us to shine by example of attitude, character, temperament, endurance, and above all, by keeping a persistent and unshakable faith in his word. Which having been impregnated by grace on our account thousands of years ago, brought to us the priceless gift of salvation through our Lord Jesus the Christ; Who walked this earth as a man of flesh and blood, badgered by the very things that we are hounded by today like the tears, fears, rejection and the various tests of life through which we build resistance, by exercising patience and tolerance on scriptural foundations, in order to be steered closer to the receptive destination of His gift divine. A gift that no other religion can authentically compare with, which costs nothing to obtain, but requires everything in one's life to maintain. Dear reader in Christ, no matter how old or new you are in the Lord, you must never cease praying for divine knowledge, wisdom and understanding. Pray and ask God for the retentive absorption of His word as you spiritually surf the pages of this unique book; for by so doing, the burdens that you have been saddled with overtime, will suddenly lighten in weight, proving more bearable as you make your journey to overcome it all by letting the truth of his word pierce through the toughened membrane of unbelief that has slowly and gradually formed around your once faithful and trusting heart, because of life's trials and adversities. The word of God beckons lovingly and reassuringly to you in the book of Matthew 11: 28-30KJV Saying; "Come unto me all ye that labor and are heavy laden and I will give you rest. Take my yoke upon you and learn of me; for I am meek and lowly of heart: And ye shall find rest unto your souls. For my yoke is easy and my burden is light. Says the Lord". How therapeutic this passage of scripture is, to the body, mind and soul of the child of God in trouble and distress.

This scriptural passage is not meant for the dead, but for the living. Rest for the soul is much more needed in this life, than in death. Because, a restless soul is not the haunting ghost or spirit of the dead that has been mythified over centuries, researched and factually documented in the twenty first century. But rather, the troubled and broken spirit of a living being/person. God is therefore summoning us, His children. He says; come to me. Lay your heavy burdens and problems trustingly at my feet and walk away in faith, and I will 'give you a break'. But wait a minute. Don't be too hasty because, right there in that scripture of reassuring promise, is a great catch. The main reason why God loving and fearing people are missing blessed assurance, and divine fulfillment supplication-wise in their lives. It is a necessary spiritually enriching catch which is, learning of God by the consistent studying and retaining of his word. That, dear reader is what God meant by "taking up his yoke (word) and learning of him". (studying it. For His word is Himself; the flesh, that came to dwell among us.) The entire concept God is trying to convey to us is that, He expects you to develop a personal relationship with him, as well as an intellectual relationship with his word.

God assures us that, being a part of his body of believers is not costly at all because His Son Jesus Christ has already accomplished the major cleaning up. Therefore our only requirement is to come to Him with arms open wide, and unburden ourselves right there in His holy realms without ceremony or standard protocol procedure. How great is that? This is a priceless spiritual package from a loving and true God, who just keeps giving, by offering life to the lifeless and rest to people who are steadily and constantly, sinking under loads of unbearable pain and despair. David the shepherd boy, the Psalmist, and the King, knew the benefits of desperately clinging to, and totally relying on God's word of truth. He shared that belief in Psalm 119:105 KJV " Thy word is a lamp unto my feet and a light unto my path." He knew that without the word of God, and without putting God in charge of his every decision, and life as a whole, he will just wind up tripping in life, by going around in circles and ending up right where he started, saddled with a life devoid of progress but rather, abounding in every regressive vice imaginable. If during his time on earth, David thought it essential to cling to the word of God, so should you and I in these troubling times of spiritual uncertainties the magnitude of which causes the repetitive questioning of the very existence of God because of the extent of devastation, wickedness, ruination and disasters worldwide. We as Christians are therefore confronted with the challenge of bringing hope not to people who have not yet tasted of God's goodness and love alone, but to those already in His hands, but refuse to be in His grip because of the shortcomings perpetrated by unbelief and doubt. We must as children of God learn to accept and embrace misfortunes and mishaps in our lives, with arms of faith and hope. In order to ensure the birth of peace and restoration for that which we have lost and I know in all practicality what that feels like, yet I live daily to exalt and praise His holy name without which I would be totally lost forever; for worldly goods are meant to be acquired and lost; but salvation is meant to be acquired and maintained with the word of truth to guarantee the swift salvaging and recovery of a soul that is hanging on the precipice of the lost, as well as keep one that is saved from getting lost.

You as a grounded Christian dear reader, are not exempt from the negative vices either. For they come to plague as well as build you up; to steer you away from future mistakes and ill considered decisions like I once made; thus preparing you for the climb unto higher heights of spiritual awareness and scriptural intellect. Quickening your faith into maturity and growth in God's word, to a higher plain where you can proclaim aloud as your predecessor David did in the book of Psalms chapter 112: 1,4a,7 & 8a. KJV. " Praise ye the Lord. Blessed is the man that feareth the Lord, that delighteth greatly in his commandments. Unto the upright there ariseth light in the darkness, he shall not be afraid of evil tidings; his heart is fixed trusting in the Lord. His heart is established." (Please personalize this verse as you read it prayerfully in faith, believing with all your heart. Don't forget to check your 'meter of spiritual establishment' against your scriptural study, and life as a whole on a consistent basis.) You will grow in Christ as you gradually digest this guide to effective prayer by the thorough study of His word, to become a spiritual giant, trampling on all stumbling blocks like the very dust on the ground until you end up standing on a platform pedestal formed from the dusty residual waste of the very trials you have overcome. This very platform, will serve as a measuring tool or instrument; the 'Christometer' (if you will.) It will define the depth of your faith and the height of your dependence on the word of God, as a Christian. When was the last time you checked your 'Christometer' ?

As you literally sip this scriptural guide, you will then realize once again that there is reassurance in God's word readily held for you, and constantly reiterating on the omniscience of your Father in heaven; God, the author and finisher of your faith. In 1Corinthians 10:13, 1:8 NIV. It says, "No temptation has ceased you except what is common to man. God is faithful, He will not let you be tempted more than you can bear. But when you are tempted, He will always provide a way out so that you can stand up under it. He will keep you strong to the end, so that you will be blameless on the day of our Lord Jesus Christ". What more can we ask for if we have such a good comprehensive crisis coverage, from the giver of life himself. I think our greatest concern should be the physical and mental ability to rise up without delay when crisis hits us in life. We must therefore bear in mind at all times that, our 'Spiritual Crisis Coverage' (SCC.) is only a tiny fraction of the benefits that we are assured of under our 'Christ Life Coverage' (CLC.), as policy holders in Him, under the divine canopy of our crisis coverage, even as policy holders in Him and of His kingdom; Amen. We may not always win physically, but in the event of a loss, under the Spiritual Crisis Coverage, the depiction of that loss turns out to be one that indubitably precedes an explicit and incontrovertible win, which can only be made manifest, and realized if we as children of God, take time to study our spiritual life insurance policy handbook, which is the Bible; the living word of God.

This constant legacy of every believer must be studied very extensively by the shiftless act of determined fellowship in Christ, and also by making conscientious efforts in spending quality time reading and learning the word of God including all the fine print. Which unlike its corporate counterpart that border's and seals legal and business documents, contracts and agreements, concealing the high interest rates and hidden charges, is plentiful with endless and abounding promises from 'the father above' (TFA). Before we delve into our core lesson, which is the sole purpose of this book, I would like to congratulate you for making yourself available for this spiritually enriching trip into the mysteries of prayer. May you keep walking back to this book for inspiration and to the Bible for scriptural study and reference, long after you have completed it, in the name of the Father, and of the Son and of the Holy Spirit, Amen.

CONTENTS

Chapter one

Self-preparedness into prayer readiness.

The act and practice of praying, being the first and foremost duty spiritually injected into every believer both old and new in Christ, takes one to a place of thought and contemplation about what this practical guide to effective prayer really has to offer that one does not already know. But do not be misguided dear reader in Christ, by the simplicity and common wordliness of this chapter's heading. As a child of God, you must always leave clearance above your spiritual perception for the steady construction of your spiritual canopy which should consist of one hundred percent unadulterated Holy Scripture, imported by the inspiration of God. Analyzing the two most similar in meaning words featured in the chapter's heading, may sound and even seem monotonous grammatically and literally. But if you give it comprehensive thought, you will realize my basis for those choices. Eighty percent of the time, we are ready for prayer, but are in actuality one hundred percent not prepared spiritually. Not in the least.

We think that since the Bible instructs us to pray without ceasing, we can just get up and pray without preparing ourselves. Well, some may argue that, if the prayer is a regular prayer like morning devotion or quiet time, self preparedness is needed. But I believe that, every time set aside for prayer no matter how long or short, regular or serious it may be, requires preparedness of self. For example; you would not observe your morning devotion while brushing your teeth and setting aside your work gear, or while applying make-up would you? And I would assume that, family-wise, all previous domestic conflicts and unrest would have been resolved before quiet time or any prayer is put into effect. We as heirs of the Father, and joint-heirs with the Son, need not waste precious prayer time with lack of preparedness. Self-preparedness towards prayer readiness acts as the potholder that protects us from the burns and singeing pains of disappointment that accompanies wasted prayer, and lost prayer time. We must learn that as adherents of God's word of truth and take every communication with him seriously. We cannot take our quality time spent with him for granted because of laziness, pride, arrogance, and sheer neglect. We need to learn to adapt seriousness of attitude towards the things of God as He reminds us through his word that, "He is a rewarder of those who seek him diligently". Therefore if we want to effectuate our prayers, then we must respect and prioritize by instituting 'Standard Spiritual Procedures', (SSP) as a form of divine protocol to expressly convey us to the presence of the Most High God. All the above can be acquired and accomplished by simply obeying God's word of truth by the right division of its sacred substance, and by according Him the due respect and divine reverence His mere name exudes. Scripture was therefore made available to us for the purpose of guidance, caution, protection, teaching, admonishment and also to transport us into the blessed and anointed halls of divine wisdom.

Scripture also alerts us constantly to keep a sharp eye out for the adversary who is always, prowling around like a hungry lion, (see:1Peter 5:8) and has already set into motion, his domino of cunning tricks to confuse the children of God by cultivating pride, behavioral complexities, a 'know it all' and condemnation attitude into you to disable your divine intuition, in order to thwart and destroy the essential components that fuel the exposure of God's love, beneficence, and utmost blessings bestowed onto us through His word, as we diligently seek Him. Hebrews 11:6 reminds us of an eminent and sure reward held in trust for us, if we devote quality time towards studying the word of God in utmost faith. You see, the adversary will only lose when all children of God in fervent and dedicated practicality are strongly versed in God's word to the point of 'Spiritual Saturation' (SS), and by so doing acquire the accurate formula for the rightful division of His word of truth.

The word of God as I term it is "Curriculum Eternale" . An expression I made up to exude the unending nature of God's word as I studied it day by day. It is the only written word that keeps multiplying chronologically, and replenishing bibliographically, while universally touching every subject, object and theme known in intellectual circles alphabetically, from acoustics to zoology; depicting extreme malleability by way of expansion, while globally breaking down barriers and boundaries of prejudice thus, bringing all things orderly under its subjection by the power of the Holy Spirit.

Let us take a look into prayer readiness by touching on some few issues. As we are well aware, no child of God is completely and perfectly versed in the things of God which are solely acquired by the ardent study of his word, yet even though it is the true perfect and perpetual legal divine document on which the Christian faith is established and secured, as well as serving as the authentic evident witness to our faith, so is the knowledge of the complaisance acquired from His word. Yes, regular church attendance is the foundation to spiritual fellowship in our faith, for the word of God instructs us to have fellowship with one another. It also instructs us that faith is nurtured by hearing His holy word. (see: Hebrew 10: 25 and Romans 10:17). But as a Christian, you must realize by now, the futility of your vague spirituality if you open your Bible only on Sundays at church. You see, as a child of God, you must refrain from limiting your auditory absorption and response to God's word solely to pulpit ministry as in regular church attendance, of healing services, crusades, and seasonal revivals. This sort of habit puts you spiritually in the high risk category of 'Extreme Spiritual Vulnerability' (ESV) rendering you spiritually gullible to biblically camouflaged philosophies and dangerously twisted religious assertions.

Self preparedness towards prayer readiness is as such, all about self assessment which is the ultimate inner cleansing of your whole being from all the negativities and hindrances that stumble blocks your prayer as it travels the tunnels of supplication to the throne of God. You must also rid your thoughts of all doubt and traces of willful anticipated responses to your prayers. Instead, allow God to lead as you follow in great expectation and in absolute trust no matter the outcome of your supplication. The Psalmist David sings it out of the depths of his soul, in the following words. "Give ear to my words, o Lord, consider my meditation. Hearken unto the voice of my cry, my King and my God, for unto thee will I pray; my voice shall thou hear in the morning o Lord; in the morning will I direct my prayer unto thee, and will look up. Lead me, o Lord, in thy righteousness because of my enemies; make your way straight before my face." (see Psalm 5:1,2,3 and 8. KJV.) David was clearly asking for God's guidance and direction. Note his surrendering and totally yielding spirit. His first priority in that scripture was to be heard of God. That is why he stressed on his self-preparedness with 'the morning' time of day. A very punctual time of day; a time of high and serious priority. He also had a flexible expectation to the outcome of his prayer; freeing his mind of all preconceptions. Hence the expression, "and I will look up." He meant that he was not going to be distracted by circumstances surrounding him. But rather set hopeful precedence as one who comprehends the anatomy and dissection of prayer by, totally claiming absolute dependency and trust in God's decision, no matter how grave, as one purely driven by his faith and hope in Him.

David also revealed his belief in the importance of ridding one's mind of thought-processed negativity, and of yielding total leadership to the God of righteousness. He also distinguished himself as an individual who knew God beyond the ordinary by showcasing his relationship with Him in carefully chosen words in order to bring call to mind, the intimate nature of their relationship by the utilization of His ancient name, 'Jehovah-Tsidqenu'. Thus portraying an important aspect and vital tool for effective prayer, by the faithful incorporation of this synonym of God, supplication-wise to invoke his Divine power of performance, and that of His attributive character, as he laid his request at His merciful feet. In the next chapter, I will walk you through this highly spiritual process, by teaching you how to apply and manipulate this vital prayer tool for your spiritual benefit. As a child of God, you must always exhibit as well as bear the fruit of humility, no matter your social status, professional rank, academic prowess, high birth and religious position. This virtue is key towards effective prayer. You must also not perceive yourself as too grand in the faith to institute prayer preparedness and readiness, by way of this virtue. Also put aside all forms of falsehood, especially by covering up your problems, thinking that getting it out in the open might belittle your spiritual status, or for fear that, others in the faith might question the strength and spiritual foundation, of your footing in the Lord. "God opposes the proud and gives grace to the humble, therefore. Humble yourselves before the Lord and He will lift you up". (see; James 4: 6b & 10).

My dear friend in the Lord, this very scripture divides the word of truth, pertaining to prayer readiness by way of humility, and by making you aware of the availability of God's grace to those who seek help from him in humility of spirit. "He will lift you up." in this particular scripture does not denote the elevation of one to a higher status of distinguished recognition alone. It actually portrays God's divine ability to unburden you of all things out of those darkness into his divine luminescence, where your first step into Godly inheritance can be taken without the fear of stumbling through recurring loss thus, keeping you within the sound comforts of 'spiritual buoyancy' (SB). My personal walk with God through his Son Jesus Christ my only Lord and savior, took me on a critical, but personal faith challenging journey of multiple as well as complex crisis which unknown to me then, would transform as well as reform and upgrade my spiritual life, by way of redefining my footing in God.

You see, a greater part of my marital life was filled with trials spun on the looms of the adversary himself through a vessel surrendered to his dark works, that I by marital association was attached to. They surged in unfathomable magnitude, in accelerated torrents, the size of which could easily facilitate the immediate amputation of my life as a whole through lack of self-preservation. But, thanks be to God, for the strength of spirit that He endowed me, even when I was a clot of blood in my mother's womb, and the strength of character instilled into my upbringing, by my loving parents; Stephen and Grace. Qualities which, upon receiving Christ were transformed from the carnal to the super spiritual. Thus equipping me with a fully throttled status of strength to fuel my body in order to withstand and to vigorously race against all the stress induced negativity I faced during the dreary nights and days of those long years of suffering and strife. At the height of my crisis, my upbringing of total humility, a value that was most important to my Father in heaven and my biological parents, spearheaded by my 'Papa' (who taught us as a family this value by example), served me greatly when I was hanging on the precipice of the twin cliffs of loss and despair. My marital problems were so intelligently and aggressively maneuvered by unbalanced and extreme transgressions secured to an unending string of conscious and deliberate degradation, disrespect, humiliation, and inappropriate sacrilegious acts of unbelievably high degrees of fiendish feats by the perpetrator with the shameless support of a man of God, geared primarily towards the ultimate destruction of not only my profound spirituality, purpose in life, but to sever the very life force given to me by my Father above; and yet I lived to testify to His glory.

Thus, with unshakable faith in God, and total reliance on his promises, I was able to resume my spiritual posture. And by his grace, love, and hope that does not disappoint, I was able to put all the negativity behind me and stood tall in God's promises, with humility of spirit while he bathed me with the spirit of boldness to appear within social circles, and not hide because of the depth of the wounds inflicted on me. I must confess that, my spirituality and my image were wounded, and so was my ego. Nevertheless, I endeavored to embrace God's gift, casting aside all pride, as this bold gesture became my platform into prayer readiness and preparedness. I believed that God who is my recompense, will restore all that I had lost physically, socially and emotionally, of which I can testify by this work, compiled by a woman who lost everything to the man who grievously and inhumanly wronged her, but had the great 'man upstairs' who rights all wrong, as a pillar of strength to lean on to greater accomplishments.

Yes! The adversary meant it for evil but God turned it out for good, by equipping me with the most supernatural praying and counseling ability, driven by a strong and faithful heart fixated on God; which I acquired during my readiness and preparedness period, preceding, actual prayer warfare, during that crisis, by consistent bible study and the fervent research into victorious Christian living tools. Dear friend, remember that, a crisis of tremendous magnitude that even renders the church incapable at times of salvaging, can propel an individual into prayer readiness with equal or more spiritual force strong enough to totally shatter that problem to bits, while elevating the victim to a status only God can furnish. Such an encounter may be God's way of grooming you into fighting your own battles prayerfully, instead of solely depending on others for spiritual support. Prayer preparedness also requires a God-driven mind, body and soul, married to the precepts of God, which can only be derived from His word. The unequivocal success of this union, becomes your shock absorbing threshold to effective prayer. The former, also requires a doggish devotion to the word of God laced with appropriate practicality, in the area of your specific prayer content or topic. For example; if your prayer is centered on a desire for healing, then you must research into the healing characteristics and attributes of God, in the Holy Scriptures. You must therefore engage in extensive scriptural study and intensive research with biblical core reference books such as; a dictionary/concordance, a literary guide to the Bible, one or two other versions of the Bible, if you own the King James Version, like the New International Version, and the New Standardized Version. You will also have to learn to memorize your research findings, which will be scriptures on healing that denote and depict God's characteristics and records of his deeds in the healing category. To be effective as well as spiritual in memorizing scripture, I can only refer you, faithfully to one source. And that is, by investing in

Integrity Music's scripture memory songs, which are without a doubt, one of the most essential and indispensable auditory tools for effective prayer. These are the basics to name a few. If you cannot purchase these books, you may gain access to them at your local library in the non-fiction section, shelved under classification numbers; 220 and 220.6. As a child of God who desires to live victoriously, you must consider a gradual investment in scriptural resources and guides, including audio visual materials, and other informative sources as well, to build your personal or family Christian library.

These informative sources will in actuality assist you by way of elaborating on God's word for your comprehension and retention methodically, from the general aspects of your prayer topic to the very specifics. Bible study and research should not be the sole spiritual responsibility of Pastors, Bishops, Evangelists and Teachers. As a true Christian you must refrain from such casual traits of 'Spiritual Idleness and Dormancy' (SID.), by sitting around all week expecting, juicy sermons that perchance might shed a tiny light of hope on your problems, or get agitated and label the preacher non effective if you are not as spiritually fed as you expected or turning your spiritual life into that of a 'miracle hunter', hopping from revival to revival expecting to be fed miracles and thriving on dramatic transformations from ten day crusades without taking time to study God's transforming word as a crusader living in Him. The word of God makes this clear in Acts 17: 28 KJV. "For in him we live, and move, and have our being." And within us He longs to dwell if only we will surrender ourselves completely to Him in deed and in truth by rightly dividing His word as we sojourn in this world the Lord our God has given us. One cannot function spiritually, outside God and his word which is life in itself. We must study His word persistently and ardently, as His workmen and not as labeled Bible believing churchgoing Christians, who I'm afraid are rapidly filling Christian churches and auditoriums these days, looking for spiritual shortcuts and 'Fast Spiritual Fixings' (FSF); but fix our whole being on him as faithful and practical believers. For if you believe in something with your whole heart as you have professed by faith, then you must by the same belief and the very hope that drove you into that unshakeable faith, exploit all possibilities and avenues relevant as well as vital towards its safeguarding, security and preservation.

Such dedication gives birth to adoration and commitment of such high degree that propels your will into a zeal that finds you fighting to keep it no matter the circumstance, risk, or cost. Bearing the status of a

Christian is not to be taken lightly. It is like signing up for military duty whereby you become a soldier in God's army with Jesus as the Captain of the Hosts, and the Holy Spirit as the intelligence unit safeguarding the entire operation in divine reconnaissance and God as Commander in Chief overseeing and coordinating the entire operation. With our status as Christian soldiers, the persistent study of the word of God serves as an aerating agent to our minds; transforming it into a fertile field spiritually ready for the cultivation of the Christ crop, followed by the sprouting of his teachings, which gradually matures into a bountiful spiritual harvest of growth in His word. I personally found out the fast way, through crisis that, the methodology of Bible study is much more effective, beneficial and fun when ritualized. An easy option especially for Christians living in developed and the developing parts of the world, where easy access to divers tools of research and in-depth study of the Word is easy to come by.

Knowledge of God's Word grants you boldness and strength derived from the deep realization of its potency and its powerful ability to stabilize one's wavering conscience. The word of God is also medicinal, therapeutic, and an utterly reliable life support system, without the clinical trappings. The in-depth knowledge and realization of God's power settles your doubts before prayer begins. Thus, summoning your faith from its hiding place of fear and uncertainty to a venue beaming with the bright lights of a future overflowing with blessedness laced with the assurance and expectancy of greatness from God. A true Christian must on no occasion, be prowling around with an impressively sized Bible and still be ignorant of the potency, knowledge, and complaisance of the substance and embodiment of God's written word. A child of God living in such ignorance can be boldly labeled a 'deserter' in the army of God. This type of Christian as I would boldly remind you, is one who possesses the ardent capability of exhibiting Christianity on the outside by regular church attendance, upholding false virtue to impress the world. But be not deceived God is not mocked. For gradually, his or her starched and neatly pressed false robe of spirituality will begin to crease and sag at the hem as well as the seam, eventually falling apart due to lack of proper care and maintenance of its fabric eventually plunging that individual into a sickly state of spiritual deficiency, which leaves them naked and vulnerable to the salivating wide jaws of the devilish roaring lion and his demonic cubs.

I therefore charge you in all humility as adherents of the true word, that you take quality time to arm yourselves with that which cuts either way, and rightly divides the Holy word into its divine truthfulness. By this I mean the fervent acquisition of spiritual intellect attained by way of the literary sword of justice and righteousness; the Holy word of God. You must take time to school yourself with this guide book, together with your Bible and concordance by taking notes, researching and getting ravenous for God's wisdom so that, your mind will be continuously and spiritually nourished, in order to keep your prayers and supplication beyond that of the carnal; enriched in spiritual depth. You must also believe that your sins have been forgiven, after repentance, confession, and prayer during your period of prayer preparedness. Ensure this fact by taking the right steps towards asking the Father for forgiveness. The Bible reminds us that, "we deceive ourselves and the truth is not in us when we say that we have no sin; and that if we confess our sins He is faithful and just to forgive us of our sins and to cleanse us from all unrighteousness." (1John1:8&9). Asking for such forgiveness from God must be devoid of egotistical notions, and pride as depicted in the following prayer sample.

"Lord, I praise you and magnify your name for your goodness and love. Well, tell you what, I hit my wife you know. I knew I shouldn't have. But your word depicts that I am the head, and I don't want her habit of talking back at me to go unchecked. I am asking for your forgiveness for hitting her. Father, you know how difficult it is to communicate with her, I had no choice but to get physical because, I had to take measures to secure my place as the head. Everybody makes mistakes, but I must admit that she has shaped up since then. I am sorry Lord, and I'll try not to repeat this act again. Thank you for forgiving me, in Jesus' name Amen". This is what I term a self-conceited and arrogant prayer of confession, trapped in ego. True confession however, should be born out of the womb of regret, remorse and repentance. A true and sincere confession, should hurt the conscience of the confessed. Then and only then, will the flood gates of forgiveness be opened by God, to wash and cleanse you from all unrighteousness. You must also remember that, after forgiveness, the Lord remembers our sins no more. It is therefore pointless to keep reminding him of forgiven sins, over and over again during prayer. let us take a short break together and sing or recite this inspirational song about the reassurance of sins forgiven by, Morgan Cryar entitled, "What sin." If you do not have the music, you may still reap its scriptural as well as spiritual benefits by reading and quietly reflecting on the lyrics before we proceed with our lesson.

It happened so long ago
I cried out for mercy back then
I pled the blood of Jesus
Begged Him to forgive my sin
But I still can't forget it
It just won't go away
So I wept again Lord wash my sin
But this is all he'd say

What an amazing display of the knowledge of God's truth, by the revelation of his forgiving power this song depicts. Try to purchase it if you can. Music is a very powerful prayer preparedness and readiness tool, which takes us to a place of divine serenity and calmness as we get ourselves ready to enter into the throne room of God with our supplications. As such, we must continually thank God for our music ministers who by divine inspiration, deliver God's word to us through spiritual lyrics, tones and vibrations. Reminding God about past sins forgiven, is a sure sign of a valuable point lost through doubt about His unchanging love for us; for doubt sprouts from the soil of unbelief. And wherever the spirit of unbelief thrives, hopelessness, faithlessness and praying disabilities lurk rampantly in every shadow.

Christians who fall victim to the above, can only be saved by the integration of an intensive faith recovery therapy into their dormant minds and bodies, based on scriptural tools, plus consistent counseling and teachings, to jump-start them from their static state by spiritual means designed to divinely trigger a metamorphosis within them to transport them into a state of alertness to their Christian duties. Dear friend, are you ready to step into prayer? If so, you must by now be equipped with 'effective scriptural eloquence'(ESE) which is in actuality the ability to speak and quote scripture effectively with boldness and accuracy, in your prayers so as to recall to God his promises. This is very essential because he who plants doubt, unbelief and fear into the minds of God's children knows scripture off-hand from Genesis to Revelation in so accurate a way that, he is able to twist its truth with his subtleties and lies, thereby sowing unfruitful seeds of uncertainty into the world. Thus, during your preparedness period, be sure to stay alert in the spirit. Keep a sharp eye out for the adversary, the corrupter of justice. For he will try to set the stage for negativity so cunningly that, your slightest lack of divine wisdom will find you falling for his devices. Yes! As he did to the Master, so will he try to do unto you. See Luke 4:1-13. Remember that he only pauses for a fraction of a season, coming back even more conniving, and evil than before. Constantly gird yourselves in your spiritual armor which is the word of God, for he is no respecter of persons. Know that as a child of God, your life long homework is to study scripture and to be well versed in the things of God, ardently and devotedly. You must view your commitment to the Father as a spiritual thesis, imprinted in the 'Christ zone' of your neurons, to be transmitted topically, according to needs, and applied at the right time for the appropriate predicament. Taking these steps renders you fearless in all things because, the one who is perfect in knowledge is with you always.

Bearing a born-again status is based on the principle of the total surrender of one's life to the sole proprietorship of God through Christ Jesus. You must know your God in the one and only way described in the bible, in the book of John1:1-5 KJV. "in the beginning was the word and the word was with God. And the word was God. The same was in the beginning with God, all things were made by Him; and without Him was anything made that was made. In Him was life; and the life was the light of men. The light shineth in the darkness; and the darkness comprehended it not." Well dear reader in Christ, how can you profess knowledge of the Father devoid of His word? How can you go to Him in prayer if you lack the conviction of His word? And how can you make demands of Him in prayer and be totally ignorant of his extensive and endless capabilities? In the second chapter, we will take an in-depth look into God's capabilities as reflected in his word, and also savor His power to deliver on a deadline, through the invocation of his names of performance, that in turn reveal his character and great prowess.

Now therefore dear child of God, may you study with zeal His living word. So that, you too will be blessed with scriptural eloquence, through divine knowledge. For it is authoritative as well as authentic. And when you are totally consumed by its power, the adversary will bow in total surrender to the Holy Scripture as it falls from your lips like coals of fire, singeing him (that old liar) and leaving him no room for negotiation, but rather clearing for him a dangerous runway that is headed straight for a fatal crash into a dismal abyss. May he (the adversary) flee before the resistance projected from your aggressively scorching biblical proclamation, Amen. Let us now agree in faith to overcome every stumbling block in Christ

Jesus our Lord and Master, by first practicing, and then finally jumping the highest bar of spiritual maturity, by allowing our prayers to graduate from the carnal to the spiritual, devoid of all guilt, pain, being unforgiving, bitterness, and self righteousness.

Chapter two

(1) God's Holy word, your master prayer tool.
(2) Pages of scriptural proclamations of comfort and encouragement dedicated to the victims and survivors of natural disasters, including a self expressive and personalized ready prayer, exclusively and expressly compiled for their immediate spiritual nourishment.
(3) God's ancient names, your spiritual responsibility to know and utilize.

(I) God's Holy word, your master prayer tool.

To be a remarkable prayer warrior, requires nothing other than being a devoted and breathless pursuant of the word of God. I have personally observed, how people get all worked up, confused and depressed, looking outside of themselves for help from physically visible sources, anticipating quicker resolves to whatever derailed them from a life of normalcy as Christians, to that of chaos and disarray because, I was once one of those people. The negativities felt by these people oftentimes, steers them towards extreme feelings of anger and betrayal by God. I know because, I have experienced it too and I am not ashamed to admit it. This anger usually stems from a feeling of helplessness and loss simply because, they have known and believed their lives to be untouchable since they have surrendered it totally to be led and governed diligently and conscientiously by the word and precepts of God. But we must realize that as long as we serve an omniscient God, he has prepared for us astounding victories no matter the gravity of our circumstances. The Bible makes it clear in Psalm 34: 19&20 KJV. that; "many are the afflictions of the righteous: but the Lord delivers him from them all. He keepeth all his bones: not one of them is broken." This scripture does not literally or necessarily mean that as Christians, we are condemned to a life of suffering and trials in order for God to be glorified. It rather reassures us that His mighty hand of deliverance is forever stretched out towards His own that is us, with love and protection as we traverse this dense realm of sin, chaos and struggles thrown down our paths by the adversities of this world. As children of the light, we are inevitably bound to run into clashes and confrontations with the powers of darkness, most of which will manifest around us in forms of variant afflictions and unexpected losses. Nevertheless, God in all his faithfulness and love promises us a safe delivery devoid of all casualty from them all. Not only are His promises sure and steadfast, but they are delivered to us as a divine source of spiritual strength to prepare us as vessels of great testimonies, as well as future counselors within the body of Christ, by way of our experiences.

Our Lord and Savior Jesus Christ came into this world as God the Father deemed perfectly well and fit, and bore afflictions and scorn of great magnitude for the redemption of mankind. He walked miles and miles in our shoes as a mortal, yet he was divine; A man of sorrows, acquainted with grief, despised and rejected of men. Yet, He did not for a moment or for an instant open His mouth in verbal retaliation even though he possessed the power to do so but kept it closed in prayer; muted in spiritual reflection and divine discipline into victory. We must emulate this virtue in our daily lives and furthermore, when undergoing extreme pressure during personal crisis. I will like to call to mind this sudden personal realization; which may not hold significance to a lot of people because of its commonness particularly to movie lovers. It is the expression 'silence is golden', which usually precedes the movie as part of the preview package. Being a lover of intelligent quotes, several of which I am usually able to grammatically dissect to extract spiritual essence, which I tend to infuse into my Christian life. This particular one stuck with me.

I knew that, the moment the movie was over everyone would have forgotten about it because, its benefit to enhance auditory response was over. But to me, it became a source of spiritual growth. This phrase as I deduced, expands beyond the theatrical halls to the world outside, positively affecting our domestic, corporate and spiritual lives when applied appropriately. Christ Jesus was crowned King of Kings and Lord of Lords after he defeated death by the simple but disciplined application of strategic silence while He focused on securing the keys of hell and of death; an action which instantly earned Him the golden crown and scepter of divine kingship. Thus the phrase 'silence is golden' was once again applied to induce the positive and the priceless, depicting its power and effect. As a believer, you must constantly be on the lookout for avenues and resources for spiritual enhancement and advancement at any location and under any circumstance. You must endeavor to seek out the most minute traces of things spiritual in the secular world as you reside and function in it; which upon discovery, must be utilized adroitly as a source of spiritual strength that in turn will secure for you a sure and steadfast footing of pure Godliness in Christ Jesus. I have always believed that at the appropriate time, the absence of verbal outpouring induces the intellectual capabilities of one's mind into its fullest throttle. The Bible declares how Jesus bore his trials with humility and tolerance laced with hope. Thus equipping us perpetually with spiritual resistance for the life of trials ahead of us. The word of God as we all know it to be, is sharper than a two edged sword(see: Revelation1:16) This simply means that it possesses the ability to propel, divide and rearrange chaos and confusion into law and order, war and strife into peace and tranquility, transforming sorrow and mourning into gladness and comfort, by divinely projecting the medicinal characteristics of an antidote fit for the complete and utter elimination of all negativities.

David the Psalmist proclaims; "Thy word have I hid in mine heart that I might not sin against thee."(see: Psalm 119:11) God's word should always be at the forefront of your conscience, to discipline, control and guide your decisions before they are transformed into action. I sincerely believe that, at the time of total surrender of the 'old man', to a new life in Christ, one is immediately awarded the 'Christ conscience' together with the 'new man package' which functions as a forerunner to one's regular conscience, by projecting signals of conviction, reprimand and admonishment, while working hand in hand, with the Holy Spirit. Whereas your regular conscience gives you the signal to decipher right from wrong without forceful conviction by leaving the ultimate choice of good and bad entirely to you, while at the same time serving as a guilt source when you get involved in negativity, it still cannot stop you from being involved in the latter because, it lacks divine conviction. In this case, you have the option to quit and get help, go on or indulge in whatever manner of negativity you choose to,repetitively with a seared conscience of course.

The latter choice renders you as an individual on the wide and broad way to the realm of dark souls. Thus, with my spiritual analysis, I can safely place the percentage of successful conviction administered by the regular conscience operating independently, in the lowest category which is why most addicts ultimately secure total liberation by the infusion of religion which in turn changes their conduct and behavior of non-compliance into that of total surrender. According to my theory, your regular conscience as a believer can have no relationship with the Holy Spirit as it performs its function of inducing spiritual conviction without consulting the Christ conscience that works as the mediator/clarifying agent; the sifting source and ultimate processor of every negativity perceived and conceived by the former (the regular conscience); which when relayed by the latter to the Holy Spirit, is then perfected and relayed back to the regular conscience by way of the Christ conscience. Again, I boldly assert that Godliness may be the only spiritual source that may one day eliminate and possibly bring the high crime rate to an incredible low if we work hard enough as adherents of the word, to spread the gospel exemplarily by way of our personal lives, as well as by witnessing to the unreached and unsaved.

As a reader in Christ you can clearly deduce that, only Christians possess this spiritual gift and benefit, which is part of every true Christian's blessed and assured 'life-in-Christ' policy; which is in fact designed to safeguard all believers decisively towards their victorious Christian goals in life. However, you must know and realize that when you cease to live for righteousness by constantly, persistently, and willfully backsliding coupled with the excessive and diverse involvement in those vices that usually accompany such lifestyles/choices, the Holy Spirit and the Christ conscience are both dismissed. To be precise, they vacate the polluted temple, taking leave in grievance, leaving you alone with your regular conscience and a fat load of vulnerability to more adversity that your feet of disobedience can barely carry.

My spiritual findings once again, describe the Christ conscience as pre-programmed and constantly set at 'auto-admonish' and 'auto reprimand'. A perfect example of the failure of the regular conscience at work independently is its inability to prevent serial crimes and extreme behaviors from commencing and its failure to terminate their recurrence. It has also been unable to disable people with incorrigible minds to keep themselves in psychological balance for the sheer lack of the two vital spiritual components. The Christ conscience and the Holy Spirit may well prevent the incubation and neurological ripening of psychotic traits from lingering or manifesting in children growing up in Christian households, and thus eradicate or possibly slow down the population of notorious killers, because of the parental spiritual covering, through Christian dedication/anointing during infancy, coupled with properly enforced balanced upbringing. Thus, the word of God reassures us that when one is saved, the whole house is saved. And children being the most innocent and vulnerable, are at the top of the household list in the eyes of God.

His word of truth makes this clear in Luke18:16. "let the children come unto me for theirs is the kingdom of heaven". To continue our lesson,we must take note that, the Christ conscience and the Holy Spirit are acquired only through the total surrender of the carnal man to God through Christ Jesus. You see, God in all his majestic glory and creative righteousness, knew and realized that after the fall of man in the garden of Eden, man needed a fore-conscience to back-up the regular one. That is why He devised the salvation plan that has been our present and everlasting source of 'Spiritual Discipline (SD.) which in effect, has benefited society and the world at large, by awarding it a considerable percentage of level-headed and behaviorally disciplined individuals. Even though medical science has detected through expert research a defective neuron in the offspring of normal parents that catalyzes and triggers disturbing behavior in some humans; a theory which I support and believe to be highly probable as an adventurous and curious intellectual in a wide range of subjects, I nonetheless believe as a child of God that, we should not be ashamed or reluctant to approach the divine manufacturer of the human product, for the acquisition of an adequate and appropriate replacement of defective parts, when there is great difficulty, in securing physiological and anatomical normalcy through medical science, where ailing humans are concerned, (When all else fails, medically, and scientifically, in the expert hands of acclaimed and qualified professionals.) At this juncture, God the creator of all things and the source of all being must be contacted for 'Authentic Divine Warranty' (ADW) information, through his holy word wherein 'Expedited Spiritual Assistance' (ESA) in terms of healing and restoration, can be procured by simply redirecting our faith and refocusing our hope and expectation towards the Father believing as we ask; and surely, that request will be delivered expressly. (refer to the movie 'The exorcist').

Now let us begin our study of the benefits of 'Spiritual Credentials' (SC), which can be achieved only by acquiring the scriptural technique of applying God's Word, through 'Divine Wisdom' (DW). The Bible teaches us to arm ourselves in the Spirit. An act which is impossible to project without knowledge of the source and acquisition of the appropriate materials needed to fashion the armor of the spirit. Before proceeding with our assignment, we must bear in mind that, using the wrong armor for certain battle situations can result in fatal or severe injury. For example: a rugged full bodied armor is most suitable for an aggressive and viciously rough man to man combat type of battle situation. As warriors in Christ, we are committed fully to the same agenda as regular warriors or soldiers (a term which is more appropriate for our times) and that is, to stand tall in the midst of the roughest and toughest combat or battle situation in order to attain victory by way of God's might and power, as well as by effective spiritually induced strategic maneuvers, as we take prisoners, (subdue/ conquer adversities), claim victories (win souls/share testimonies) attend to our casualties and protect our territories (apply relevant, effective and productive follow-up ministry), claim and reclaim more territories (win and re-win souls worldwide), while securing justice and honor (defending our beliefs and our faith in the secular world). Therefore as warriors in Christ, our battle gear though invincible to the naked eye, is more effective on the battlefront because, it is immersed within the right division of God's word of truth, through the Captain of the host, the Lord Jesus Christ Himself, who had it forged within the refining fires of immense sacrifice, to secure for us great victories, by His divine power and sure protection. I will like you to recall to memory, as we discuss spiritual soldiering, the words of this popular hymn entitled, "Stand up; Stand up for Jesus".

> Stand up! Stand up for Jesus
> Ye soldiers of the cross
> Lift high His royal banner
> It must not suffer loss
> From victory unto victory
> His army shall He lead
> 'til every foe is vanquished
> and Christ is Lord indeed.

I love this hymn to which I marched for years in my Ghanaian primary school, from morning assembly to the Chapel for Worship; not realizing I had been signed up in Christ's army then, and that I was being groomed at an early age to uphold and defend the precepts of my Faith. I love its bold depiction of Christ's omnipotent power, and the bold declaration of His inevitable conquest. Analyzing it spiritually, it serves as a reminder to all Christians about their automatic sign-up in Christ's army, not only at the venue and time of salvation in adulthood, but even as infants and children with no voices, when they are dedicated and baptized in Christ Jesus whereby, they are saved and covered by the very faith laden decisions of their parents and guardians. It also serves to all Christians, their divine militant detail on the platter of Godly commitment, specifying their prerequisite; the sure and essential alertness to spiritual duty, while at the same time making them aware of their spiritual enlistment right away. It stresses on alertness first and foremost because, no matter what circumstances surround you, when you are alert, your senses are at their perkiest, and as such, physically accords you a perfect and upright posture. Therefore, 'Stand up' in this hymn simply signifies a Christ armor clad soldier at attention, chin up, and ready to defend the Gospel, draped with banners inscribed with Christ's Kingship standards, coat of arms and crest; denoting His divine royalty, supreme sovereignty and eternal righteousness.

This banner also depicts the Christian's outward and shameless declaration of belonging in Christ's army by the act of totally surrendering his/her life to God in Christ, as well as to the zealous dissemination of the Gospel by way of outreaches and strategic witnessing at the slightest chance or opportunity, to keep it alive so that, the adverse squalors and philosophies of this world would not drown it. Therefore as Christian soldiers, in this religiously and spiritually competitive world, where other creeds/religions are fervently claiming the spiritual ownership of the Son-ship and the Godhead, we must be ready to campaign even in the midst of spiritual battle, by reversing all the discrediting avenues through comprehensive Godly evangelism devoid of extremism; for in so doing, we attract new converts and strengthen the weak amongst us, by the spiritually balanced application of the word of truth on which our Faith was built, as we claim spiritual territories non-violently with love, so as to secure this global victory with Christ the Lord of hosts at the forefront. As we continue our discussion about the power in knowing the word of God, we must bear in mind that pursuance of God's word is like a political campaign, in which the constituents are the resource pockets by which a sure goal and a winning future is demographically effectuated. There has to be total contribution towards a collective and effective goal, for the birth of a positive outcome by the sound strategic utilization of effective spiritual campaign tactics, with the sole propaganda to study and apply the word of God, in all practicality so that, the said constituents will be spiritually and securely fed through expert scriptural avenues which in turn will project a positive outcome the type of which yields in bountiful folds, a divinely accrued substantial spiritual surplus, to be made available at all times, for the spiritual nourishment of the unreached in the hinterlands. This success will serve as a tool for erasing all traces of doubt, loss and suffering, among the vulnerable within the Church, as well as serving as the steering compass leading us into ultimate victories, that will in turn affect others outside our Faith, and the world at large, by drawing their attention to our teachings,(which of course should be inclusive and not divisive) capturing their minds, and swaying as well as persuading their conscience to embrace Christianity.

In world politics, winning constituents in the majority, and subsequently an election, induces media attraction and attention worldwide. The winner is celebrated and inevitably assumes prominence in status by being known by name, title, position, by media ratings, press conferences, interviews and reviews denoted in highly soaring approval ratings and percentages. As Christians, we on the other hand acquire divine strength and resistance. We become spiritually eloquent, and scripturally intellectual in God's word, as it reflects in our diction, deeds and accomplishments. Possessing this superb expertise of knowing God's word in depth, runs parallel to knowing Christ, which is the sure and only way to attain one's credentials of spirituality in the Christian world. (knowing the Christ, thus becomes the square root of knowing God's word in depth and living it through unshakable belief.) Thus knowing God's word and believing in it, takes us to a place of absolute trust, and tremendously unshakable faith, during prayer. Thus, rendering our supplications effective and fruit yielding. "And the word was made flesh and dwelt amongst us..." See: John 1: 14 KJV. God loves that quality in a believer. The constant integration of His Holy word in your prayer, clings to his robe of providence because, you prayed by speaking and recalling His words of truth to him in faithfulness and love. He therefore recognizes you, as one who is acquainted with the endless extent of His capabilities. I can testify by experience, how my personal growth in His word of truth served as a bumper guard against my physical and psychological well being when a great crisis struck my life.

I had only been married for a year when negativities invaded the relationship by high degrees. At first, I was thrown off balance by the mere thought of what might happen each day. I likened my tests and trials to the quests of Hercules as they worsened and expanded in malicious magnitude since they occurred rapidly in constant, intentional and calculated succession. As I lived this nightmare during the subsequent years, things got really bad and out of hand. I am talking about being bombarded by all the negative vices that fuel marriages to the volatile climax of divorce. I felt especially alone and betrayed when I discovered that, my closest friends were part of this conspiracy. I resorted to resentment and got very vengeful but then I suddenly came to the heartfelt realization that, God was with me, and that he was my only friend. I revived intimacy with Him. Our relationship then grew by leaps and bounds through the power of his Word; the sole medium of our communication, running parallel to my ardent faith and trust in his power to deliver me from the implacable turmoil that was speedily drowning me. Through the power of His firm and steadfast word, and my parent's profound love and support, I was reborn again. I fell totally and immensely in love with the Father, who in turn comforted my soul and body by equipping me with strength and a sound mind which then enabled me to continue running my business without flaws of any kind. In addition to my spiritual equipage, I also sought counseling through the church, which was (gender biased a very sad trait in the African culture that is unfortunately transfered into many a Church.) and subsequently through community law enforcement when the situation graduated into violence and abuse. I took this latter step even though many Christians from my part of the world condemned and shunned me, for the reasons of not believing me, and that of reminding me by their actions, of my place in this marriage as an African woman. During this period of silence, and abandonment, my very demise became spiritually ripe and golden for the divine development of my faith to a higher level in Christ. I therefore continued to enhance my spirituality, by intensively linking up with the divine network of the Trinity through which I plunged into God's arena of expedited deliverance, by immersing my self totally into the study and practical application of His word. I acquired my credentials with the Bible as my supreme source of inspiration, together with Christian audio-visual materials and scriptural core reference books. During this time, whenever I felt beaten down (mortal as I am) I listened to my vast collection of integrity music's scripture memory songs, pertaining to my emotional need at the time, and applied my librarianship background towards extensive scriptural research. My Parents who were alive at the time supported me,and my family friends the Yoda's never left my side. I lost two pregnancies during this marriage and to this day have remained the only childless one among my siblings. Yet, I live to testify with gladness and not with resentment; as I summon from the depths of my soul, "...a thousand tongues to sing, my great redeemer's praise; to profess the glories of my God and King, and share the triumph derived from the graciousness of my Master and my God, who through His love, assists me to proclaim His might and power with this literary work; to spread through all the earth abroad, the honor and wonders His very name doth wrought...Hallelujah hallelujah."

As a result of these uninterrupted spiritual sessions I discovered the profound therapeutic characteristic of God's word as I clung fervently and desperately to it, constantly seeping and absorbing into my embittered system every nectar of divine antidote it offered for my parched soul and the various ailments that tormented my body, which I can assure you were many. I discovered through God's word that, I did not need to feel sorry for my self by the act of self-scrutiny but rather, pity the perpetrators of my pain and hardship, for what they had done and for the magnitude of the wrath that the God of justice will rain on their heads for touching me, His anointed. Yes, know you not that the God we serve administers justice? He is a God of righteousness and will not be provoked. I then resolved to live and not die in the mind, soul, and body, but to declare the works of the Lord. God taught me to rid myself of all the bitterness and the gall, as I forgave those who had hurt me, difficult as it seemed at the time. And as always the word of God in (Isaiah 54: 5) assured me of my future. It says; " For thy maker is thine husband; the Lord of hosts is His name, and thy redeemer the Holy one of Israel; the God of the whole earth shall he be called." This scripture became my source of sustenance, until my marriage finally ended in July of 2004, after eight years of physical, mental, emotional, and verbal abuse, numerous miscarriages, and tremendous spiritual battle. On the day my marriage officially/legally ended, it had spiritually ended years ago because of the profound, incorrigible, and continuous marital contamination drawn into it by my spouse at the time. I would like you to know that, being a fervent believer does not necessarily guarantee complete and utter success by way of worldly expectation; because on that day, even though I walked out of court with nothing, in terms of compensation because my ex was clad in the deceptive robes of "no income" fastened with buttons of self impoverishment, the Lord bathed me with strength to replace my anxieties, joy and gladness for all my pain, and also endowed me with beauty for all the ashes of humiliation and disrespect I endured at my perpetrators hands.

I also carried a backpack laden with great spiritual expectations with me on that day. Yes I was leaning on an infinite sustenance and my blessings though invincible to the naked eye, were hid with Christ in God, as I walked out of court with great contentment, and assurance from a Father who is constant and true, by the power of His word. My marriage ended yes. But that did not mean my prayers were not answered, or that I was not good enough. It was because, I was too good and too bright a light in that darkness, and had to be transported by my creator into a worthy environment where I could shine, glow and bubble in order to reach my full potential, as well as fulfill my quota, as The Father above has designed. God knew that I was unequally yoked. And He came to ease that yoke off my neck to save me from destruction by freeing me from the crushing weight of that heavy burden of subtleties and lies, into a life of great expectations. Listen and listen well dear reader in Christ. When crisis pitches its tent in your life, stop analyzing the situation carnally. Instead, immediately sign up for divine therapy with the Most High God the greatest analyst, by way of His unfailing word, together with the incorporation of Christian resource avenues, retrieved from centers and organizations where people with great scriptural and spiritual credentials, like Pastors, counselors, Evangelists and ready help programs on radio like 'Focus on the Family', and Christian book shops, laden with divers audio visual materials, can help you secure the appropriate hold on your life, together with the afore mentioned people, who can prescribe the adequate antidote capable of strengthening you on your way to recovery and victory. The following is a prayer sample for a person in distress; it exhibits the typical signs of emotional turmoil, through confusion, and depression.

"Lord I thank you for this day that you have made that I might rejoice and be glad in it. (salutation of gratefulness and thanksgiving.) Blessed are you Lord God Almighty. From everlasting to everlasting you are the same. Elshadai, I give you glory. I worship you in the beauty of holiness. I declare your majesty and sovereignty in great exaltation o Lord God whose majestic power echoes throughout the earth, filling it with everlasting love. (praise, worship and adoration.) I come before you father, broken in spirit but strong in faith and hope. I stand on your word that promises peace and tranquility (Jehovah Shalom) and also greater peace because, I love your law. I also receive from you expressly, a life of victory over the adversities that confront me because, you have assured me that your love will shield me from all things that are offensive to my well-being. (see: Psalm 119: 165) I am standing on the promises of your word as I cast my burdens upon you for sustenance, knowing fully well that you will never give me cause to doubt you or cause me to experience fear and uncertainty. (see:

Psalm 55: 22) I also stand on the promises about the plans that you have laid out for my future, even before I was a clot of blood in my mother's womb; which as you said, will surround me with hope and prosperity. (see: Jeremiah 29: 11-13) My soul waits for you Lord, like them that watch for the morning, as I hope daily in your word. (see: Psalm 130: 5-6). Lord apportion me with wings of eagles, to soar above all adversity, as I wait on you. Renew my strength to enable me overcome my trials and tribulations without weariness of the body, spirit and mind. Furnish me dear Master, with the stamina to boldly walk towards my life's goal. (see: Isaiah 40: 28-31) Thank you for endowing me with your divine hope that does not disappoint, because of your love that has been shed abroad in the hearts of all believers by the power of your Holy Spirit given unto us. (see: Romans 5:5) Father, I thank you for your unfailing love and divine assurance that compels the faith to bring my request before you by prayer and supplication with thanksgiving, as my heart and mind is bathed in the serenity of your peace that transcends all things, through Christ Jesus my Lord and Savior. (see: Philippians 4: 6&7) (Note the ardent utilization of the art of spiritual as well as scriptural presentation in this prayer and supplication) I open my arms o Lord my God in faithful anticipation, and my heart, in pure dedication for you to fill with your bounteous blessings. Thank you for what you have done in my life, what you are perfecting at the present, and what you will be performing, in your generosity and perfection, for your glory and my redemption. May you the only God who answers by fire, (see: 1King 18: 24) project your performance power by manifesting its extensive blessings in my life for all to see that you are God indeed. This I pray with blessed anticipation, through your son Jesus Christ, Amen." (a conclusion of faithful anticipation and thanksgiving) (AOP)

Child of God. By praying like this, you end up touching on all the essentials of effective prayer. Which are, acknowledging God's reverent presence by a salutation of praise and thanksgiving, which in turn summons the presence of the Holy Spirit and thereby moistens the prayer environment for the effective germination of prayer seeds. And secondly, your pronouncement of praise worship and adoration, which waters the tiny prayer sprouts, followed by the spiritual presentation of your supplication, incorporated with the word of God, which in turn defines the scriptural depth and authenticity of your need devoid of all carnality. And finally, your faithful and grateful anticipation denoting thanksgiving, and absolute trust, belief, and rest assurance in His promises. Please note that, the last portion of your prayer is most critical as it represents the spiritual richness of the soil into which your prayer seedlings are to be transplanted, to take firm root, to grow, bloom and to yield a sustaining healthy crop and bountiful victorious harvest.

"My people perish for lack of knowledge." (see: Proverbs 29:18) this Godly admonishment, does not literally denote perishing as in death. But rather, denotes failure and stagnation in every aspect within all the positive factors that enhance our spiritual lives to their highest standards of progress and prosperity. The word of God instructs us thus; "If any of you needs wisdom, you should ask God for it. He is generous and enjoys giving to all people. So He will give you wisdom. But when you ask God, you must believe and not doubt. Any one who doubts is like a wave in the sea, blown up and down by the wind." (James 1: 5-6a NSV) You see, scripture becomes more effective through prayer because, it gets amplified to a greater degree of potency, when personalized. But you must be cautious not to add to, or subtract. But to simplify the texts by spiritually induced comprehensive elaboration in order to grammatically enhance its benefits, and to provide assistance and ease for its absorption, to its ravenous seekers and readers. The following is another prayer sample. It is a prayer asking for God's divine providence by an individual confronted with a need of extreme urgency. As you read it, please take time to find the essential portions incorporated within and record them for future reference in the subsidiary pages of the prayer guide, allocated for 'Notes'. God bless you.

Let us pray. "Worthy! worthy ! is the Lord God Almighty. The whole earth is full of your glory. The heavens declare your Glory and the firmament proclaims your divine majesty forever and ever. Father, I come before you with arms of want and needs calling on your divine providence. King of kings and Lord of lords, I lay my request before you the omniscient God and deliverer. Relieve me of this need by blessing me financially. Shower your blessings on my occupation by throwing it into the light of prosperity. Help me shine in my area of expertise. Bless the work of my hands and let them be fruitful; yielding in multiples of folds. Take me out of the wilderness of want and establish me on the shores of plenty. For " you are the Lord my God, the Lord my redeemer, the Holy one of Israel who teaches me to profit, and leads me unto the divine paths of abundance." "Save me now I beseech you o Lord! o Lord I beseech you; send now prosperity." (you may affirm the last sentence, seven times or repeat the last three words in the same fashion) I open my hands to receive your bounteous blessing with praise and thanksgiving, in the name of your son Jesus Christ, who lives and reigns with you, and the Holy Spirit for ever and ever, Amen." (please read Psalm 118: 25 and Isaiah 48: 17, in reference to the scriptural texts used in this prayer sample.)(AOP)

Dear reader in Christ. Why wouldn't the Lord show up with divine deliverance, disbursement and performance power on your behalf when you go to him armed with the knowledge and the fullness of His word of truth? With a prayer such as this devoid of vain repetitions, there exists no doubt within God about your knowledge of the extent of his Divine generosity and providence. " For has He not said time and again; "Is my hand short, that I cannot deliver?" (see: Isaiah 50: 2) A prayer for provision structured with such dedication and total reliance on God, will surely yield fruits. For it is not the length of your prayer that effectuates its response from the father. But rather, the spiritual depth and scriptural authenticity of its projection and wording, married to the Godly dedication of the heart from which it is being outpoured. Let us now move on to another degree of prayer. this time, let us focus on the twelve synonyms of God by opening our hearts and minds for God to cast and forge them in readiness to absorb the power they project, as each of them reveals His divine characteristic by displaying their transcending and indispensable merits as essential prayer tools. Before we proceed, I will like to elaborate on the word 'name'. What is a name? My choice of definition derived from Webster's dictionary is as follows; "name adjective; having an established reputation, (name; performers). Name (brands)." If I may guess what you are thinking, you are probably wondering why a common thing like a name, a title which every living and nonliving thing possesses, should be researched. Of course I know that everybody has one. Yes, and it is one of the first early childhood developmental skills that humans acquire by way of cognitive responsiveness and as such, I am therefore very much aware of it being common to all. But every being with a name does not possess divine synonyms together with the ability of exuding its potency by way of divine performance and power, carried out with expert precision and perfection like 'The Guy upstairs'. By taking a second look at the definition, please take note of the key words; 'reputation' and 'brand' and keep them in mind as we continue our lesson. Secondly, may I encourage you to memorize the following text/quotation that I originally put together to secure your apprehension of the subject to be discussed? Thank you.

"HIS DIVINE POWER, CHARACTER, AND REPUTATION, PRECEDES EACH NAME. AND THE BLESSINGS THEY CONVEY TO THOSE WHO FAITHFULLY AND PRAYERFULLY INVOKE

THEM, ARE FOREVER BRANDED IN ENDLESS LOVE AND PURE BENEVOLENCE." (ANQ)

Knowing a person, and the actual act of calling them by name, are two different things altogether. The latter being less formal and as such, more personal than the former. The degree of intimacy that one has with a person known to them by name depicts, a certain rate of intensity by way of closeness or level of intimacy in the relationship that exists between the two. When we go to the Father (God) in prayer and supplication, we call him by other names like Alpha and Omega, etc. but judging the extent, importance and intensity of the covenant we made with him through Christ Jesus and subsequently by that spiritual marriage and self-yielding covenant, we must be seriously lacking in intimacy, commitment, deficient in esteem and trust to be so self-limited in the arena of adorable and reverent terminologies, accolades and appellations relating to His divine performance functions and characteristics. Let us pick our example from the secular world since that will be easier to relate to. For example a platonic relationship between two individuals holds little or no endearments. But in the type of relationship where intimacy that extends beyond the platonic exists, everything changes to a level of extreme emotional sensitivity. Expressions and terms of endearment are rampant as well as intimacy, which is often expressed in varying levels and degrees. As the relationship intensifies, they(feelings) are emotionally projected from each person by way of affection and love to enhance the physical and psychological growth of the relationship. Trust is abundant and not taken lightly. So also is devotion, dependency, reliability, extreme and utter dedication, selflessness, protection and sacrifice. All these components of intimacy are thus transformed into attributes of faithful commitment. These are the essential ingredients that people expect to savor in the brewing pot of deep/intimate relationships.

Shall we now focus on the most beneficial as well as rewarding of all intimate relationships which is, one between a person and God. Between you (dear reader) and The Father to be precise. Imagine how blessed you will be in every area of your life if you can just grasp the depth of the riches to be acquired if you know The Father God beyond the platonic. Like the secular intimate relationship, you must work on it to ensure its growth without any negative interferences by the dedicated study of His word which is your only channel to "meeting the family" so to speak. The Bible teaches us that, "...the people who know their God shall be strong and do exploits." (see: Daniel 11: 32). The word of God instructs us all by these words of truth. However as your literary teacher in the Lord, may I be bold enough to ask you this question. Do you know your God? To what extent or degree do you revere him? Are you aware of his sublime capabilities and the divine extent of His benevolence? Do you know that your total trust and dependence on him should inevitably generate within your very being, the ardent desire to invoke his ancient names of power and performance? The very names that established him as the 'Ancient of Days', the one true God who possesses all things and dispenses at will His eternal wisdom which spans for generations, hand in hand with the divine knowledge of centuries unending? I bet you do deep inside or you wouldn't have purchased this book to bring it out.

Being born and raised in Ghana West Africa, called to my mind one of our traditionally rich customs set aside for our Chieftains, Kings and Queens, whenever they appeared in public for royal gatherings we call 'Durbar'. At these gatherings, each chieftain is ushered in by their respective Chief linguists and royal entourage by way of profound and distinguished uttering, appellations, and proud declarations of conquests past and present, laced with honorable accolades of distinction and prowess. At this particular moment, the entire atmosphere at the durbar is transformed into that of regal serenity and obeisance as each Chief is transported to the Durbar grounds in ornate palanquins of gold and velvet amidst the cheer and homage to their respective thrones. I will like to reiterate the sudden injection of power and recognition their mere presence exude as they make their way through the portals of royalty, drowned within the pump and circumstance. These are people from very old families, of high birth with titles of royalty spanning centuries that they constantly strive to live up to all their lives. As you may realize, theirs is a commitment of great proportions which has to be upheld in the highest of esteem. For you see, they cannot be Kings and Lords and suffer the loss of power over the entire jurisdiction of their households, estates, and regions as that will lead to dishonor and ruin. God on the other hand is almighty. He is a spirit and must be worshipped in spirit and in truth. (see: John 4:24) To rightly divide the truth in this scripture, is a good reason to invoke His synonyms of authenticity, performance and astounding capabilities that has been limitlessly exercised since the days of yore, which also are His code names of power, performance, character, and that of divine status which when appropriately invoked during times of prayer, supplication and extreme crisis or need, 'power alerts' Him to your problem which

He in turn projects with love towards their expedited eradication. Using God's ancient names stamps 'urgent' and 'priority' on your prayer scroll as it cyclones its way towards His majestic footstool where He immediately upon receipt, comes to your aid directly or dispatches the appropriate *Angel to expressly perform your needs in purity, perfection, accuracy steeped in divine haste. (*an in-depth knowledge and insight into the ministry of Angels is available in the fourth chapter of this book.)

Another secular example where a special name used for an appropriate need draws attention and immediate response is as follows. If the President of the United States paid a visit to your neighborhood, everyone of course will like to see him and possibly speak to him, or shake his hand because he is a very important personality in the country, and the world at large with an established name and status. Now picture yourself in the midst of that throng as a person who grew up with the President as a child. But has never revealed yourself to him or contacted him even though you've had several opportunities to do so, simply because you do not know how and where to begin. "what is the point. He might not even remember me." you say to yourself . " I might end up being disappointed and embarrassed." Yet deep inside you know it is something you must do because you believe he undoubtedly will love to hear from you. Well, 'tell you what! You have two options. You may mingle with the crowd and call out to him like the rest of America and the world does, and wave to him from a distance like everybody else. "Mr. President! Mr. President!". Trust me. It will not make any difference to him. But why is that? Doesn't he care? Yes he does care very much. But giving the level or depth of acquaintance between you both, you are not making an impact as a childhood connection because, because you sound like everyone else. You will never attract his attention, by that mode of appellation. He will not budge. But just wave to the crowd at large including you, as standard protocol demands because millions of people nationally and globally call him that. Your second and best option is to boldly compose yourself and yell out that special name you called him when you were boys growing up together. The name that denotes something very peculiar, significant, positive, nostalgic, and important. Now dear reader, you must put your lesson into action. But what do you do? You ignore everyone and every protocol procedure. You know it is now or never. Reflecting about how he might probably have ruled you out as deceased or something close to that. A thought that is highly probable since he has not heard from you for decades not because you do not call out to him, but because he cannot hear you. You also know and believe that despite his position and status he still remembers what good friends you two were. but because, you are not appropriately keeping in touch by utilizing the right techniques of contact, he is gradually forgetting you. (this may happen to you as a praying Christian for a long time; the Lord will not hear you if you are not praying effectively) yes! Your continuous lack of appropriate contact and approach has you completely forgotten by him. But today you have finally decided to do what you should have done a long time ago. You confidently call out that name. The name that nobody in the crowd knows. The name that the President has not heard used for the longest time. You watch as his eyes bulge out with excitement. "who called me by that name?" He bellows, interrupting his own speech. "Listen whoever called me so and so, would you move up out of the crowd towards the podium where I can see you?" The rest is up to the secret service of course to check you out and shake your pants for authentication and safeguarding of the CIC. Well you certainly got his attention didn't you? He will certainly bypass all standard procedures to grant you audience. You are instantly elevated from mob status to where you should have been a long time ago. A dear friend at his side. He may even go on to grant you more favors like squeezing in between his busy schedule to give you the opportunity of a one on one audience with him, to listen to matters that need to be addressed in your community; and of course the days that followed found him dining with you and your family whilst visiting your community to view first hand your issues. Thus by the appropriate method of re-acquaintance you have strengthened a lost friendship and blessed others as well. I hope you grasp the general idea projected by this sample story. You may try it out one day when I am President of Ghana:) (just kidding but who knows, it could happen why not!)

As we all know, one of the most popular verses in the Bible teaches us to ask and in order to receive. Often times we do not receive because we do not ask. And even when we do, we sometimes ask amiss. (read Luke11: 9). But what does it mean to ask? Well, I will define asking in my own words as: "The act of verbally, projecting one's wants, needs, aspirations and innermost desires, into a request to another, with a clear sense of anticipation or expectancy of some sort, to be carried out by way of a projected response, result, or an answer." (ADA.) My dear friend in Christ, this works the same way and even better in a spiritual way with God our Father who is perpetually seated on His throne just waiting and watching out for your prayerful desires to come tumbling at His glorious feet. Believe it or not, He will fish out your prayer scroll from amongst the trillions floating about in His throne room simply because it has his brand name of performance on it. You see, He sits daily in benevolent royalty and in eternal majesty granting spiritual audiences. That means, not by physically appearing to you but through His divine responsiveness to your prayers by His great power of expedition exercised when attending to the supplications of His children. Brother and sister in the Lord, if you are one who prays ceaselessly; judging by the number of prayers you as an individual projects into God's throne room daily, then it should be easy for you to imagine what God will sanction to be stamped on your prayer scroll by the heavenly record keepers,(The *Dominion Angels) to certify His receipt of your prayer requests as they are spiritually processed and as they make their way to the divine 'in' tray, on His desk of providence. 'approved'! Of course. Simply because, you prayed differently than all the others. Yes! And that is exactly why this book was written to guide you towards how to pray effectively by the right division of His Holy word of truth. Let's pause our lesson and attend to this urgent prayer request for assistance that God has laid on my heart, for the victims and survivors of the very recent as we also remember past natural disasters and our fellow humans still reeling from the devastation and loss, as well as those still slowly recovering physically, spiritually and psychologically from them, as they rebuild their lives all over again.

Specially inserted pages of scriptural proclamations of comfort and encouragement, dedicated to the victims and survivors of recent and past natural disasters. Including a self expressive and personalized, 'ready prayer', exclusively and expressly compiled for their daily 'Immediate Spiritual Nourishment.' (ISN)

I will like to further reiterate God's names of performance, for a specific prayer need involving a great crisis in urgent and speedy need of 'Advanced and Expedited Spiritual Intervention' (AESI) to spiritually propel the wheels of aid and support through help from heaven and its manifestation here on earth. Since there have been numerous disasters globally, I would like to pray in that direction as it is the most Christian thing to do. I will therefore lead you into effective prayer, using God's special names of performance as we pray for the families, communities, countries and all who have been adversely affected by these disasters physically, socially, financially and psychologically. During this prayer, we will also remember the souls of all who lost their lives in the wake of the disasters including the families and loved ones they left behind. Let us also remember the children who have been traumatized by these terrible disasters including all the new born. We will also pray for the families of the sick, disabled and elderly who lost their lives during these disasters who were in healthcare institutions all over these disaster areas. We will also pray for the Leaders of the countries affected as they work to bring these difficult situations under complete control. As we do so, let us remember the health organizations, the evacuation crew on site, especially the fire service personnel and those in charge of social assistance, relocation and recovery. In conclusion, we will pray for the riddance and the subjection of all feelings of loss, pain and hopelessness weaving its way around these devastated nations as a result of the disasters they have encountered, by calling on God the provider and healer; Jehovah-Jireh and Jehovah-Repheka, to divinely assist through our prayers, with the restoration, and recovery of these nations as a whole.

Now dear reader in Christ, this is the time to propagate the word of God through prayer for our fellow men, women and children facing the most extreme of needs. Which are of course matters of great priority in the areas of safety and sure recovery by attaining healing of the mind, soul and body as well as stability from the disastrous circumstances that have come to unexpectedly plague them. Let us go to the Father of restoration in prayer and call on His brand name that denotes His divine characteristic as the superfluous horn of providence, to bring them these gifts that they are in dire need of at present, as well as those they will be needing for years to come, as we offer them not only relief laden humane support, but spiritual assurance and support drawn from the scriptural application of the word of truth, and its appropriate disbursal within bundles of hope, comfort and encouragement, in the name of the Father, and of the Son, and of the Holy Spirit. Let us pray.

A prayer for the recovery and healing of the victims and survivors of natural disasters worldwide.

"Father we come to you grieved in the spirit, hurting in mind, and broken in heart, seeking help, aid and assistance on behalf of your people trapped within the hardship and crisis following the disasters that they encountered. You alone are Lord over all situations. Yahweh and Jehovah art thou o Lord God of Abraham, Isaac and Jacob. I ascribe all glory, honor, and power, unto you o Lord of Hosts. From everlasting to everlasting you are the same. As Jehovah–Shamah, watching and guarding your children with love and protection from on high. We invoke your divine assistance and that of leadership by your power to perform on behalf of our brothers and sisters in crisis asking you to guide them spiritually as well as physically out of these turmoil as Jehovah-Tsebaoth the Lord of Hosts. Transport them o God, to the safe and prosperous shores of healing and recovery. We bring before your healing presence; Jehovah-Repheka all those who have been adversely affected by these disasters. Father, dispatch your *Archangels and Powers of Light to encompass them within their healing wings of your *Archangels and Powers of Light, as you render every form of loss they have suffered restored by your supreme power of providence, and by your divine power of restoration. May all the adversely affected citizens and people of these nations in turmoil emerge from your healing throne, fully restored in spirit, soul and in body. Dispatch o God, your *Cherubim and Seraphim to administer therapeutic melodies in heavenly tones and vibrations to divinely calm, purify and replenish their troubled minds, by freeing them from all suffering they may experience psychologically, physically, socially and financially as a result of these disasters. Father, bathe them in your divine waters of peace and endless tranquility. Jehovah-Shalom; giver of peace encamp them within the shelter of your peaceful tents overflowing with tranquility and serenity.

We pray for the souls of all who lost their lives during these crisis. That they too may find eternal rest in heavenly places in Christ, as they soar above the tragedy of the circumstances of their passing into the divine realms to find peace in His everlasting arms of love. We also lift up the families and loved ones they have so unpredictably and unexpectedly left behind. Father guide them towards your constant and ever present hope and comfort in you as they deal with their losses under these difficult and trying conditions. Endow them with your pure comfort and restoration even as you did in the days of yore for your servant Job. Visit and restore unto them all their losses in millions of folds as you inject into their very beings, supernatural faith and belief to know that, what you have promised, you are also able to bring into performance and fruition. For you o God are the supplier of needs and the stable answerer of all requests. Yes! you are Jehovah-Jireh the provider who furnishes tables of nourishment in the wilderness and brings into existence rivers in the most arid of desperate situations. Manifest your powers as the God whose extensiveness in providing for His children are limitless as well as boundless, overriding all negative situations and crisis, while spanning across all borders and jurisdictions.

"suffer the children to come unto me… For theirs is the kingdom of heaven." (see Matthew 19:14) those were your words of divine love and affection, as you rebuked your disciples for the sake of the little ones who found a place of safety at your feet, while you were on earth. We therefore stand on that promise and invoke your divine and infinite power of performance as Jehovah-Raah the good shepherd, as We pray and lift unto you these precious little ones affected by these national crisis. For the missing, we pray that they may be rescued, recovered and delivered to their families on the wings of your courier Angels. Father touch their little minds and hearts with your feathers of divine therapy, to calm as well as cleanse their memories of all negative scars by healing them physically and emotionally. May you also stabilize all the newborn, both full term and premature, caught within the uproar and confusion with health and vitality. Surround them with minions of Guardian Angels Father, and bless all the healthcare personnel and volunteers; from the Chief Surgeons to the orderlies who work around the clock attending to these precious ones as well as the other patients. Endow them with patience, tolerance and tireless stamina. Replenish them in strength and in wisdom to wisely as well as professionally resolve all clinical complications, or difficulties that may arise as they tend to their patients. Exhibit your might that transcends all situations o El-Shaddai; and let your glory illuminate to reveal all the darkness surrounding the sites where these crisis occurred. Father, bring them under the subjection of your divine power to vanquish and of conquest as Jehovah-Nissi, and throw them into complete and utter evanescence. In your divine nature of righteousness and pure justice as Jehovah-Tsidquenu, bring comfort and compensation to all the families who lost sick, disabled and elderly loved ones.We also lift up all the relief organizations in charge of evacuation, social assistance, relocation, resettlement and recovery that by your divine power as the Lord Most High Jehovah-Elyon, you will equip them with strength and tireless commitment as they go about their daily duties serving their fellowmen. Protect them from accidents and random contamination and infection o great physician of yore, and enshroud them in fabrics of divine protection so that no harm will befall them during their complex and strenuous duties. We also lift up their families and loved ones before your throne of divine providence. Induce into them the moral support needed from them by their loved ones as they carry out their civic and humane duties.

May you be ever present Jehovah-Shamah with the leaders of these countries. Father empower them with strength and endurance, as Commanders-in-Chief together with the entire membership of their cabinets and administrations as they work in unison perfecting strategies and plans of recovery towards the reconstruction of the cities, villages, hamlets as they work hard to foster the swift resettlement of the citizens affected by these great crisis. Endow these leaders with divine wisdom and expert knowledge, by furnishing them with the most effective and beneficially stable rescue, recovery, relocation and resettlement strategies for their affected nations. Father Almighty, exhibit your total and supreme control as head over these situations, as we invoke your divine performance power of omnipresence, to instill into them, tremendous outpourings of peace and a spirit of unification, during these crucial times in their lives when they have obviously been torn apart at the family hem and community seam, due to their national crisis. Equip the inhabitants of these nations with the strength of character impregnated with tolerance and self control of great spiritual dimensions strong enough to propel them at large into retrieving positive sustenance from your throne on high, while enabling them to work and live together as a people of one nation, united to strengthen each other. Receive our heartfelt supplication o Most High God, as we present them on behalf of our fellow men, women and children, for they wait on you with grateful expectation, in faithful anticipation. For these and other needs known to you, omniscience God do we pray. In Christ Jesus' name. Amen." (AOP)

+++++

Scriptures of comfort.

Isaiah 49: 13

"Sing, o heavens; and be joyful o earth; and break forth into singing, o mountains: for the Lord hath comforted His people, and will have mercy upon His afflicted." (KJV.)

Psalm 9: 18

"For the needy shall not always be forgotten: the expectation of the poor shall not perish forever."(KJV.)

Psalm 16: 1, 5, 6, & 11

"Preserve me o God: for in thee do I put my trust. The Lord is the portion of my inheritance and of my cup: thou maintainest my lot. The lines are fallen unto me in pleasant places: yea, I have a goodly heritage. Thou wilt shew me the path of life: in thy presence is fullness of joy; and at thy right hand there are pleasures forever more." (KJV.)

Psalm 18: 2, 4, 6, 16, 27a & 28, 31.

"The Lord is my rock, and my fortress, and my deliverer; my God, my strength, in whom I will trust; my buckler, and the horn of my salvation, and my high tower. The sorrows of death compassed me, and the floods of ungodly men made me afraid. In my distress I called upon the Lord, and cried unto my God: He heard my voice out of His temple, and my cry came before Him, even into His ears. He sent from above, He took me, He drew me out of many waters. For thou wilt save the afflicted people; for thou wilt light my candle: the Lord my God will enlighten my darkness. For who is God save the Lord? And who is a rock save our God?" (KJV.)

Psalm 27: 14

"Wait on the Lord: be of good courage, and He shall strengthen thine heart: wait I say on the Lord." (KJV.)

Psalm 34: 1, 17, 19, 20 & 22.

"I will bless the Lord at all times: His praise shall continually be in my mouth. The righteous cry and the Lord heareth and delivereth them out of all their troubles. Many are the afflictions of the righteous: but the Lord delivereth him out of them all, He keepeth all his bones: not one of them is broken. The Lord redeemeth the soul of His servants: and none of them that trust in Him shall be desolate." (KJV.)

Psalm 119: 50.

"This is my comfort in my affliction: for thy word hath quickened me." (KJV.)

Psalm 145: 14.

"The Lord upholdeth all that fall, and raiseth up all those that be bowed down." (KJV.)

2Corinthians 1: 3, 4 & 7.
"Blessed be God, even the Father of our Lord Jesus Christ, the Father of mercies, and the God of all comfort: who comforteth us in all our tribulation, that we may be able to comfort them which are in trouble, by the comfort wherewith we ourselves are comforted of God. And our hope of you is steadfast, knowing that, as ye are partakers of the sufferings, so shall ye be also of the consolation." (KJV.)

Philippians 4: 12-13.
"I know both how to be abased, and I know how to abound: everywhere and in all things I am instructed both to be full and to be hungry, both to abound and to suffer need. I can do all things through Christ which strengtheneth me." Amen. (KJV.)

+++++

A ready prayer laden with compilations of comforting and encouraging scriptural affirmations expressly written for the devotional benefits of the victims and survivors of natural disasters worldwide. (all pronouns are personalized for individual prayer sessions or group praying convenience.) May all who have been affected receive divine comfort and consolation by this supplication derived and forged from the word of truth, for all time.

The Lord is in this place with me/us, even under my/our most difficult circumstance(s).

Despite my /our pain, loss and desperation, i/we will listen for His voice to comfort, counsel and to provide me/us with the answers, i/we so desperately need.

He will send His Angels to bring me/us gifts of healing and restoration, as He has done in times past.

The uncertainty(ies) of my/our troubled heart(s) is/are settled and stabilized because, He alone is capable of delivering on a deadline.

I/we will say of the Lord that, He has been and still is my/our fortress and safe haven in the midst of this adversity.

Shield me/us o Lord, with your faithfulness, for you are my/our rock and my/our high tower.

Fashion in me/us a heart(s) that is/are thirsting to trust in you no matter how grave the circumstance(s).

Father of all nations; faithful throughout all generations; lifter of my/our head(s).

Jehovah-Shamah; the ever present God, author and finisher of my/our faith, I /we give you the glory. For in all things and at all times, you know my/our needs and supply them as you see fit.

I/we exalt you above this crisis o Lord; that i/we may emerge from this dark pit stronger, bolder and bigger in faith and in character than i/we was/were before.

May i/we be strengthened by your hand so that, i/we may be able to comfort others who are too broken in spirit to lift up their heads.

Endow me/us with the emotional capability to deal with the loss of loved ones and acquaintances so that, my/our survival during and after this crisis, will serve as a testimony to bless them in loving memory.

May the babies and the young ones who have been traumatized find healing, positive growth and serenity in the care and counsel given to them.

Shower me/us with confidence and hope as i/we temporarily relocate to various places and erase the trauma and nostalgia that constantly plague me/us until your appointed day of our resettlement into my/our city/cities of residence.

Endow me/us with gratefulness to count my/our very survival as a tremendous blessing even though i/we have lost so much.

Bless the works and tireless efforts of my/our President (s), our Mayor(s) and other leaders of my/our country, the voluntary and relief organizations, law enforcement and the army, celebrities and all whose stretched out hands of assistance and benevolence brought me/us provision and comfort.

Bless the Lord o my/our soul(s) and forget not all His benefits; who heals all my/our disease(s); who redeems my/our/ life/lives from destruction; crowning me/us with loving kindness and tender mercies. Who satisfies my/our mouth with good things, so that all my/our loss(es) is/are recovered through His divine provision.

Bless the Lord and all His Angels whom He dispatched by His supreme authority, to save my/our life/lives, on that tragic day.

Bless the Lord o my/our souls and all that is within me/us, bless His holy name.

I/we give thanks unto the Lord; for He is good: for His mercies endures forever.

Let the citizens and people of .... (please verbally insert the name of your country/city/district/ or county in distress in the space provided) now say that, His mercies endures forever.

Let the families of the survivors say that His mercies endures forever, and is able to bring them to a place of solace in the midst of woe.

I/we called upon the Lord in great distress; and the Lord answered me/us and set me/us in a large place.

With the Lord on my/our side, i/we will not live in total fear of my/our future.

The waters of death surrounded me/us. But In the name of the Lord, i/we rode on the wings of *Angels to safety.

For i/we know and believe that those who rode the same divine wings even in eternal slumber, have been transported from this life of turmoil, into that of glory and peace, as they vacated that receptacle which was susceptible to handicap, disabilities, injuries and various ailments, on that fateful day when they were spiritually transported on the mighty wings of the *Cherubim, accompanied by heavenly rhythms and tones eternal.

For by this trial, have i/we come to know, as i/we take my/our days, and live my/our life/lives one day at a time that, God's strength is made perfect in my weakness. Therefore, at the moment and time or times when I/we am/are at my/our weakest, then am I / are we strengthened from deep within, by His divine power.

Not only has the Lord been my/our strength and song; but He has also become my/our salvation and pillar of recovery and rejuvenation.

The right hand of the Lord has delivered me/us.

I /we shall not be depressed, confused, disoriented, afraid, or entertain negative spirit-dampening thoughts of despair, hopelessness and of self-destruction, as long as His word reassures me/us of joy in the morning, even after a night of weeping and distress.

By God's power, I /we will be strong for my /our dependents.

I /we will not die, but live and declare the works of the Lord by my/our testimony(ies). Because in Him my /our future is bright and not as bleak as I /we physically view it/them to be.

The gates of restoration have been widely flung open for me/us. Therefore, with hope at my /our heels, and faith leading me/us on, I /we will enter into them with boldness, bearing a winning attitude to claim a stable and prosperous future for me/us and mine. /ours.

May the divine presence of the Lord always be with me/us and shower me/us with peace, as i/we daily acquaint myself/ourselves with Him.

For I/we know and believe that, underneath all the physical, emotional, financial and personal losses, are His ever opened and everlasting arms of love are stretched out in parental readiness, to lead me/us to the glimmering shores of blessings divine.

I/we will be strong in the Lord, and totally rely on the power of his might throughout the duration of this crisis and even when the imprints of its aftermath linger. For He has not endowed me/us with the spirit of fear and uncertainty, but that of love, and the confidence to forge ahead through His insurmountable power, with a sound mind. Amen."

Author's prayer of blessing and that of proclamation over the lives of all victims and survivors of natural disasters worldwide.

"May the Lord guide you always and satisfy your needs. May He strengthen your human frame into exuberance, like a well watered garden and like a spring whose waters never fail, as you transit from recovery and relocation into resettlement, and comfort you in mind, soul and body. May he grant you perfect peace and refreshed memories, as you begin life again, not on your own, but within his loving grip overflowing with divine providence. Amen."

+++++

Upon the global victims and survivors of natural disasters do I make this proclamation; standing on the authority of the rightly divided word of truth, as recorded in the book of Isaiah.

"I implore you in the name of God Almighty to " Arise and shine for your light is come. For the glory of the Lord is risen upon you. And even though the waters came rushing, and winds came rustling, and the earth gave way covering and laying your lives, homes and investments to waste, so also shall the Lord rise up to your aid out of all this confusion, loss and turmoil to dispense truth and equity into your countries, cities, counties, regions, villages and towns, by His mighty hand of righteousness. For the Lord has already provided a way out for you from this crisis by first sparing your lives. Yes! He is bringing profound and insurmountable blessings and restorative measures the world has never seen before, to your borders and shores. He will appoint to you His children who weep in different parts of the world, divine comfort during the course of your grief and loss. He will shower your countenance with contentment when depression raises its mournful head around you. He will anoint you with the oil of joy and of gladness to wash away your pain and loss and equip you forthrightly with garments of praise. Your heavily laden spirits and grief invaded minds will be lightened. Finally, unto you do I prophesy that, sooner than you think will you stand tall in the gardens of restoration by faith and belief in prosperous bloom. Where all eyes will bear witness and tongues declare you as; "trees of righteousness; the plantings of the Lord and the forever blessed of God." So that His name might be glorified by the profound testimonies of your soon to be transformed into peace, prosperity and stability lives." Amen.

Dear friends in Christ. I am glad we paused during our lesson and made prayer room for our fellow humans in crisis, by the express compilation and dedication of these pages of prayer to fill the spiritual void created. May our brothers and sisters be joyfully blessed in the Lord, as the hope in Him.

Shall we end this chapter by furthering our spiritual knowledge, while studying the synonyms of God, as they throw light into the depths of His Divine character and performance power. I would like you to retain deep focus and keep one word in mind throughout this lesson. Our key word for this lesson is the word 'invocation'. Invocation as a word, has for centuries indigenously revolved around religious rituals and spiritualism, which was not necessarily Christian. However, it is not entirely a word originated from paganism, as most have been led to believe over the years; making a fair percentage of Christians wary to the extent of grammatically refraining from its usage entirely. To invoke according to Webster's definition is: "The act of calling on for aid; as in prayer. For example; to invoke God's blessing." Invocation by my understanding and definition is: ("The summoning of a higher being or spirit in whose capabilities, performance and accomplishments, one firmly believes; to aid and assist with a situation or need that requires supernatural or 'expedited Spiritual Intervention' (ESI) while exercising tremendous anticipation and 'Unshakable Faith' (UF.), in order to swiftly propel the desired results into physical manifestation." (ADA). As Christians, we must be cautious by not letting our 'spiritual credentials' (SC.), fall short of our ability to dissect secular literary expression as we function daily. To ensure this, we must cultivate the 'good Christian habit' (GCH) of researching into words and phrases that have been adulterated and portrayed as pagan or taboos over the centuries, by projecting them into positive realization and balanced awareness into our faith; For by so doing we position them rightly, where they fit in the Christian faith and in our lives as a whole. We must never hesitate or limit our 'spiritual intellect' (SI) when uncertainties arise, or question their use and function, as a result of our own 'spiritual weakness' (SW.) such as the repetitive lack of ardent Bible study, scriptural research and the refusal to enhance our intellect by any means available, without which one cannot achieve a 'practical Christian status' (PCS) which is undoubtedly packaged within a certain degree of theological knowledge.

Thus the harnessing habit of this 'spiritual Know-how and ability' (SKA) is very vital as far as safeguarding our very persons; the very precious receptacle wherein our faith and belief are contained. This investment is as sacred as it is vital for it shields us from vulnerability by offering us spiritual protection which keeps us from being confused when the world throws upon us challenges, inquisitions as well as its strong opinions, adverse perceptions and exertions which most times than not, throws us off our scriptural pedestal, due to our own laziness, ignorance and the deliberate shunning of our 'spiritual responsibilities.'(SR) There are in fact different types of invocation carried out for different reasons. This simply means that, It is what you invoke and your manner of invocation, that makes it pagan or not. Remember dear reader in the Lord that, the adversary has a counter version of everything scriptural, spiritual and of all that exhibits Godly magnificence and Christ-like virtue. How could that be? You might ask. Because, it is his best and only handy strategy effective enough for propagating his adverse mission to confuse and corrupt the minds of those who are ardently seeking God. This is the sole reason why I have been keen on stressing and encouraging the indispensability of working spiritually hard to attain scriptural intellect, and insisting on the benefits of investing quality time for core Biblical research, as well as enforcing the dire need for the acquisition of scriptural research materials, for 'intensive Bible study' (IBS), throughout the pages of this book; because it is the only reason I am alive to share with you this literary work.

When you invoke the Spirit of God for aid and assistance, you are transported spiritually and supernaturally to a place of 'immediate divine acquisition' (IDA), by His performance power. Invocation projects from within you, a stronger surge of belief beyond expectation, which usually induces the manifestation of miracles and expedited transformation of circumstance, by the swift conveyance of visible results, and that of great benefits ready to be reaped in blessed abundance by the invoker. It is a very useful and potent prayer tool during extremely fatal situations. It is also beneficial to the very sick and ailing who cannot talk or exhibit physical mobility. People in such situations can invoke the Spirit of God by simply invoking His synonymous names of Divine performance and character, through mental prayer. For example: a believer involved in a car wreck waiting for emergency medical assistance, can invoke the spirit of God by the spiritual act of thought processing His name Jehovah-Shamah; by faith and more *Angels will be dispatched by the Father to assist and backup those already at work. If the victim is in shock and still conscious or partially responsive, it will only take a speck of faithful thought processing towards that particular area of need and spiritual direction, to invoke 'Godly spiritual backup and intervention.' (GSBI) Yes dear friend it only takes a whisper because, the name or functional appellation used serves as a 'prayer concentrate' (PC.); a saturated spiritual concoction of dire needs and expectation in itself which wholly and divinely qualifies the very thought of invoking as an act of pure faith in itself. Which in turn, proves powerful enough to induce the 'expedited divine manifestation' (EDM) of aid, healing, recovery, rejuvenation and restoration.

Well brother and sister in Christ, now that you are all versed in the prayer of invocation, you may have access to your tools of divine appellation, as practically handy as you have never had before in any published inspirational or Christian book. I am greatly honored to present to you as a fervent and committed servant of the Most High God and a believer in the Holy Trinity, His names of power and of performance, as depicted by His character and brand, which I have previously also defined and described as: the synonyms of God for the sake of literary brevity, applicable comprehensive ease, user friendliness and easy retention.

They are after all, God's code names of performance, as projected by the power they exude. Welcome to the store house of 'divine performance.' (DP.) Be blessed in knowing Him intimately by His ancient names.

"Acquaint now thyself with Him and be at peace: thereby good shall come unto thee". (see: Job 22: 21 KJV).

+++++

(III) God's ancient names; your spiritual responsibility to know and utilize.

SYNONYM: Jehovah-Yahweh.
MEANING: The Lord.
FUNCTION: Lord of all creation.
PURPOSE: Divine Supremacy; Godhead.

SYNONYM: Jehovah-Elohim.
MEANING: The Lord is God.
FUNCTION: The one and only True God.
PURPOSE: The Divine one.

SYNONYM: Jehovah-Elyon.
MEANING: The Lord Most High.
FUNCTION: Omnipotent God.
PURPOSE: Limitless source of Divine Power.

SYNONYM: El-Shaddai.
MEANING: The Mighty God.
FUNCTION: Omniscient God.
PURPOSE: Procurer of all Success.

SYNONYM: Jehovah-Repheka.
MEANING: The Lord is healer.
FUNCTION: God of restoration.
PURPOSE: Recoverer of lost causes.

SYNONYM: Jehovah-Jireh.
MEANING: The Lord will provide.
FUNCTION: God of providence.
PRUPOSE: Supplier of needs.

SYNONYM: Jehovah-Tsidquenu.
MEANING: The Lord our Righteousness.
FUNCTION: God of Recompense.
PURPOSE: Divine Adjudicator and constant vessel of Exoneration.

SYNONYM: Jehovah-Tsebaoth.
MEANING: The Lord of Hosts.
FUNCTION: God the Mighty in Battle.
PURPOSE: Holy General; Divine Commander-in-Chief.

SYNONYM: Jehovah-Nissi.
MEANING: The Lord is Conqueror.
FUNCTION: Divine Banner of Victory.
PURPOSE: Triumphant Master over all adversity; Shelter in the Storm.

SYNONYM: Jehovah-Shalom.
MEANING: The Lord is Peace.
PURPOSE: God of serenity.
FUNCTION: Father of Tranquility.

SYNONYM: Jehovah-Shamah.
MEANING: The Lord is There.
FUNCTION: Omnipresent God.
PURPOSE: God of stability.

SYNONYM: Jehovah-Raah.
MEANING: The Lord our Shepherd.
FUNCTION: Gatherer of All Nations and Peoples.
PURPOSE: Ever-loving Father of All nations and Peoples; Divine Enforcer of Racial Unity and Equality; Holy institutor of Ethnic and Cultural Diversity.

Welcome to the ready reference guide to God's names of performance, with each name displaying variance in criteria, function and purpose, with supportive scriptural texts provided for comprehensive study, absorption, retention and spiritual enhancement. Experience God's nature as revealed by His Names; The only prayer tool drenched with divine catalytic elements driven by holy abilities that speedily convey our prayers and supplications to the throne room of God, boomeranging them to us, laden with performance power. Utilize them and be blessed by The Ancient of Days.

The Name 'Yahweh/Jehovah'.

This synonym of God denotes His spiritual nature and divine status as:
(1) The Great I Am.
(1) The Divine symbol of authority.
(2) The Holy source of final verdicts.
(3) The everlasting hand of assistance and protection.
(4) The mighty hand of deliverance from divers bondage.
(5) The Divine settler of disputes.
(6) The only subduer of all powers in words and in deed.
(7) The sole and authentic symbol of The Godhead, and highest universal authority.
(9) The self-sufficient and self existent God.
Scriptural reference: (Genesis 2:4; 13:4; 21:33.) (Exodus 3: 13 &14.)

The Name 'Elohim'.

This synonym of God denotes His spiritual nature and divine status as:
(1) The Divine Father of blessings and bounty.
(1) The only source of everlasting goodness.
(2) The possessor of limitless abilities.
(3) The spiritual guide to a life of fullness.
(4) The reflection of Divine majesty and power.
(5) The eliminator of all evil and suppression.
(6) The crippler of the wicked and their devices.
(7) The spiritual embodiment of the Trinity.
(8) The Divine replenishing vessel for the rejected, forgotten and needy.
       Scriptural reference: (Genesis 1: 28; 17: 3&6; 30: 17,18, 22 & 23.)

The Name 'El-Shaddai'.

This synonym of God denotes His spiritual nature and divine status as:
(1) The eternal symbol of self sufficiency.
(2) The eradicating instrument of negative obstacles and stumbling blocks.
(3) The breaker and reverser of curses.
(4   The realtor of goals and dreams.

(5)   The purest source of reliance.

(6)   The Divine source of revelation power.

(7)   The spiritual hand of fulfillment and constancy.

(8)   The supreme tote and propeller of good fortune.

(9)   The initiator and keeper of covenants and promises.

(10)   The Divine accelerator of conquests, and guarantor of triumphs.

(11)   The Divine incubator of success, and eliminator of failures.

(12)   The purest and enduring divine source of affluence.

(13)   The Divine source of all honor and power.

Scriptural reference: (Genesis 17: 1-9, 19 & 21) (Hebrews13:8)

The Name 'Elyon'.

This synonym of God denotes His spiritual nature and status as:

(1)   The Divine embodiment of praise and worship.

(2)   The possessor of heaven and earth.

(3)   The God and creator of the universe.

(4)   The Name above all names.

(5)   The ultimate spiritual source of universal ownership.

(6)   The sole and authentic praise worthy God.

(7)   The awesome and adorable one true God.

(8)   The one and only supreme God.

(9)   The most loved Deity.

(10)   God Most High.

Scriptural reference: (Genesis 14: 18 - 20)

The Name 'Repheka'.

This synonym of God denotes His spiritual nature and status as:

(1)   The Divine healer of infirmities.

(2)   The Great physician of yore.

(3)   The rejuvenating and replenishing vessel of defective body parts and organs.

(4)   The reverser of clinical death sentences, through the Divine remission of diseases.

(5)   The Divine possessor, supplier, and acquisition source of unknown antidotes and remedies for the ailing.
(6)   The designer of all anatomy and expert forensic.
(7)   The Divine diagnostic source of all hidden maladies of the human body.
(8)   The river of Divine healing.
(9)   The ultimate storehouse of health and vitality.
(10) The unfailing hope of *mankind. (All humans)
(11) The Divine source of all life.
(12) The sole holy authority and Divine dispenser of eternal life after death.
(13) Bread of life.
Scriptural reference: (Exodus 15: 25&26) (Isaiah 53:5) (John 3:14 &15.)

The Name 'Jireh'.

This synonym of God denotes His spiritual nature and status as:
(1)   The sole source of Divine providence.
(2)   The allocator and realtor of wealth.
(3)   The Divine bestower and sure guide to prosperity.
(4)   The sacred stock reserve and controller of all profitable mergers and acquisitions.
(5)   The ultimate furnisher of titles and status' of prominence.
(6)   The Holy outfitter of wealth and honor.
(7)   The restorer of lost assets and store house of abundance.
(8)   The supplier of needs.
(9)   The only virtuous and Divine universal Chief Executive Officer of all prospective assets, accounts, and resources.
(10) The sole spiritual channel of eternal amplitude.
Scriptural reference: (Genesis 22:1-14.) (Psalm37:23-25.) (2Corinthians 9: 8,11&15.) (Luke 22:35).

The Name 'Tsidqenu'.

This synonym of God denotes His spiritual nature and status as:
(1)   The Divine avenger of the wronged.

(2) The giver of closure, to lost causes and painful experiences.

(3) The sacred pacifier of troubled Hearts and minds.

(4) The sanctified settler of doubts.

(5) Lover of principle, and despiser of immorality.

(6) The holy disbanding force against all corrupt leadership.

(7) The sacrosanct and ever wise adjudicator of mankind.

(8) The supreme hand of justice.

(9) The pure and holy source of all righteousness.

(10) The Divine paragon of freedom, justice, and equality.

(11) The ultimate and Divine source of recompense.

Scriptural reference: (Psalm 19: 1), (Matthew 6: 26, 28-30), (Jeremiah 23: 1,2,3,6, 11&12).

The Name 'Tsebaoth'.

This synonym of God denotes His spiritual nature and status as:

(1) The supreme embodiment of all leadership.

(2) The vanquisher of all crisis.

(3) God the Mighty in battle.

(4) The King of glory.

(5) The Divine overcomer of all anguish.

(6) The spiritual forerunner and decisive vessel in times of evil and adversity.

(7) The Divine eliminator of fear and uncertainty.

(8) The ultimate spring of courage and boldness.

(9) The supreme subduer, silencer, and Divine eradicator of all wrongful opposition. (10)The sole Divine authority and effector of veritable submission.

(11) The mighty fortress and sure defense.

(12) The strongest deliverer.

(13) The Lord of Hosts.

Scriptural reference: (Joshua 5:13-15.) (1Samuel 1:11; 17: 45-47.) (Psalm 84:12.) (Isaiah 2: 12; 14: 27; 28: 29; 31:5; 37:16; 44:6.) (Romans 9: 29.) (James 5:4).

The Name 'Nissi'.

This synonym of God denotes His spiritual nature and status as:
(1)   The sovereign spiritual embodiment of all conquest.
(2)   The Divine banner of victory.
(3)   The eternal presence of power and victory.
(4)   The ultimate standard of Divine authority.
(5)   The sole prevailing power over all adversity.
(6)   The spiritual source of insurmountable protection.
(7)   The Divine and progressive source of direction.
(8)   The prevailing source of refuge, and fortification during physical attacks and crisis.
(10) The reverent and constant banner of love.
(11) The ultimate Divine shelter in the storm of life.
Scriptural reference: (Exodus 17: 1-16*) (Numbers 2: 2), (Psalm 20: 5), (Song of Solomon 6: 4).

The Name 'Shalom'.

This synonym of God denotes His spiritual nature and status as:
(1)   The Divine embodiment of ultimate peace.
(2)   The endowment of Divine freedom.
(3)   The Divine reliever of stress.
(4)   The provider of sleep.
(5)   The Divine source of calm and serenity.
(6)   The Divine river of soothing and calming waters.
(7)   The ultimate power of stability and resettlement, during crisis.
(8)   The Divine channel of solace for the mind, soul and body.
(9)   The sure and present source of repose and reassurance during national and personal crisis.
Scriptural reference: (Judges 6: 4, 5, 8-10, 23-24) (Psalm 119:165) (Isaiah 55:7-13) (Luke 10:2-6) (Romans 15: 33) (1Corinthians1:3) (Ephesians 2: 13&14) (1Thessalonians 5: 23)

The Name 'Shamah'.

This synonym of God denotes His spiritual nature and status as:
(1)   The ever-present God.
(2)   The faithful companion of the lonely.
(3)   The sure and present aid for the troubled.
(4)   The friend of the friendless.
(5)   The Divine source of endless sustenance.
(6)   The spring of living waters.
(7)   The bread of heaven.
(8)   The ancient of days.
(9)   The unseen guest at every meal.
(10) The silent listener to every conversation.
(11) The eliminator of all anxiety.
(12) The ultimate booster of mankind's*(humans) morale.
(13) The Divine infuser of all confidence.
(14) The supreme and sole spiritual source of reliance.
Scriptural reference: (Ezekiel 48:35), (Genesis 14: 18-19), (2Samuel 6: 12-19), (Jeremiah 3: 17), (Revelation 21).

The Name 'Raah'.

This synonym of God denotes His spiritual nature and status as:
(1)   The embodiment of love and protection.
(2)   The authentic source of Divine parenthood.
(3)   The sole Divine protectorate of all people.
(4)   The endowment pool of unconditional love.
(5)   The caring master of all beings.
(6)   The spiritual guide to all righteousness.
(7)   The restorer of hurting souls.
(8)   The comforter of the heavy in heart.
(9)   The spiritual guide to all who stray from the path of virtue.
(10) The Divine resistance of people in difficulties and crisis.
(11) The Divine eliminator of fear and uncertainty.
(12) The nurturing mother figure.
(13) The endowment source of eternal salvation through Christ Jesus His only son.

(14) The Divine source of security, protection and credibility against slander, harassment, discrimination and abuse.

(15) The pure and everlasting reservoir of spiritual and Divine anointing.

(16 The restorer of joy in times of distress.

(17) The solemn and total embodiment of goodness, grace and mercy.

(18) Divine nourishment for the hungry soul.

(19) The Divine and immaculate lover, adorer, and protector of children.

(20) The good shepherd

Scriptural reference: (Psalm 23), (John 10: 27-28), (Psalm 147: 5), (Genesis 48: 15), (Genesis 49: 24), (Psalm 78:71), (Isaiah 40:11), (Jeremiah 31: 10), (Ezekiel 37: 24), (John 10: 11, 14 & 16), (Revelation 7: 17), (Hebrews 13: 20-21).

Holy holy holy, Lord God Almighty
Early in the morning my song shall rise to thee
Holy holy holy, thou art most Merciful and Mighty
My Lord God in three persons
The Blessed Trinity.
Holy holy holy, dearest Lord God Almighty.
All thy works shall praise thy name on earth and in the skies above.
Yes! the seas will break waves that echo its greatness.
The Cherubim and Seraphim bow before thy throne in eternal worship
For thou w'ert and art and evermore shalt be Lord of all.
Holy holy holy, I hail you my Lord God Almighty
together with all the Saints I adore thee while I live
and will join them in death as they
cast down their golden crowns around the glassy sea
Holy holy holy, merciful and mighty
God in three persons
Blessed Trinity
Holy holy holy, Lord God Almighty
Though sinful men may never see or acknowledge thy glory
My lips shall proclaim none other but thou as Holy
For I know and believe that besides thee there's none other
As perfect in love, in power and in purity as thou art.
Amen.

(Words adapted from my favorite Hymn.)

Chapter three

Praying in tongues: How essential and beneficial a tool is this unique gift towards effective prayer?

Praying in tongues. Also known as the baptism of the Holy Spirit, is the fervent desire and sure or prospective ability of many a born-again Christian in the world today. However, if you never speak in tongues that is; in an unknown language inspired by the Holy Spirit, God's love for you will remain the same and your soul will nonetheless be transported into heaven by Angels when you pass on, as long as you have received Jesus Christ in your heart as your Lord and Savior. Dear reader, can we then safely assert that the gift of tongues is not that big a spiritual deal? Of course not. Why? Because, it has its spiritual role and place as a prayer tool in our Faith to grant you and I direct oratory, as well as communicable access to God, surpassing all Human comprehension. The word of God makes this clear in the following passage: "For he that speaketh in an unknown tongue speaketh not unto men, but unto God: for no man understandeth him; howbeit in the spirit he speaketh mysteries." (1Cor. 14: 2 KJV). Personally, I term speaking in tongues as the extra, or the bonus given to believers after salvation. However, not everyone has this bonus, and I believe not everyone will have it because of the varying levels of the desire and praying for its acquisition among believers.

At the place and time of salvation, the Holy Spirit which is a Divine personality sent from the throne of God, is dispatched to live inside you. The function of the Holy Spirit is to comfort, guide, instruct and convict you as you live in Christ, into all righteousness. I believe fervently that, the Holy Spirit achieves and carries out its Divine purpose, with its divine component that I call the 'Christ conscience' which operates at the forefront of one's regular conscience, sifting through decisions, thoughts and actions, relayed to it by the regular conscience, for the Holy Spirit to process by distilling and clarifying them into pure thoughts, before relaying them back to the regular conscience, all convicted and purified. The latter (the regular conscience), is easily contaminated and susceptible to evil tendencies without the constant monitoring and pure convicting nature of the 'Christ conscience' which is a direct component of the Holy Spirit. (I hope you got that.) As explained earlier in this book via the Word of Truth, when God made man in His own image and likeness, He gave him a conscience to guide him. But after his fall in the Garden of Eden, God the Father decided to furnish man with a spiritual backup; the Holy Spirit, but only made it available to man upon total surrender of 'the old man' through repentance in Christ, to act as a lens of some sort for the regular conscience by sifting through the debris of negativities it harbors working with the 'Christ conscience' respectively, that dwells within it as the sifting chamber. Thus leaving bad or evil thoughts hard to process into live negative ideas and actions of evil and destruction by the regular conscience, for man to physically carry out. (This spiritual finding sheds light as well as emphasizes the authenticity of Christ's existence in the beginning of creation, that many doubt and challenge in the world today.) You can now realize how vulnerable to sin one's life would be guided only by the regular conscience. Sin exhibited or portrayed in this state of existence (with a mind controlled solely by the regular conscience) spans from that of a conscience plunged into the infectious state of unbelief,(which is a sin in our Faith), to that which is seared to sin, leading to its susceptibility to engage in high crimes and adverse deeds. Therefore, do not be surprised if a very successful, respected or very nice mannered person is termed a persistent sinner. Because sin has many faces and is manifested in divers degrees.

To receive the gift of speaking in tongues, you must acquire as well as possess a fervent belief and a strong yearning laced with unequivocal conviction devoid of all doubt. This criteria of spiritual mindedness propels the Holy Spirit into furnishing you with utterance whereby, the gift is orally manifested. However, some Christians have cheapened and robbed this unique gift of the Holy Spirit of all it's spiritual depth and authenticity by speaking falsely and orally projecting fake uttering under pressure to fit in with other believers. I have found out as a Christian that, this sort of blasphemy has been incubated by the persistent yet untimely laying on of hands at spiritual gatherings on nouveau Believers who are not able to, or even spiritually ready to possess the gift because they lack the understanding, the desire, the zeal and the belief that propels its forthcoming. Most of these believers, fall under the category of the newly saved, who ignorantly expect to have the gift as automatically and as quickly as the Holy Spirit was dispatched to them at the juncture of salvation. My life of experience in the Lord, which is almost two score years of walking in His statutes and learning of Him, stumbling and recovering my spiritual footing, and my personal experience in said arena, has led me to this conclusion as well as suggestion. I strongly but humbly suggest the ardent teaching of the substance, nature and benefits of acquiring the gift of the baptism of the Holy Spirit, instead of practicing the former, that is laying on of hands, in order to enhance the comprehension, that fuels the growth, maturity and ultimate blooming of the bud of belief and yearning in the non-tongue speaking Christian, so as to propel it into full bloom. Church leaders should also allow and encourage members to go through that spiritual metamorphosis themselves, only after they have been fed the appropriate dosage of the serum of comprehensive belief and desire-propelling spiritual nourishment, by way of relevant Bible study and teaching within that specific criteria. I never had the chance; but wish this for others, for the growth and greater good of the Church of Christ.

Speaking in tongues should in no way and under no circumstance be falsified or induced under forcible carnal pressure from other Christians and Church leaders. I went through that experience and hated it; (there was too much pressure and too much force almost like a sort of oppression which made me cave in (when I saw everyone uttering except myself) and just utter falsities just to be left alone from the constant screaming in my ears and pounding on my head.) Thus, I was left alone with a haunting sense of falsity, deception, and guilt within myself which affected my faith and relationship with God, instead of being strengthened yet again by its acquisition into Christian growth. It was the single most unsettling and worse experience I had church-wise; yes I hated it that's why I am writing about it; and I know there are others who feel the same way that I do, or have felt this way but are afraid to expose themselves for fear of not fitting in with the Christian crowd; but I live for Christ and not for mortals.

Trust me; you are better off not speaking in tongues, than speaking falsely. For every time you fake it, you distance yourself from God and mock the Trinity. In God there is no force, but freedom and liberty of authentic spiritual expression especially when it comes to speaking in tongues. Thus to this day I do not speak in tongues due to my excruciating experience as a young Christian, which deadened and twisted my desire, yet I am spiritually, as well as scripturally fit to square it off on the divine canvas of conquest with any adversity that puts me to the test, by praying with understanding; and as such have edified countless others in and outside the fold. Therefore do not be hasty in grading my place in Christ, or mistaken in your judgement of my scriptural depth, for I will nonetheless meet you, and you, and you in paradise. Thus, if you desire this gift of the Holy Spirit, then you must take on the additional task of fervently praying for its manifestation, while breathlessly yearning to receive it. You must also exercise spiritual patience by learning to wait on God, and not be hurried into its manifestation by the spirit of pride and covetousness simply because everyone else in your church possesses the gift.

Do not feed your starving ego with the concept of; "well, I should be the one endowed with this gift because, I have been in the Lord longer." Such thoughts projected into attitude and thereafter into action, are sinful in the eyes of God. His word of truth admonishes such behavior in (Gal.6:7) "be not deceived; God is not mocked: for whatsoever a man soweth, that shall He also reap." (KJV.) Learning tongues carnally certainly may result in severe consequences, as (Gal. 6:8) clearly states; that those who defy God's leadership and guidance in life, may end up making ill considered decisions, that may in turn adversely affect them in life. But those who lean toward God for direction, are swarmed with perpetual benefits from His eternal throne on high. "Trust in the Lord with all thine heart; and lean not unto thine own understanding. In all thy ways acknowledge Him, and He shall direct thy paths." (Prov. 3: 5&6 KJV). As a true believer, you must not regard yourself as too intelligent to yield to instruction as God's word demands. V.7 goes on to admonish us; "be not wise in thine own eyes: fear the Lord, and depart from evil." Relating this passage to our subject lesson, diverts us from the evil of falsifying the gift of tongues. Just think how rude this particular sin must be to God. As you are well aware, the gift of tongues is Holy Spirit induced. The latter being the Divine entity of the Godhead that functions primarily to instruct us unto all righteousness, and as such, endowing us with the spiritual intellect of heavenly dimensions and a mind of goodness. Thus falsifying this gift will mean leading and instructing the Holy Spirit, instead of vice-versa. Imagine how insulted a Brain Surgeon will feel when his patient tries to school and instruct him in neurology, and you will realize the point I am trying to put across. If perchance you are reading this book and are speaking such falsified tongues, please cease doing so immediately. Get down on your knees instead and beg for God's forgiveness and thereafter resolve to the right way to receive this gift. If you do not feel the need for its desire due to lack of spiritual comprehension and that of scriptural information/resources, which has in turn limited your apprehension of its abilities and benefits, start researching about its effect on your spiritual/ prayer life by finding out its vitality through biblical study and also by way of other scriptural publications relating to this subject matter from the general aspect of its spiritual acquisition to the specifics of its divine function and purpose. You may find a variety of books on the gift of tongues and also on the functions and purposes of the Holy Spirit at your local library's Religion section for lending, or at your local Christian family bookstore for browsing and purchasing. But I do believe that not all are, or will be endowed with the gift to speak in tongues. It is and will always remain a subject of great debate and controversy among Christians and non-Christians alike. But I am glad I comprehend the divinity of its acquisition, and believe that it is not for all to attain; for though I possess it not, I nonetheless am very contentedly rooted spiritually as well as scripturally in my walk with the Almighty as a Christian. Amen.

The new testament unfolds, as it reveals the practical and spiritual ministry of the only begotten Son of God, our Lord and Savior Jesus, The Christ and that of the Holy Spirit, so clearly to all who are willing to absorb the teachings of God through His word of truth. Jesus longs to baptize us all with the Holy Spirit; but it is our fervent desire and the magnitude of our belief, and the depth of our zeal that induces its spiritual incubation and physical manifestation. In (1Cor. 14: 39KJV). The apostle Paul instructs the Church as follows; "........................Forbid not to speak with tongues." This also sheds light on the fact that speaking in tongues is not necessarily a prerequisite for attaining the title Christian. When Jesus baptizes you with the Holy Ghost, you receive instant power from on high to function properly by walking in God's precepts. Paul depicted praying in tongues as an essential tool for self-edification. Thus he means that it is self-satisfying and beneficial more to the individual uttering it than anyone else. Hence it's irrelevance in securing one a more prestigious place in the eyes of God. " He that speaketh in an unknown tongue edifieth Himself." (1Cor. 14:4a) But what exactly is edification? I define it as; "The moral and spiritual act or attitude projected by an individual that serves to positively benefit one's self, as well as effecting the same, on others influentially by the exemplary depiction of good and positive outcomes." (ADA.) Speaking in tongues edifies you into greater faith whereby propelling you to focus on God, instead of on the circumstances surrounding you. Thus it has its place in our Faith. (1Cor.14: 2&18 KJV) The Bible further elaborates on the speaking of tongues; "For he that speaketh in an unknown tongue speaketh not unto men, but unto God: for no man understandeth him; howbeit in the spirit he speaketh mysteries. I thank my God that I speak in tongues more than ye all." That was Paul the apostle speaking to the Church at Corinth. This passage in scripture theologically depicts the possibility of some in the church, being able to manifest the gift of speaking in tongues, while others spoke less in tongues, or did not manifest the gift at all. Yet, they were still a church, spiritually united and wholly functioning in Christ Jesus, rightly dividing the word of truth. When you desire the gift of tongues and pray for it believing, then you must give substance to that belief by the potent injection of faith into the whole yearning process in order to receive your gift. If it does not happen, then you are not meant to have it.. that's my take on this subject. You may argue it out and discuss it within your Book Club; it should be fun and very interesting as well as edifying. God bless you.:)

Speaking in tongues as I define it is; "The outpouring of profound spiritual utterance, infused by the power of the Holy Spirit into a believer who in turn spiritually projects it out of a fervent yearning, desiring, vessel drenched with the genuine belief and faith to receive its gift." (ADA) Yet a lot of Christians are using this Gift homogeneously by excluding the other Divine entities in the Trinity. They have also totally ignored the study of God's word because, they possess a higher feeling of accomplishment and that of an advanced spiritual height due to the Holy Spirit Baptism. To such believers, speaking in tongues is the ultimate goal in their Christian walk, and attaining it certainly climaxes their spirituality. They therefore use tongues to avoid praying with understanding, which actually takes a lot more than 'babbling', as it requires the fervent study of God's word of truth and the continuous acquisition of scriptural acumen. Thus they utilize their gift of tongues to avoid the very scriptural study that led them into its acquisition. As far as they are concerned, it is a well accepted 'Spiritual Detour'(SD.) to all their prayer needs, and that of Bible study. As a Christian, I have encountered dozens of believers who have vowed not to pray with understanding and have carried out this practice for decades. They are the Christians of the millennium who cannot pray when called upon in a gathering; who even upon endeavoring to do so, end up praying in tongues thus, edifying themselves and excluding all others. Some Christians use their gift of tongues to gain respect in the body of Christ, while others use their theirs to attain spiritual status and also to gain popularity in the fold. And I have to state that many a Christian women in the fold are attracted to men who exhibit such negative showmanship, thereby encouraging its incubation. Such weakness of the flesh, camouflaged in robes of spirituality, must be avoided at all times. It is a great sin against the Trinity and a blasphemy of immeasurable consequences which should be avoided in order to ensure a balanced footing in the Faith. "Search the globe for a firm and steadfast believer. And you will find one who spends time studying the word of truth and is not moved by circumstances but praises and talks to the Father in Psalms and hymns and in spiritual songs, laced with supplication and outpourings drawn from the very depth of their heart and soul; performing their one and only duty as adherents and defenders of the Gospel of Christ Jesus, by rightly dividing the word of truth." (ANQ)

The Bible teaches us that there is a time and place for everything (see: Eccl. 3:1-8) There is a time to speak mysteries, and a time to pray with understanding. And projecting one's faith and belief into effective prayer and ministry serves as a clear example. When you go out witnessing, you cannot knock on peoples doors and start babbling in tongues. Why? Because, carrying out your dutiful Christian ministry in such an unadvisedly manner, will result in a poor outcome. Either they respond to your call nervously by setting the family dog on you, or have you secured in a straight jacket by the appropriate authorities because of your uncontrolled and senseless racket. (Wow how funny, that was a rhyme wasn't it?) I guess my funny side just crept its way into this book.(giggle) Well, shall we continue with our lesson please. You see the Apostle Paul was quick and precise to realize and recognize that weakness in the church at Corinth. A weakness that renders some members in the fold to shift all their 'Spiritual Focus' (SF.) on one spiritual area unguardedly while ignoring the other areas. Thus creating chaos and disorder as a result. He reprimanded the church at that time saying; "let all things be done decently and in order." (see; 1Cor. 14: 40 KJV). As a child of God possessing the gift of speaking in tongues, you must also learn to trouble the other spiritual waters that flow concurrently with the Holy Spirit, which are; God the Father and God the Son; by bathing spiritually in their blessings and benefits respectively, or otherwise be rudely awakened one day to discover your faith and entire spirituality falling out of balance and spilling leaving you drenched in a great mess due to 'Wrongfully Applied Spirituality' (WAS.)

Now my dear reader in Christ, if you have this unique gift administered by the Holy Spirit, then may I humbly implore you to refrain from devaluing its potency by wrongful utilization and application, as a short cut to regular prayer because you find it easier to use than finding words of understanding and putting them together to make prayer sense. If you practice this habit continually, you will lose your praying capabilities altogether. Remember that when you go to God in prayer, you must enter His presence in an orderly fashion, armed with reverent outpourings of praise, worship, adoration and thanksgiving seducing Him with scripture by way of speaking it (scripture) with all boldness, 'Divine Accuracy' (DA.) and surety, while incorporating tongues where necessary, If you possess the gift. Also note that, it is always described as the 'gift' because not all will attain it. Yes! Some will prophesy, while others dream 'Dreams'. For the sum of all these spiritually endowed components projected within the body of Believers from The Father above, shall be the Holy manifestation of the sacred substance wholly within the Church of Christ. Amen.

David the psalmist is my favorite person in the bible because, despite His grievous shortcomings, like most or all of us mortals as we are, he knew how to talk to God in a way no one else in the Bible did. David was a being of scripture. He was consumed and embodied within it's substance. He also possessed the spotless ability and know-how of effectuating its potency by seducing God with it, and by interlocking God's word of truth together in a systematic yet spiritual format that always caught His attention. All God fearing people must always keep in mind that even though God is omniscient and has knowledge of our needs and desires before our requests hit His throne room and are conveyed to His feet of glory, He nonetheless longs to be asked; because, it makes Him feel known to us as the sculptor of our lives and needed by us as our Shepherd. A lot of religious skeptics, make this same criticism. They wonder why God does not provide for us automatically if He is so loving good and omniscient. Well, so are parents. They love their children and provide for them but they are always appreciative of the fact that they ask them for things that they are no doubt going to acquire for them anyway. This gives them a sense of being needed, as well as providing them with a sense of dependence from them as offspring and fulfillment from them as parents and providers. For example; it is more socially strengthening, acknowledging and enhancing to one's family relationship, if a child would ask his or her parents before opening a new video game package, and to accord them a sense of appreciation and gratitude, even though the package was intended for them. However, this expectancy does not render parents, incompetent and incapable of appropriate nurturing and love. Asking to receive, denotes respect and reverence, while opening up a sure avenue of assurance for future providence. It also demonstrates the acknowledgement of authority and headship on the part of the beneficiary for the benefactor, together with a sense of appreciation and value, by not taking parents love and provision for granted.

Therefore during certain needful circumstances, you must learn to cry out to God; wailing your supplications onto Him like David in (Ps. 25: 1-20 KJV) "Unto thee, o Lord do I lift up my soul. Oh my God, I trust in thee: let me not be ashamed, let not my enemies triumph over me..........................let integrity and uprightness preserve me: for I wait on thee." Keep this in mind dear reader in Christ; as much as the gift of speaking in other tongues is a beneficial component to effective prayer, it is in my opinion, and according to my scriptural findings an essential component to effective prayer during certain specific situations; but not a mandatory one. Being that, the potency, relevance and of course the spiritual depth and girth of your supplications are not adversely affected when conveyed to the prayer halls of heaven by way of praying with understanding. However, tongues are very effective in situations that call for prayers and proclamations of aggression. It is also very effective during healing and deliverance sessions where dark entities have to be eluded and confused before total riddance and eviction from their borrowed receptacles or abodes. When the need arises for 'Spiritual Ferocity and Aggression' (SFA) for during prayer tongues become the prayer tool that expedites the absolute eradication of said dark entities, hand in hand with aggressive scriptural proclamations poured out by way of praying with understanding. So you see, praying with understanding is effective during and under all praying circumstances, but praying in tongues has its limitations supplication-wise. As a Christian, you can live a full Godly life without this gift of the Holy Spirit, and yet be spiritually secure by not being adversely affected (by its absence from your spiritual life) as far as your place in Christ here and in eternity is concerned. However, it is a good 'Christian Asset' (CA) to attain spiritually. So, desire it, yearn for it, and get totally consumed by its attainment. It is a gift that not all will receive because the recipient of a gift should be deserving of it. Are you? Or do you think you can possess it by negotiating with the Holy Spirit? May be you are thinking about outsmarting the Holy Spirit by inventing and navigating your own 'Spiritual Detour' (SD) in order to expedite its acquisition; but how do you go about outwitting the sole divine source of all intellect? You tell me!

For the readers who possess the gift of tongues, I congratulate you in the Lord and offer a word of caution, please remember that because the adversary possesses a counter version of tongues, you must in all spirituality exercise caution and discernment as you pray in mysteries by totally focusing on God and immersing your whole being into Him at the time of prayer; as the slightest thought of negativity during such times can alter and derail one's tongues. Thus giving room to adverse contaminants in the form of strayed uttering invading your prayers. (in tongues.) On the other hand when you are fully focused, you are taken to higher heights of mysteries and growth in the baptism of the Holy Spirit whereby, your tongues are spiritually updated to denote your spiritual growth in the spoken mystery criteria. For the readers who truly desire this gift, beware of the luring and trappings of false Prophets. Do not allow just anyone to lay hands on you to receive the baptism of the Holy Spirit until you are sure of their 'Spiritual Grounding and Scriptural Credentials'. Which I term the (SGSC) clearance. As always, pray to God for the wisdom of discernment when you are confronted with such delicate choices and important decisions to make. You must realize that as a Christian or as Christians, our spirituality is measured by our 'Scriptural Credentials' and divinely bestowed intellect, as well as our exemplary lifestyle and virtuous choices. Which also fully compliments and equates our personal relationship with God. Once again you may realize that your only source of acquiring adequate and accurate information regarding a Prophet or a Minister or any person within the family of Believers, for the purpose of an (SGSC) clearance points and directly leads you to the word of God; which in all aspects of precision is The Word of Truth. " By their fruits, ye shall know them." (see: Mt. 7: 16)) It is said that we must not believe what we see in movies to be real. But some of what we see in movies are actually eye openers to the realities of life and also that of our lives spiritually.

If I can recall to your mind the movie 'Child's play' starring the possessed doll 'Chucky', if you watched that movie with your 'Spiritual Thinking Cap' (STC) on, and not as a regular horror movie fan, you would have realized that the most spiritually significant thing or focal point of that movie was how 'Chucky' could speak in adverse tongues that sounded so authentic, authoritatively spiritual yet demonic to the very core. Dear friend in Christ; are you speaking mysteries unto God, or have you been mystified into speaking other tongues induced by adverse powers mimicking God because of your arrogance, covetousness, self exaltation, big ego and 'Spiritual Pomposity' (SP)? As you pray for the gift of tongues or as you continue to edify yourself with this gift bestowed on you by the sacred component of the Trinity, do so in all Godliness and reverence. Rid your thoughts of all pride, arrogance and covetousness so that your status, as far as this spiritual gift is concerned, may be hidden and safeguarded forever with Christ in God the Father, and directed by the astute instruction of the Holy Spirit. Amen.

Here are some scriptural references for your research benefits and for the further apprehension of The Gift of Tongues.

John 7. 37-39 , 14. 16 & 17.
Acts 1: 8; 2: 1 – 4, 16 – 18, 38 – 39; 8: 12, 14 – 17, 9: 17; 10: 44 – 46; 19: 1 – 3, 6.
Luke 11: 11 – 13; 24: 49.

THE LORD'S PRAYER (The Model Prayer)

"But thou when thou prayest, enter into thy closet, and when thou hast shut the door, pray to thy Father which is in secret; and thy Father which seeth in secret shall reward thee openly. But when ye pray, use not vain repetitions, as the heathen do: for they think that they will be heard for their much speaking. Be not ye therefore like unto them: for your Father knoweth what things ye have need of, before ye ask Him. After this manner therefore pray ye";

"Our Father which art in heaven,
Hallowed be thy name.
Thy kingdom come.
Thy will be done in earth,
As it is in heaven.
Give us this day our daily bread.

And forgive us our debts, as we forgive our debtors.
And lead us not into temptation,
But deliver us from evil:
For thine is the kingdom, and the power, and the glory,
For ever. A-men."

(Read: Matthew 6: 6 –13 KJV.)

Chapter four

Angels; knowing and incorporating their ministry into your prayers.

Welcome to the chapter that enlightens your spiritual intellect and broadens your divine perspective on the most fascinating beings that God created aside of mankind.* what or who are Angels, and why did God create them? Why are they in existence, and what are their functions and purposes? Where and how do they fit in with our spiritual lives and most precisely our prayer lives? I know your mind is full of inquisitions of this nature, but if you will just be serene for one moment, I will walk you through the Angelic armory of prayers and supplications, as we reap the spiritual benefits of these beings that God created differently from humans to do His bidding, to perform specific duties, and to serve purposes, for our benefit. The key word that runs alongside the main subject of our discussion that you should keep in mind is the word, 'SUMMON'.

Mankind as the Bible refers to all humans; was created in the image and likeness of God. Angels on the other hand, were created in His purity and holiness for a pure purpose. They were there with Yahweh/Jehovah in pure existence before we were created. Genesis chapter 3 verse 24 served as their first introduction/debut in the word of God as follows: "So He drove out the Man; and He placed at the east of the garden of Eden *Cherubim, and a flaming sword which turned every way, to keep the way of the tree of life." Here in this scriptural passage, the Angel's first duty by way of function and purpose was revealed; first as guards, and then as protectorates of God's valuable asset, 'the Tree of Life'. But what are they really; these beings called Angels? They are celestial beings and visitants, who glide on spiritual pinions. They are completely perfect in their attributes of protection, knowledge, love, healing and solace devoid of individual personalities like human beings. Angels interact on both the spiritual and physical levels with great force and power, driven by legendary strength and the ability to take apparent form. Their basic purpose is to guide us in our walk with God. To which when we yield in obedience, helps us fulfill our quota in life. This they do as well as attending to their God-given assignment as protectorates, healers, guardians and boosters of morale. (see the movie: 'Angels in the outfield' starring Danny Glover and Tony Danza) it might give you an idea or enlighten your vision on these beings of pure light. Angels may also take human form for our pleasure. But mostly operate in specific functional and purpose driven groups called 'phyla'. Believing and praying for their assistance alone (a spiritual process of invocation that is referred to as "summoning" when referring to Angels,) propels their accessibility. It becomes the magnetic force that accelerates their attraction to the one praying for their assistance. Being in existence devoid of personalities and preferences, projects their purity which is depicted in their intense ability to love. Thus illuminating and expanding the embodiment of their purpose of protection and assistance.

Angels possess the closest identity to God, next to Christ, and the Holy Spirit. They are thus laden with pure thoughts and emotions that nurse no negative vices like rudeness and uncertain temperament. That is why the notion of the existence of a dark Angel could not be possible. Rather, there are dark forces. Angels reside in the heavens in utter bliss and perfect love. But may at times take human form in order to get in touch with or get through whatever feelings we may be conveying to them in our prayers. This enables them to perfectly guide and assist us appropriately and satisfactorily. Guardian Angels operate this way. Gliding between the blissful realms of heaven, and our adversely dense realm, the earth. Angels also represent all races on earth. They are therefore, an authentic depiction and reiteration of the pure embodiment of equality, perfection, and the peaceful co-existence of all races as God our creator intended, as they represent pure unity, strength and love and as such, carry out their duties devoid of racial bias, and discrimination when summoned or dispatched by a needful human and God respectively. This representation of racial equality without boundaries or restriction in Angelic ministry is exhibited by them in all purity by their ability to attend to humans of all color and ethnic origin because, within them exists a pure nature with no room at all for prejudice of any form or kind even though physically, they were created by God possessing different racial characteristics and perform different roles by way of functions and purpose phyla-wise. Thus, the probability of you being visited or served by an Angel bearing your very own racial characteristics is nil. Not possible. Which means if you are Caucasian you will be attended by a Black, Native American, Mexican, Asian or Eskimo Angels. You know your race and as such expect an Angel outside it. If you doubt God's law pertaining to this subject, then you are not of His fold and as such, whatever is attending to you is not of God, but from your own willful extraction.

This dear reader, is a Godly fact; and a true Child of God should have no problem with it. Which is why people who harbor adverse racial sentiments and detest those outside their race could never qualify as God fearing, as Children of God, or as Christians no matter how much they are loved and respected or revered on earth, and no matter how strong their affiliation with big Churches and renowned Men of God. For they are to God Almighty in opposition to His creation and an affront to His image and likeness, by their very thoughts and actions. Racism is therefore, an outright rejection of God's Supremacy and as such a capital sin in every Faith. The Bible teaches us that, if we do not love the people that we see on earth, how then can we profess to love God whom we have not seen so fervently. For our righteousness is like filthy rags before God. (See: 1John 4: 20&21 and Isaiah 64: 6) Let us not forget that we will be judged on love which is the embodiment of the very nature of the God we profess. (See: 1Corinthians13) The inspirationally gifted in song ministration Cheri Keagy, sings about loving and giving to each other as being 'what matters most' in our lives as children of God, in her album of the same title. I once heard someone on television compare having the disease Aids to being born 'Black'. I couldn't believe my ears. Very offensive to people of my descent, but more damning to the soul of the utterer. Yet, it may surprise others who think like this person that being born Black; of African descent was the best thing that ever happened to me. I love being an African and I am very proud of my Continent, culture and my people. I greatly treasure my roots and family tree which would have been totally impossible if I was born of another race. You see, God saw it fit to place me in Africa within my family. And chose for me, the parents he saw fit; and I say, He chose well for I am very content and comfortable with what I am, which is a human created in God's image and likeness; an African woman; A descendant from that great Continent of continents, from whose precious bowels 'nouveau great continents' of our era has enriched themselves; where The Lion of the Tribe of Judah; The root of David was chosen and drawn by the omniscient Lord God Almighty. What more can I ask for? Africa is to me the Greatest continent in riches, the source of civilization, awarded with being the birthplace of all mysteries pertaining to the beginning of creation and blessed with wealth and beautiful people with varying shades of bronzen, mahogany, and ebony rich dark skin tones with wooly hair that inspires endless creativity and transformation. A perfect variation in God's beautiful garden of racial diversity. Do not be afraid of the diversity we bring to the congregation of nations and peoples. Remember Child of God, "Embracing racial diversity is the foremost ticket to Godliness; for it proclaims God's Supreme Majesty as Father of all Creation." (ANQ) you cannot profess to serve Him if you think he has made a mistake for; "We all are one; the same person. I'll be you and you'll be me." Our great and gifted Songwriter, Philanthropist, and civil rights activist brother Jimmy Cliff, proclaims in song. Expect your Angel soon.

Angels are endowed with faces and skin tones that differ as that of people. But are completely identical in stature. They are also androgynous; without sexual distinctions of any kind. A characteristic that reflects the very aura of the pure innocence embodied within their very existence. As heavenly beings, they manifest tremendous beauty as very tall and stately beings exuding brilliance in the form of very radiant light. Angels may be distinguished by purpose and function. That is, by 'phyla' and by the tint or color exuberance on the tips of their wings. This same color is emanated around the outer fringes of their aura, in the form of a soft radiating but almost blinding glow, around them. This glow which is very luminous, is generally depicted above their heads by artists as a spherical disk popularly known as 'Halo'. Even though they are androgynous beings and may appear masculine or feminine, Angels possess no distinct genitalia; a characteristic that I term 'gender exemption', which once again exudes their embodiment of pure innocence and perfection to the core. Angels do not possess the merging abilities that other counter beings like dark forces and demons exhibit to perpetuate their own powers and enforce their reality; as this will greatly interfere with, as well as contaminate their sole existence of complete devotion and servitude of utter purity to God.

As messengers in human form, their presence is brief, but full of power and energy. God created them with wings for fast acceleration, during flight and transition. Another function of their wings is for our protection against harm and for encompassment during ministration to shield us from adversity and intrusion. (we will learn more about the function of Angel's wings further in this chapter.) Angels also work in tandem amongst themselves, and are the first to sense danger by awakening our instinct and also by alerting us with their voices. Thus acting as guides. These voices alert us in our minds and not our ears; the voices of instinct, if you may call them so. They also exude advanced divine telepathic abilities that project persuasion of the highest degree laced with the highest level of apprehension where our needs are concerned. Thus displaying their purposes of healing and love without our need to relay it to them. As such, the power and truth of what they are capable of imparting, must never be underestimated. As we continue this lesson, I will reveal to you how to derive spiritual benefit from this divine prayer tool and source that solely comprises sheer purity, by following these spiritual guidelines.

In order to summon Angels for aid and assistance, you must incorporate them into your prayers by requesting their presence from God, through our Lord and Savior Jesus Christ and your Heavenly Father God, will dispatch them to you expressly laden with gifts of aid and healing within their wings. For "Are they not all ministering spirits, sent forth to minister to them who shall be heirs of salvation" ? (see Heb. 1: 14KJV). And "Were they not created by the Almighty for our benefit to provide us with expedited aid in all purity and perfection as divine commuters, heavenly delivery personnel, couriers and spiritual 'gophers' of God, speedily dispatched and laden with tremendous gifts of love, aid, assistance, healing and protection, within their wings?" (ANQ) Angels also offer unconditional love. A characteristic only God Almighty can deliver without competition from any other counter sovereignty. Even as God made Angels to project this pure and loving nature, they exude no emotions and yet were nonetheless created by the same God to perpetually offer a pure and constant flow of love to mankind*. (humans) Angels have no life spans. For they have been in existence with God before we were created; even as Christ also was within the Father, as the divine component 'God the Son', of the Holy Trinity; until God deemed it crucial for Him to be sent in flesh to dwell amongst us. To take on the burdens of our sinful nature by dying for us, so that we through His precious blood shed for the remission of our sins, may by the sincere act of confession and shameless declaration of Him as Lord and Master of our lives, through utmost surrender, might die to sin and live for righteousness and by His stripes, secure healing of the body, mind and soul, now and hereafter. (See: Genesis 3: 22-24) Angels only exist to carry out God's purposes in heaven and on earth. Like the Archangel Michael (Warrior Angel) who fought with his Angels (The warring phyla) against the great red dragon when war and rebellion broke out in heaven. (See: Rev. 12: 7 – 9) Another Angelic instance in the Bible was about the three Angels, (Messenger Angels) who appeared to Abraham in human form to expressly deliver the message of the birth of The Son of Promise. See also: (Gen. 18: 1-14). (Notice first and foremost how Michael and his Angels carried out their duties as warriors of heaven for God very swiftly with great precision and brevity. Michael carried out his duties, together with other Angels assigned by God, possessing the same capabilities by function and purpose, known as phyla; all of whom are Archangels, with Michael at the forefront as the General executing their purpose with the swiftness of eagles. A very typical characteristic of Archangels. Also note and compare it with the sudden appearance of the three Angels unto Abraham. Observe the brevity with which they delivered their message together with their sure departure by way of body language. (V. 16) "And the men rose up from thence, and looked toward Sodom: and Abraham, went with them to bring them on the way." You must realize that, no matter what their function, purpose, and category depicts and dictates, Angels always carry out their mission driven by a pure force of love for mankind, and for God of course, whom they serve with unshifting devotion and unadulterated dedication. Their source of joy does not emanate from humor or self satisfying indulgence. But from the pure joy projected from the very essence of their being. Their level of intelligence is identical, but that of their strength and power is not. Even though they are all identical except two* of the angelic phyla. (you will learn about them as this chapter unfolds.) in their ability to traverse and transcend both heavenly and earthly realms to aid, calm, and to guide us as they fulfill their roles as divine couriers of the Trinity, we must understand as believers that, the word Angel itself denotes and substantiates all things that are immaculate, sacrosanct, pure and good. Therefore, the misconception of the existence of dark or evil angels, is totally false, irrelevant and unscriptural; As there are only dark forces who feign angelic characteristics which as children of God, we must be able to discern as long as we remain alert in dutiful submission, as well as in studious immersion to and within His Word of Truth.

Let us go back to the source of this misconception. Please turn your Bible to (Rev. 12: 7 – 9) paying expert attention on verses (7b, 8 & 9) KJV.

"...and the dragon fought and his angels, and prevailed not; neither was their place found any more in heaven. And the dragon was thrown out, that old serpent, called the devil, and satan which deceiveth the whole world: he was cast out into the earth, and his angels with him." Now allow me to dissect this passage of scripture for your comprehension once and for all as I am led by the Holy Spirit into all righteousness and wisdom. In the beginning, was an Archangel called Lucifer. He was the music director of the heavenly choir and of course in charge of songs and praise; who during his ministry as an Angel of God, grew strange feathers that were out of place, and thus were nonaligned with the ones created for him by God. These feathers of pride and self exaltation planted by the great deceiver after being allowed by Lucifer, contaminated this Angel's pure self; and thus led him into recruiting others for a 'coup d'Anges' if I might term it so or more precisely, a rebellion that led to war in heaven. Now, dear reader, let us go back to verse (7), which on the whole makes mention of the dragon twice, without mentioning the Angelic name 'Lucifer' for a special reason. You see, studying Theology on my Papa's knees as early as my formative years revealed to me that, this dragon was the same serpent in the garden of Eden, which deceived Eve into eating the forbidden fruit after which, God cursed it. From that moment onward the serpent became an adversary of God and all the goodness and purity His creation exudes in heaven and on earth. After all those centuries, that same old serpent grew bigger physically aging as well, with lies and deception; and spent all its time restlessly touring God's universe, on a destruction and contamination spree sowing seeds of corruption, deception and ruination, on its own until Lucifer an Angel of God, corrupted and contaminated his existence of purity, by allowing a merge into His pure self by the serpent (through pride, by wanting and assuming to be like God) who by now has grown older, bolder, and more cunningly and convincingly vile, with the dark plotting wisdom of centuries. Now as you will recall earlier in this chapter, I talked about merging abilities, not being a part of the Angel's characteristics, when created by the omniscient God; because of it's marring effect of contamination and corruption, of their very existence of purity.

We are also very much aware especially those of us who watch the national geographic channel, and the animal planet that, all the extremely or the very ancient of reptilian species bearing close resemblance to snakes, are termed dragons by Zoologists universally. So there it is; we have a great big dragon, (that serpent from the garden of Eden, now grown

71

older, developing toughened scales and features like horns and claws, ugly distorted and twisted over centuries) that gained access to heaven because a resident, an Angel of great position, broke the law of purity by allowing a mergence into its pure self. Thus transforming into the Devil itself. Right from that day, Lucifer together with his army of rebellious angels, lost their feathery wings for webbed ones. The latter lost together with their new master, their place in heaven due to their role and association to the evil cause, and were transformed into demons, imps, principalities, and powers of darkness. They did not fly or glide down on spiritual pinions as dark angels. No! No! No! They were cast down; remember this now and always. "Cast down" thrown out, in dishonor and shame as adversaries, and opposing evil entities. For they became the very embodiment of all evil and darkness. They lost their place in heaven because of pride, that progressed into self glorification, over confidence, and rebellion, as well as contamination of the worst sort by consorting with the old serpent to get back at God, which was followed by a great big fall from their divine height of pure distinction and power, to the dismal depths of desolation and degradation. Take note of how, the name Lucifer was less used as it changed to satan, the devil, the old serpent, the old liar, the great red dragon in the Bible, and also names like; the corrupter of justice, the great conniving manipulator and other character descriptive names in theological books. You will also realize the persistent use of the adjective 'old'. You may be wondering why? Because, satan has been there from the very beginning of sin using man and woman in the garden of Eden. The devil due to the androgynous nature of it's former self may manifest either as man or woman, and is capable of exhibiting flawless beauty, or project the most horrid appearance at will in a split second to confound the living, as well as accomplish fiendish and unbelievable feats to spiritually displace the Child of God who dares question its authority and power. It can also speak with multiple voices that mimic all life sources from the very young to the eldest of humans and animals of all types. Twisting the truth with lies to derail Men of God and Exorcists. But after all these showmanship, it loses and only gains power when we stray from our God-driven paths and allow a contamination through continuous sin. And unnecessary indulgence in sources and avenues that trigger its adverse yearning to thrive. But thanks be to God for His love and His word of truth that continuously guides us back into the sheepfold of light when we stray from the verdant pastures of Godly teachings and scriptural discipline; Yes thanks be unto God The Father, Jehovah-Nissi the Conqueror of yore, who furnishes us with ultimate victory through our Lord Jesus Christ. Now will you ask the Lord to endow you with the divine ability to absorb what you have read so far, before we proceed into deeper Angelic teachings by saying a short prayer on your very own? Talk to God as a friend; He is waiting for He longs to hear from you. Thank you.

From the preceding paragraph, we as Christians can learn a few spiritual as well as scriptural values that, light cannot dwell with darkness, on any occasion or at anytime. This is quite simple. Either your light is on, or you resolve to stay in the dark. The devil only gains total power and control over your life, if you grant him access through the entertainment and conscientious indulgence in wicked practices and negative vices devoid of repentance and remorse, overblown with arrogance, and pride. We must realize that since the old liar, satan and his army were all once Angels, who had no life spans because they lived no lives, they are still out there as long as the Gospel is spreading, and people are accepting the Lordship of Christ, and are yearning to know more about Him, while striving to live according to His Statutes, as they patiently await the blessed hope of His glorious appearing. (see the movie: "The devils advocate"; starring Al Pacino and Keanu Reeves.) And please do not fail or hesitate as a Child of God to educate yourself with selective movies that contribute positively to awaken your spiritual intellect about the darkness of this world, by the imparting of valuable information as you research spiritually as well as scripturally. Just keep your spiritual antennae up and you will pick up those valuable and informative frequencies to edify yourself as well as others in the Fold. Do not for a second take some movies with spiritual streaks lightly. Keep your spiritual antennae up or upgrade it with one of higher divine frequency by extensive scriptural research and studies. Arm yourself in the spirit. Do not lose grounds because the adversary never rests. I will also like to reiterate that, the adjective 'dark' that usually precedes the adversary and his demons denotes their purpose, actions and mission of evil and wickedness; and not their physical appearance. Also bear in mind that, after the rebels were cast out of Heaven they landed on earth deceiving men into corruption, oppression, mental and physical enslavement, and wars stemming from intense hatred, greed and prejudice. The adversary has done well in endowing men (his followers and worshippers) with unaccountable wealth and syndicates of worldly advocates to protect and aid them for fanning his limitless and wicked devices. But God has done excellently providing us His children, even better tools of divine guidance and fortification, for our protection and sustenance. We must also remember that, after merging with the dragon, Lucifer and his band of rebellious angels retained their outward characteristics of comeliness, but lost their Angelic names and titles including their pure nature of 'gender exemption', but twisted it so they can manifest however they please gender-wise.

Thus the adversary can either manifest as male or female. Very beautiful, handsome, ugly and vile. They also acquired the ability to merge into other beings, from the dragon they teamed up with. Thus, contaminating the normalcy of the lives of those people by a condition known in religious circles as 'possession'; a condition sneered upon and ridiculed by the adversary's agents amongst us, into confounding humans and planting the seed of deception, unbelief and doubt about the existence of evil beyond sin. This condition of possession which also manifests as well as mimics uncontrolled clinical psychosis of the rigorous and catatonic kind, as well as manic outbursts in some people, has many confounded and as such, has the adversary grounded in promoting its dark devices, while devout Priests and seasoned Men of God, who expose and weaken him through exorcism are pushed further and further into the mocking realms of utter ridicule and dishonor, only to most times find themselves labelled within the outlandish category of medieval spiritual wackos. I must admit that some of these troubled and sick people or patients respond to medical science very well by consistently undergoing expert professionally monitored drug treatment and psychotherapy. But a majority, I am afraid are hospitalized for life purely because their ailments are spiritually rooted and are as such, outside the medical professional's area of expertise. This is not because they are not good at their profession, God forbid; (I believe and strongly support medical science. Heck! I have several accredited Physicians in my family who are accomplishing great feats helping the sick in their specialties by God's Grace.) but because, these people have a spiritual problem, which is the reason why I used the term "troubled" (with a spirit) as well as "sick" (with an ailment or disease) respectively. The sick need healing, but the troubled must be liberated; set free from the entity that bothers them. Amen? (see; The movie; "The exorcist" starring; Linda Blair and also, "the possession" starring; Timothy Dalton.) Some of these people are also released to families who do not know what to do with them. Thus, we have people walking this earth who have spent their whole lives in bondage to strange infirmities that have no medical classification, definition and diagnosis. Who within the highest probability, may be possessed by dark entities. While at the same time, we have people depicting the best personalities, and calm outward appearances who extraordinarily, intellectually and successfully have answers and explanations for every wrong they do, while artfully and doggedly, by manipulation and cunning, are able to wriggle their way out of all the evil and chaos propagated by their very hands, causing the innocent to pay for their wrongdoings. These sort of people, I term 'agents' of the old dragon. Because they dedicate their entire lives, fanning, contributing and reveling in the negatively concocted and instigated devices of the adversary. But thanks be to God; for His limitless providence towards us through His holy word that protects and furnishes us with wisdom and knowledge, while keeping us in the full posture of spiritual alertness, to rightly study and divide His word of truth. I thank God also for providing us with the Holy Spirit, who instructs us into all righteousness and sagacity, while convicting us and morally purging us. All praise be unto His name for according us the ultimate sacrifice through His Son our Lord and Savior Jesus Christ, who divinely purchased us with spiritual currency, by the shedding of His sacred Blood, that garnishes the top of this spiritual sundae, bursting with scriptural sweetness. Let us thank God for His throngs of Angels waiting to be dispatched, like the colorful sprinkles on top of a desert waiting to be savored as heavenly ambassadors, ready to do His bidding in our favor, while operating under the purity and perfection of His divine tutorship and leadership.

Angels are the pure component of the material that compliments our complete divine armor in the Faith. That is why we must learn to form the spiritual habit of adorning ourselves with them the right way, in order to receive adequate protection as we journey through this dense world. We must also be alert as believers by remembering that, we openly declared war on the devil the moment we accepted Christ; and that, he will definitely stay alert for centuries writing his counter spiritual dissertation with which he proposes to perpetually harm and confuse us; God's Children. But by the power vested in us as Heirs of the Father, and joint Heirs with the Son, we will fight him with the Light and with Truth. For "God has not given us the spirit of fear, but of power and of love, and of a sound mind." (see 2Timothy 1:7 KJV) Let us continue our lesson on Angels please; During visitation, Angels do not come in singles but in throngs of tens and of thousands, and in flights and bands; traversing by order of phyla, which is; (categorically by function and purpose), depending on the type or nature, urgency and gravity of the situation at hand. A clear example is the visitation of Archangel Gabriel to Zechariah and Mary respectively in

(Luke 1: 5 – 80). And to the Shepherds in the fields at night heralded by a band of Angels. (See: Luke 2: 8 to 15) Angel Gabriel also appeared unto Daniel alerting him about the end time prophecy (see: Daniel chapters 8 & 9). He also appeared to Gideon under the Oak of Ophrah. (see also: Judges 6: 1 – 22) exhibiting its function as the Archangel in charge of Heavenly communications. "If you summon them, they will come." The stunning fact about summoning Angels is that, one must apprehend the fact that, they are many in number; functioning for specific situations and clearly carrying out missions for definite purposes. As such, the summoner (you) should be well equipped with the knowledge of which one to call for what function, and to what purpose. You should nonetheless be perceptive of the physical characteristics of each and every one of them, in order to identify, reap, as well as spiritually savor the benefits of their existence in its complete totality. Shall we now take an in-depth look into the realm of Angels, as characterized by their phyla*. As in category or level? Thank you.

Guardian Angels.

Guardian Angels are the most populous category of Angels. Existing in their trillions, which precisely renders them utterly countless in number; thus making them the most likely category or phyla by way of probability to first manifest in your life as a Child of God. They are commonly referred to by humans as, 'Angels'. They in all physicality and spirituality, radiate the love and glory of the Holy Spirit in comeliness and are of course "gender exempt"; appearing by manifesting pure brilliance in white light that is almost fluorescent yet dreamy in nature. This same light emanates from their white silver tipped wings, as well as outlining and revealing an underlying beauty from within. They shine with the brilliance of the sun. And may be closely likened unto the softened but jeweled purity of the pearl.

Their purpose.

They carry out their purpose as guards for humans by protecting us at night when we sleep, as they fixedly and devoutly watch over us during this time when our bodies are at rest, motionless, and at their most vulnerable. Guardian Angels may not be summoned but prayed to because, they are always around and at their most perkiest at night as we are most susceptible to physical and spiritual harm at this time. Yet they are effectively active at other times as well. Their primary purpose is to protect us. And they will go to intense extremities to fulfill that obligation. The most amazing thing about Guardian Angels is that, they have the ability to transform (not merge). An ability that other categories of Angels do not possess. A Guardian Angel can wrap itself by divine ectoplasmic means around a human being ejected from a fatal car wreck by inertia, leaving him or her inexplicably unscathed. They also possess tremendous power of agility and can move massive objects from harms way, just to fulfill their divine purpose. For example; a Guardian Angel may lift a skyscraper or a huge building away from the path of a highly destructive tornado, and lift cars away from the paths of fatal accidents. All these powerful feats are carried out by them with the precision of divine molecular disbursement on earth; a realm far denser in terms of adversity environmentally, as well as spiritual negativities, than their natural heavenly habitat.

Their dutiful purpose is driven by the Divine Power of God the Father, the Holy Conscience of God the Son, and the 'Spiritual Intellect'(SI) and credentialed astuteness of God the Holy Spirit, to guide and aid them with Divine power of such magnitude as can only be conveyed by the Holy Trinity itself. Guardian Angels are also the heavenly beings that protect children, by relaying pure links of attraction because of what they both have in common; which is in the form of pure innocence of mind and that of the body. A relationship that I have witnessed first hand, by the Grace of the Almighty.

When my Early childhood business commenced in the summer of '99, everything was slow. I opened my home for business with two infants; a boy and a girl. The former was almost seven months old and the latter a little over a year. After a couple of weeks into the business, i started feeling this strange coziness in the primary childcare area, which was situated on the lowest level of my home. A coziness that I can almost describe as engulfing and comforting, and was always accompanied by extreme excitability in the little ones. Thinking that they might be feeling uncomfortable at the time, I would at times check the vents or turn the air condition thermostat up a bit. I also sometimes, wondered if the weather outside had gotten more humid. I must reiterate that I always kept the thermostat at the most comfortable, constantly without tampering with it, and that is why

I wondered at the time if I was experiencing hot flashes at an early age. (I mean) I thought about everything. But never for once did the thought strike me to look lower into the faces of my two tiny companions or to even associate their random giggles and hand waving to anything spiritual. I must admit that they became excessively active when the coziness was present, but all the while I was leaning on my own understanding trying to professionally fix things for their comfort.

This went on for about two weeks and on the Wednesday of the third week, the younger one of the two who was very lazy most of the time, did something out of the ordinary. He started crawling, faster than usual towards the rear exit; as he got about two feet to the door, he stopped and effortlessly stood up in a funny way with his chubby hands in the form of a clasp as if someone was aiding him by hand. He did all this looking hopefully up as far as his little neck could stretch; the older baby then dashed over there almost knocking me out of the way with excitement while casting a similar upward glance at the door. I joined them at the rear exit, and quickly pulled up the blinds hoping to spot an intruder if there was any, just then the older one muttered a sad "uh oh" and instantly burst into tears as if someone had trampled on her toy but to my surprise, she resumed to her happy self almost as fast as she got upset, laughing with glee after I moved out of her way. I must admit that I was a little bit baffled but then again, I said to myself; "well, they are just being themselves; they probably saw a butterfly, a bird, or something that I could not see like a bug on the rug or something crawling on the glass panel door. I then quickly brushed the whole incident aside, or "stacked it into the toy chest" if you will. I wondered what it was all about when they made that corner their play spot the ensuing days. Don't laugh when you read that I even thought about setting a plate of goldfish crackers and pear juice out there for whoever the summer time Santa Claus was. Then on a fine day appointed by the Lord of Hosts, the light of the whole matter was revealed to me during a phone conversation with to my baby sister Alexandra; A prophetess of God. "Well, she retorted, after listening to my story. "Have you considered the presence of Angels"? Just then, the thought struck me, as I recalled little things that had occurred at the daycare, centering on the recreation room and also the rear exit. I remembered the constant cheer exhibited by the little ones in my care, and the absolute cessation of one's colic symptoms, coupled by other positively inspiring developmental progress and adequate responsiveness that I in turn received from the little ones, as they alerted me to the presence of Guardian Angels in home.

I knew then and there that, they had permanently pitched their tent because of the children. I also realized in truth that, they inhabited the house in large numbers because of the constant pitter patter of little feet, commuting in and out of it for care when parents and guardians are at work. I resolved to be more spiritually alert and receptive from then on to this day, according Angels a special place in my prayer life. I hope you do the same; for you too will be blessed tremendously by incorporating them by function and purpose into your spiritual life. For they love to serve our needs as God the Father intended.

Communicating / Ministering Angels.

Each of us is assigned a Ministering Angel, serving us privately and Individually. Yet, these personal Angels can also be sent or asked by us to aid and protect others who need them. All we have to do is to ask God the Father and more will be dispatched. There are at least five or six Angels of this phyla(Ministering) around one individual at a given time. But a spiritually conducive environment is extremely essential for their manifestation. Ministering Angels are God's helpers; couriers who deliver aid to us in this world of uncertainties and strife. They are telepathic and as such, can hear our voices without verbal utilization or exuding audible sound. Their powerful presence alone becomes our source of calm, protective shield and healing. They are also body language communicators endowed with the divine ability to read our thoughts; but only with our full permission. That is, when we give them access to our thoughts. This process of spiritual auto transmission becomes a consistent pattern of communication between us and them; rendering the act of verbalizing our thoughts to them totally unnecessary. Ministering Angels are easier to access by way of communication than Guardian Angels who are perpetually laden with bigger itineraries as guards and guides of our lives. They tend to be extremely occupied with their primary business, which chiefly involves the intensive responsibility of commuting back and forth from one realm to the other while keeping a sharp eye out for us in case we stray from our God given paths. They also spend most of their time relaying issues concerning our life's choices back and forth to the Godhead and The *Holy Council (revealed later in this chapter) respectively. Their thought process is centered exclusively on us. Bathing us continually in pure love and protection. Their pure dedication to us stems from the openness of the channels of communication that consumes their entire being; and as such, we being the direct recipients of their functions and purposes, need not do much like fasting and other spiritual acts of self purification, in order to gain access to those sacred channels.

It may please you dear reader in Christ that, they love to communicate; for even though they possess the ability to auto transmit thoughts and agendas with us, conversation is nonetheless their main source of power; and they will exercise it on a daily basis with you devoid of formalities. Thus, rendering their apprehension of our needs as purely one hundred percent guaranteed. Yes! God our Father knows what we need before we ask Him. But together they work concurrently in Divine tandem, devoid of discretion. However, there is pure reverence projected in stature, in power and in authority between them both. Ministering or communicating Angels are very observant and alert; and may relay our uncertainties and secret thoughts to God the Father, even though we may have them pre-programmed in our minds as classified thoughts being 'kept' from God the Father. They are also perceptively watchful and totally fixated on us; watching our every move with pure dedication.

Why certain Christians / people in general do not use Angels as tools of protection and aid by way of prayer.

(1) Because of the total ignorance of some about the personal nature of Angels, and their longstanding belief in Angels as recorded spiritual characters of the Bible and other religious literature, who have served their purposes long ago and as such function no more.

(2) The widespread lack of knowledge about the random and immediate availability of Angels and the potency of Angelic ministry as a vital prayer tool.

(3) The constant lurking of the spirit of unbelief in some about the divine reality, truth and authenticity of their existence.

(4) Because, it is a scriptural subject and a vital prayer tool that has been pushed unawares into the background of Christian teaching; overshadowed by our fascination with ministries that offer 'fast spiritual fixings', thus

keeping the children of God largely dependent on religious leaders for prayer substance instead of being religiously and scripturally self-reliant by cultivating the priceless habit of ardent Bible study and extensive spiritual research, in addition to pulpit ministry offered in present day churches. Some patterns of Christian teaching have also resulted in its scriptural deficiency whereby, new believers in Christ learn every aspect of the Christian way of life during teaching, as well as of fervent prayer constituting all the 'Vital Spiritual Essence' (VSE) that steers the Christian's life into victorious living without being instructed, taught or schooled comprehensively about Angels and the spiritual benefits derived from incorporating their ministry into the believer's daily prayers and lives as a whole.

(5) Because, Angels have been commercialized over the centuries by the corporate system through the conscious act of 'Constant Spiritual Devaluation and Degradation' (CSDD), a system which has resulted in them being depicted as seasonal celebrity icons only at Christmas time; after which they are totally discarded or stored in attics and cellars; forgotten like the Christmas tree and ornaments until the next year; and as such have been limited spiritually, by function and purpose in the lives of many a Christian.

(6) Because, some Christians regard Angelic ministry to be limited to the functions and purposes carried out by them in the word of God; after which their services are finished and done with.

(7) The ill-cultivation in some of our minds about their divine existence, and lingering doubts about the adequacy of their ability to satisfactorily as well as spiritually serve us due to lack of appropriate scriptural teaching in the Fold and extensive spiritual research on our part.

(8) The constant confusion about where Angels fit in heaven with the Godhead, aside of the Holy Trinity. (Answer; The Trinity is God the FATHER, SON AND HOLY SPIRIT) and Angels are His Divine Servants created in His ultimate purity of mind to carry out His prompt bidding as well as that of His Children (us). They serve as the domestic household staff of Heaven; ranging from the Librarians, Stewards, Secretaries, Housekeepers, to Valets of a great house governed by a man of great wealth and title.) You see, heaven is the greatest, most beautiful, most ornate, and most magnificent of all great houses owned by the greatest landlord, who

bears the highest title in heaven and on earth. The King of kings and Lord of lords. He created these beings in His pureness and divine magnificence, to serve His purposes and those of His Family as The Great Lord of the entire universe.) So dear friend, there it is; spiritual wisdom at your finger tips. I hope this chapter throws great light on the ministry of Angels, and adds the appropriate measure of 'Spiritual Zest (SZB) and Boost' for your utmost praying benefit.

Angels defined again.

"They are sentinel figures. The anointed Divine tools of aid and protection depicting spiritual looking glasses, holy walls of fortification, shields of truth and sanctified swords that execute pure justice on behalf of The Most High, against all forms of negativity and powers of darkness when expressly dispatched for duty from on high by our summoning." (ANQ)

What can Angels do for you; how can they serve you?

(1)Angels can replace negative thoughts that plague you by installing and restoring your thoughts with positive and productive ones, as well as establishing flourishing suggestions to be carried out that in turn, serve as an easy way out of disturbingly hounding situations you may encounter.

(2)Angels can eliminate depression by way of 'Pure and Divine Psychotherapy' (PDS); a divine skill that denotes their excellence as the most effective, most discreet and highly sensitive therapists. Our only conducive duty is to avail our thoughts to them by asking and we will receive our due in pureness and complete abundance. You must realize that, asking is the 'Ultimate Divine Fuel' (UDF) that drives an Angel into action. The word of God makes this clear to us in (Luke 11: 9a); "Ask, and it shall be given you;"

(3)Angels also possess the 'Divine Expertise' (DE) to enforce the erasure of cellular scars; that is, the permanent removal of all imprints of past maladies both physiological or even psychological ones, from the human anatomy and cellular structure to the most minute detail. An example of this is the complete and utter eradication of built up scar tissues as a result of surgery or the complete eradication of symptoms and triggering agents of depression and other mental ailments from the body system. You may call on the *Archangels of healing to eradicate the problem and to bathe the area in their healing waters of light. They are also able to heal you of any infirmity if you are specific by way of request and if you harbor no weakness and stagger not in faith, by being fully persuaded that they are capable of the specific divine duty you requested of them, fully believing.

(4)Angels can strengthen you by injecting supernatural energy and zeal into your very body when you are at your physically weakest. A clear example is found in (Lk. 22:41 – 44) when Our Lord and Savior Jesus Christ received Strength in the Garden of Gethsemane while weakened by intense agony on the night He was betrayed. Yes! Angels carried that out; for remember that he was flesh and blood at the time for a divine purpose. Verse 44 rightly divides this truth in the following words: "And there appeared an angel unto Him from heaven strengthening Him." Amen? And I believe that that angel was either of the Principality or Thrones of light phyla. Why am I sure of this? Because, Jesus prayed using the key word 'Father' and these two angelic categories are the only ones whose functions and purpose depict as well as project the parental embodiment of God. They are also the closest to Him and as such are stationed by His throne always. Like a Duke and Earl are to a King or Queen. Which even further authenticates the fact that, Royalty is a Godly institution. Designed during the times of the prophets and carried on into the new testament presenting our Lord and Savior Jesus Christ as a Child born from the line of King David. Thus revealing to us The Father above, pre-installing the ultimate physical manifestation of the birth of Jesus way back by anointing a King from the house of Jesse out of whose line the Savior shall come. Wow! I love the Bible; it is indeed the word of Truth for it rightly divides this in the following words; King of kings and Lord of lords. What more can I say; there it is:)

Aside of the above facts; Angels sometimes need boosting when confronted or called upon for aid with a situation that does not conform to their functional ability. For example, when *Guardian Angels, (whose sole purpose is to protect) are confronted with a summoning pertaining to a fatal malady or situation, they will have to call on the *Archangels; (the Powers of healing and of Light,)for assistance. If the situation is too grave, they too will have to ascend to a higher Phyla or category of Angels like the *Angelic Thrones of Light, or the *Angelic Principalities of Light, who in turn will alert the *Angelic Council of light to the situation for Immediate Spiritual Intervention (ISI). *Guardian Angels, as you can deduce by this example, may not be able to call on the *Council of Light directly, but they do have full authority to call in *The Calvary (The Angelic Military Reserve) without mediation and help from other Angelic phyla. (I hope I have not confused you) Please note how all the Powers of Healing are denoted and typified by the complementary title 'Light'. I am stressing this because, almost all Christians I have met even several Pastors, associate the titles 'principalities and powers' to the devil's hierarchy of demons, which is a clear example of how the father of all deception can mislead God's children, by installing counter beings and establishing them with similar titles, to be better known than the good ones God created who are equipped with tremendous power, force and divine aggression powerful enough to incinerate them at a touch. That is why we as Christians must study and research tirelessly or be misled by the adversary for all time; causing us to miss our blessings. Also do not forget that, Guardian Angels are less effective as couriers of The Almighty because of the nature of their functional purpose of being ever presently stationed at our sides. However, their assistance is vital for the relay of what goes on around us, to the Archangels, who then forward the messages to the appropriate Angelic phyla. (whose primary functional purpose requires total mobility and does not require them to be around us like The Guardian Angels.) Ministering Angels on the other hand may relay messages that require no functional purposes outside theirs; like a call for help about a fearful situation. The Word of God further teaches us to practice random acts of kindness; which when carried out in unpretentious and selfless constancy, may one day find us entertaining Angels unawares.(see: Hebrews 13: 1&2) (see also: Genesis 18: 1-16)

Angelic appearance and manifestation in human form; is this spiritually possible? Dear Author, please clarify and elaborate on this mind baffling inquisition.

Yes! Dear reader, Angels do take on human form, if the situation at hand calls for such form of manifestation. This is an experience shared by many. Angels manifest this way to enable them deliver peculiar messages from God that require such manifestation and also to enable them experience or feel what we relay or have relayed to them from a realm much denser (spiritually contaminated) than, theirs. This they carry out by 'Divine Transformation' (DT), and not by mergence, like the powers and principalities of darkness do by way of possessing others and objects(bodies of living or dead humans, toys or objects) to carry out their dark missions. The act of merging as previously explained in this chapter is totally out of character, purpose, function, and existence in the Angelic realm because of its ungodly and contaminating effect on the purity of their pure source of existence and by way of their function and purpose. Please note the phrase, "take on human form." This depicts an act of pure transformation and not of a transference which graduates into mergence are you with me? I am sure you are. Note that, the latter graduates into a possession; which is the evil manifestation of the rulers of the darkness of this world, in human beings, other forms of life and objects by the taking over of their faculties as in; minds, bodies, and as such their lives in its absolute entirety. However dear reader, on no occasion should you discredit, underestimate, or underrate the power of Angels in your prayer and life as a whole. You must also refrain from the temptation of using them as a last resort during times of distress and urgent need. But rather learn to incorporate their pure and powerful ministry into your prayer life; and you will experience the unchanging beneficence of the Hand of God, which is the pure source and purpose of their very existence in your life. When Angels take on human form as the situation demands, they do not linger but carry out their mission with precision, brevity and haste, bathed and propelled in pure love and servitude to God for the safeguarding and sure providence of us His children.

Why some people who experience Angelic encounters and visions never make mention of them.

Angelic encounters and visions are quite rampant among humans but people who have these experiences entertain thoughts and feelings of embarrassment in revealing them by way of testimony. This is because, they cannot perceive the possibility of marrying these experiences or encounters to their intellectual and professional status and social standing, let alone daring their counterparts to believe their unique experience. Others are too scientifically minded to spiritually perceive such an existence or encounter; They just have to have a logical explanation for every incident in life or else get guilt-ridden and infected with the virus of gullibility. But the word of God makes such false perceptions clear in; (Romans. 11: 33KJV. "O the depth of the riches both of the wisdom and knowledge of God! How unsearchable are His judgments, and His ways past finding out!" you cannot use scientific and technological logics and findings to define and measure the divine magnitude and extensiveness in power of the creator of the universe and all it contains. Likewise can you not challenge the sole and reputable manufacturer of a particular product about the authenticity of its warranty, in relation to its uses and durability. For example: it is senseless to travel to your vehicle manufacturer's plant, to supervise the manufacturing of the replacement parts needed for the repair of your vehicle, simply for the mere reason of establishing its authenticity. As a consumer, (a purchaser and user of a product or thing) your ability to satisfactorily walk away with said product, item or thing is purely based on the reputation of the product manufacturer; which can be established through consumer ratings, years of experience on the market, brand name status, and other sources. Your security is your manufacturer's warranty and the mere fact that you are able to return it to the originator and qualified personnel for maintenance.

How can one in the case of Angelic appearances and manifestation psychoanalyze the greatest manufacturer of all time. 'The Big Man upstairs", who controls every living thing. Verse 34 goes on to say: "for who hath known the mind of the Lord? And who has been His counselor." Certain people explain Angelic appearances as illusive flickers of light, and as results of physics experiments and spectrums. Simply because, they are afraid or nervous (as my late Mama used to say) of being "Rip Van Winkled"; as in being ridiculed as people once sound, who have snapped in the neurons. As a result of this, they have refused to believe that a sudden feeling of well being and hopefulness is or could be an Angelic intervention. The fact is that, If we serve an all-loving God, the source of all providence, wouldn't He have love laden subjects in His service to wait on us with pure dedication, daily furnishing us with our fair share of 'Spiritual Warranty' (SW)? And wouldn't they be categorized by rank and file, in terms of duties, responsibilities, function and purpose, to meet our every need? Creating a spiritually charged energy field to attract Angels, should be propelled by one hundred percent, unfaltering and unadulterated belief coupled with faith, devoid of such negative air pockets such as; that of doubt, wavering, and pessimism. Surrender, belief and faith are the key virtues that led us to that destination of salvation in Christ Jesus, who is one with the Father God and the Holy Spirit. Therefore dear reader, affirm the presence of Angels by sharing with others, testimonies of your visionary as well as personal encounters with them. Experiencing Angelic presence or manifestation is a sure confirmation of your hope, belief and aspiration from God. "… and hope maketh not ashamed: because the love of God is shed abroad in our hearts by the Holy Ghost which is given on to us." (see: Romans 5:5 KJV.)

Here is a scriptural text that depicts Angelic power and authority, by way of category, function and purpose, carried out with 'Divine Authority' (DA), instituted by The Lord of Hosts. I was led to this scripture by 'Divine Revelation' (DR) propagated by 'expert spiritual sight' (ESS) during one of my 'intensive individual prayer sessions' (IIPS) after one of my 'extensive spiritual research' (ESR) sessions, at the time when the state of my marital crisis had escalated to the mean heights of unjustified hatred, wickedness, and betrayal interwoven by series of lost conceptions which occurred as I would later find out because, I was being slowly poisoned by the perpetrator because he was involved with another woman with whom he had planned a family. But I lived for my Father in heaven sustained me to bear witness and testify of His goodness. Amen? This scripture is one of my favorite 'Aggressive Proclamations' (AP). As you read this scripture, notice the role of the Angel featured in its text by way of function and purpose. I will also reveal the phyla or category to you as our lesson progresses. Now, dear reader. Prepare to board the ship laden with God's word of promise with an Angel at its helm. Our scriptural text is taken from (Exodus 23: 20-27 NIV.) "See, I am sending an Angel (Archangel) ahead of you to guard you along the way (depicting the protectorate primary function of all Angels.) and to bring you to the place I have prepared. Pay attention to Him and listen to what He says. Do not rebel against Him; He will not forgive your rebellion, since my name is in Him. (the truth about Angels, as beings created in God's pure nature; depicting His name of performance as Jehovah-Tsidqenu the Father Almighty who executes pure righteousness and justice.) If you listen carefully to what He says and do all that I say, (purpose of Angels; as messengers of God and also revealing one of the functions and purpose of the Archangel phyla-wise.) I will be an enemy to your enemies and oppose those who oppose you. My Angel (denoting God as the Master and creator of Angels.) will go ahead of you (denoting God as the divine light of the world as well as on our paths, by way of his word of truth, which the Angel was carrying; also exuding God's divine luminescence as He leads us in the paths of righteousness as, the Good Shepherd; Jehovah-Raah. Please read Psalm 23: & 119: 105) and bring you into the land of the Amorites, Hittites, Perizzites, Canaanites, Hivites, and Jebusites, (the nations dwelling in utter darkness immersed in divers negativities) and I will wipe them out. (God's character of performance as Jehovah-Tsidqenu and Nissi revealed once again as the righteous and conquering hand of justice.) Do not bow down before their Gods or worship them or follow their practices. (God's expectation of total commitment and faithfulness coupled with obedience from us.) you must demolish them and break their sacred stones to pieces. Worship the Lord your God, and His blessing will be on your food and water. (purpose of the Angel; pure protection from all forms of harm preconceived and intended against the Children of God.) I will take away sickness from among you, and none will miscarry or be barren in your land. (The purpose of the Archangel; as a healer, phyla-wise girded with the pure function of hope and restoration.) I will give you a full life span. I will send my terror ahead of you, (The word 'terror' denoting another Angel of the 'Carrion' phyla or category, the bearer of dark tidings to dark souls, who also purposely dish out retributive fate to the apostate and the wicked.) and throw into confusion, every nation you encounter. (God projected as the Highest and most intelligent enforcer of 'Divine Security and Surveillance.' DSS.) I will make your enemies turn their backs and run." (God, displaying and carrying out His nature as Jehovah-Nissi; The Conqueror.)

Dear reader, I earnestly believe that, such help is already prepared for all countries, tribes and people in need of 'Divine Intervention' (DI), if we will only pray persistently, crying to God for assistance. For one day, our Angel will show up from God, with a 'Systematic and Strategic Divine Itinerary' (SSDI) given by God, laden with strategic plans to vanquish adversities, from The Lord of Hosts, (Jehovah-Tsebaoth) laid out by His divine hand of justice and sending His terror ahead of our armies to deliver righteousness on our behalf, while bringing down our foes into peaceful submission. Thus, a great many goodness will follow all nations who live in obedience to God's word, without rebellion.

God also disseminates His goodness to us through His Angels, when we are faced with crisis and disasters of great magnitude; like those of September 11th and the recent hurricanes that struck the United States; the mudslides and earthquakes, and others in countries like China and Haiti, and the tsuname in Japan, famine in Somalia, and other disasters around the globe. Angels, from the Master are able to deliver 'Divine Psychological Scar Erasure' (DPSE) to victims of such crisis when propelled by utter belief in their performance power driven by God Almighty; for there is nothing too difficult for God, the Sole Master of the universe who teaches us to hope without shame because, His tremendous love is able to overshadow our problems. Yes! "He is the rock, and His work is perfect: all His ways are judgment; A God of truth and without iniquity, ruling with pure justice and in righteousness." (see Deuteronomy 32: 4) you must know that, every negativity enforced into manifestation by the adversary leads to crisis and loss in this world; but God the Father has designed His own counter strategy to shatter and vanquish such wicked manifestation from taking over the minds of His Children, psychologically and physically, by way of Angelic ministry; For God is not a man that He should lie; neither is He a mortal, that He should repent: for He keeps all His promises and is true to His word. (see also. Numbers 23: 19.) our duty and only part to play is to believe that what God has promised, He is divinely capable to perform.

Such a belief will then propel the Angels into manifesting in bands and throngs, in their thousands, millions, and trillions, to calm all the hurting people and their families at large. The Angels accomplish this mission by anointing victims with the oil of rejuvenation, recovery and contentedness, thus restoring lost causes with pure defeat and pure provision; and by also raining down pure justice on all their offenders and perpetrators, both physically and spiritually; as the victims are bathed and renewed in pure serenity. Dear friend, may the road of Angels we have traveled together in this chapter, enrich your minds and hearts into pure belief; and into knowing that, Angelic arms are stretched out waiting to clasp and hold yours as you give them access to administer to you their divine services, with pure devotion, by the power of the Most High God, Amen. But here is a word of caution for you. While utilizing the ministry of Angels, do not get too focused on them, by giving them all the glory and power that should be awarded to the Almighty. For Angels though created by God for the function of ministration by way of protecting His own, receive their power to function and to perform by divine endowment from God; thus they cannot replace the Godhead who loves us and created them, as well as us. Please remember that as heavenly beings, God created them to be ministering spirits and couriers for His services and also that of mankind, devoid of sexual distinctions, ethnic and racial barriers; the very embodiment of Godly perfection made readily available to us by God as militant reserves and armies exuding pure light and goodness by freeing us from the powers of darkness. Therefore let us as believers of the word of Truth, by the power and authority of the Holy Trinity, stay firmly on our tracks of spirituality, as we incorporate their functions and purposes into our prayers and supplication.

Angelic services are very advantageous to our needs when we are thrown into situations and circumstances where, we are too broken in spirit and in body to pray, but can only whisper. In times like these, just call them by function and purpose and name; and they will show up as the divine couriers that they are, to deliver you on or before the deadline; to the praise, honor and glory of the great I Am, (Jehovah/Yahweh). You may now enter into the light of Knowing your Angels, in their fullness and existence; as we observe them by name, Phyla(category), nature, function and purpose. Be blessed; for you are about to receive knowledge of the purest source, the very embodiment of the luminescence and love of God the Father Almighty.

Guardian or Ministration Angels:

This category of Angels are more in number than any other in the heavenly realm. They are by far the most populous, numbering in trillions. Their purpose is to be protectorates, as they function as givers of warmth (like that of the sun) and givers of hope by calming our fears and phobias into total riddance. (Please refer to author's Angelic encounter and compare her narrative experience to this Angelic phyla.) They are typified in appearance by their silver tipped wings and the emanation of this same silverfish glow all over their aura(from head to toe and all around). They are likened by nature to pearls; a pure white softness, engulfed in a silvery but shimmering and glowing, soft finish. They are also known as the "ever-present Angels" because of their constant presence around us. They manifest in bands and never singularly as most people have believed throughout the centuries. Their perpetual presence offers to us pure protection. For example: they will wrap themselves around your vehicle during a fatal collision; forming a divine shock absorbing ectoplasm like that of a cocoon but denser, to save your life. Their devoted sense of protection or protectorate nature stems from pure devotion and extreme dedication. They will therefore go to extremities to protect you. They are also actively present in their numbers around us at night when we sleep, as we are at our most vulnerable at that time of day when we are physically and mentally at rest and as such motionless. "Thou shall not be afraid of the terror by night, nor of the pestilence that walketh in darkness... For He shall give His Angels charge over thee to keep thee in all thy ways. They shall bear thee up in their hands, lest thou dash thy foot against a stone." (see: Psalm 91) This is the most authentic record and blessed assurance from the Father Himself, reminding you of His Divine Protection over you, by way of Angelic ministry. What more can you ask for as a Child of God, and what else do you need to propel and induce you into believing, in order to fully reap the benefits their services bring? You tell me!

Archangels:

These particular Angels are divided into three groups. They are: The Archangels of Battle; with Michael as their General. The Archangels in charge of Heavenly communications (communicating the heavenly decisions and tidings sanctioned by God to earthly beings, with the Angel Gabriel as their Head Communicator, and The Archangels in charge of music and praise, With Lucifer as the Music director and Head until he lost that position, through contamination propelled by pride, selfishness and rebellion. Aside of this group, there is a general sector in the Archangel phyla who administer different functions and purposes, entirely different from the above. But all the above, are similar in characteristics as in physical features and stature. Archangels are really huge in stature, almost colossal yet, very swift and enduring in nature, like wolves. They can project and exude tremendous strength and ferociousness when circumstances or the situation at hand calls for such aggression. Their purpose of healing is portrayed by the green orbed healing scepter that they carry in pureness of equipage; bringing hope and sure healing to the desperate and afflicted respectively, by way of function. They also possess calming, refreshing and cleansing abilities, like the rain. Bringing hope to those in dire need of it. They are typified by the blue tint on the tips of their wings, which is also visible on the outer fringes of their aura. Like all Angels, they are genderless, and racially diverse. Exuding a nature that can be likened to the pure calmness and serenity of the aquamarine stone.

The Cherubim:

They are the Masters of song ministration, equipped with voices so soothing and sweet like that of the canary. Their primary purpose is to sing joyously eliminating sorrow, tenseness and restlessness. They are secondary healers. Their function is to rid us of sleeplessness (insomnia), mental agony and depression. They are in existence to exude everything purely musical; and are therefore beings of pure melody. The Cherubim can be recognized by the rosy tips of their wings. A color that is also duplicated all over their aura. They are likened to the quartz stone which they use as a spiritually alerting object to signal us of their presence during prayers, visions and dreams. The Cherubim are slightly larger in stature than the Seraphim.

The Seraphim:

Like the Cherubim, the Seraphim are also extremely musical. Serving their divine purpose as ministers of songs. They possess all the characteristics of the Cherubim, except for their size and a slight difference in function, by way of projecting the recollection or remembrance of our dreams and visions, to help us move on to another day's function and nights sleep, in order to help us accelerate our social advancement as well as spiritual growth without fear and anxiety. They can be identified by the rosy tint on the fringes of their wings and aura. Like the Cherubim, they are also typified by the quartz stone that denotes all the different refractions of the tones, rhythm and vibrations portrayed in their music.

The notable differences between the Cherubim and Seraphim that also unites as well as compliments them in function and purpose.

These two Angels are typified by wings standing high above their heads that spreads down closer to their bodies, than that of the Archangels. Please note that the colors of Angel's wings though intended by God for recognition, are also fashioned to represent their powers and function. They also serve the purpose of name tags or identification tags to aid us in recognizing them when they come to serve us. The Cherubim differ from the Seraphim by size and their tremendous melodic ability to sing. While the Seraphim are notably perfect in abilities of tones, rhythms and vibrations. Thus together, these two remarkable Angelic beings are capable by marriage of their differences in the vital musical components which constitute melody and rhythm within which tones, vibrations and pitch reside, to compose a divine score laden with cadence so holy, that exudes the most heavenly of all music in perfect and pure harmony, for the sole purpose of the sure and complete healing and rejuvenation of human minds and bodies, invaded by infirmities and maladies. Together, they functionally portray the pure melodies of the Sacred Choirs of the Heavenly Hosts. (read: Luke 2: 8 to 14) That was them in Chapter 13 and 14. I always get goose bumps when I read that chapter, especially the latter verses. Because I could clearly hear my Mother's voice singing those verses as composed by Handel. You will get the idea of what the Shepherds heard that night by listening to Handel's Messiah by the London Philharmonic Orchestra and Chorus; the version I was brought up with. The University of Maryland Orchestra and Choir has a wonderful rendition too, you will love it. It will transport you to heaven I promise you. I have had the pleasure of experiencing heavenly music by listening to the Classics right from the womb, thanks to my late parents. For my ears got attached to the sound of classical music when I popped out from God into Sub-Saharan Africa and have loved it since. They have over the years become a part of my spiritual collection and serve as invaluable prayer tools. Handel's Messiah particularly, has been to me a comprehensive way to soar spiritually on musical scales, into the instructive divine realms of scripture memorization.

My intense love for classical music has always been my therapeutic leanings especially during trying times because of the divine soothing element they infuse within me; but in times past, cost me physically and emotionally, since it also constantly reminds me of being battered by my ex-husband for playing it. I mean I had no other way out, since I was banned from praying at home; it thus served as an outlet for supplication. But it angered him like everything else about me. And how could I exist without being true to myself. How bizarre; imagine that. When I called my parents about the ban, they comforted and advised me, but both arrived at the same conclusion; "Queen,(for they often called me that) playing classical music will help you tremendously; you do have your 'Handel' collection don't you?" It may sound unbelievable, but being unequally yoked, extends far beyond the biblical. I suffered for finding an outlet in classical music for my pain. ha! What's an African girl expected to do huh? Beat bongo drums all the time? There's a time for that, but I needed at the time, to soar to a place where I could pour out my heart in secret to the Master, since I was under intense pressure and verbal restraint. I mean I had two auto accidents before it all passed; though I am considered an expert defensive driver by friends and a tough personality by my siblings. So now, I am devoted to the divine refiner Himself who loves it when I sing his word of truth to Him, and associate with people who accept me as I am. I will always remember playing and singing along to the entire 'Messiah' album with my late Mama, who was endowed with the sweetest voice, while my Papa at times joined in with his rich baritone voice. (now I am shedding tears.) I was blessed with them, oh yes! That is why I am able to extend that blessing to you. What was planted inside me is what you read in this book; and they (God bless their souls) put it there, with sound and firm instruction and guidance as loving parents. In Child Development School, one quickly learns that the first five years of life are the most crucial. (formative years) For whatever seeps inside is retained and embossed into the Child's psyche for ever. In Library school, one immediately learns about the importance of determining the binding quality of a book, by examining the spine which of course holds the entire book together; being the most important part of the book's structure. My parents bound me thus, by according me the best spine they could both harness within their perfections and imperfections as the mortals they once were, striving to touch the divine. I am as such, an extension of their lives, for they live within me; I am a living testimony of their life's work; reflecting my upbringing even to the scriptural literary core. I know and believe they sweetly repose in Abraham's bosom with the Angels; the heavenly Hosts; Enjoying the melodies, tones and refractions of the Cherubim and Seraphim in utter bliss until we meet again. But as for me, I will indulge by listening to inspiring music here on earth, rightly dividing the word of truth through extensive scriptural studies, striving to be Christ-like in virtue, while incorporating Angelic ministry into my prayer life, until the Lord calls me home. And to you dear reader,

I encourage thus. Summon an Angel; will you? They are waiting; idling on puffy clouds with nothing to do. Alert them with your belief in their capabilities through faith in God, and they will show up in bands and throngs with healing and aid within their wings. Amen?

"O thou that tellest good tidings to Zion
Arise shine for thy light is come.
Get thee out into the high mountains
O thou that tellest good tidings to Jerusalem
Lift up thy voice with strength, lift it up; be not afraid
Say unto the cities of Judah
Behold your God.
O thou that tellest good tidings to Zion
Arise shine for thy light is come.
Arise! Arise! Arise!
Say unto the cities of Judah
Behold! Behold!
The glory of the Lord is risen upon thee."

In homage to the musical genius
GEORGE FRIEDRICK HANDEL
Who Rightly divides the word of truth with his incomparable legendary composition 'Messiah' to the Glory of God, of which this Anthem is a part of; extracted from the book of Isaiah chapters 40: 9 and 60: 1 respectively.

The powers of Light:

Like Archangels, these Angels also possess the healing purpose primarily by power, but on a higher and more direct scale. Thus, they are able to function without need or use of the green orbed scepter of healing, used by the Archangels. Which simply means, they use nothing as a point of contact. This reiterates their sole and primary function of healing which in all totality, drives their entire being. They always manifest for express and pure healing duties and functions, bringing only their Powers of pure healing, rejuvenation and restoration within them. They fulfill their duties as Ministers of situations that are too critical and complex for secondary healers like the Archangels, by physically engulfing the patient or victim(s) within their enormous wings. The powers of light have the divine capability of enlarging their stature from the average or medium to the colossal. Their swiftness to attend to a healing situation is likened to that of a falcon. They are also armed with the purest form of perseverance and determination, instilled in tireless devotion, and installed in endless love that denotes their peaceful purpose of existence. They are likened to the moon; an element of nature, signifying their mothering aspects and instincts. The green color of 'Divine Healing' (DH) is their identification tag or badge; emanating on the fringes of their aura and on the tips of their enormous wings in greenish white, through which one can perceive blue neon-like flames shooting out in spray-like fashion. This is what people usually testify feeling. That sensation of electrical currents coursing through their ailing parts and bodies, during healing crusades and services where they usually manifest to assist Men of God, so that the Father, and not man might be glorified.

When called upon for healing, the Angelic Powers of Light transmit divinely transfused electromagnetic force, laden with high spiritual healing voltage, set within divinely propelled currents, laced with instant restorative and expedited eradicating force of great magnitude, that pierces the patient's body or ailing part directly, while keeping the patient in pure security and protection under their magnificent wings. This sort of protective shield devised for the patient by the Angelic Powers of Light, serves as a sort of 'Spiritually Sterile(SSE) Enclosure', designed to keep the patient safe from 'Adverse Spiritual Hindrances and Contaminants' (ASHC), while the divine healing and 'Spiritual Surgical Procedure' (SSP) is in progress. Their powerful healing abilities, can ward off, eliminate, and regress any illness, chronic condition and malady into complete and utter remission. As a Child of God, you must realize that illness is nothing but the invasion of the human body in part or whole by negativities, when it (the body) is left unguarded by our doing, or when particles and clusters of adverse physiological imbalance and hindrances are planted therein by the adversary, to trap the children of God into a state of hopelessness in order to propel them into the realm of doubt about the authenticity of God's power and existence as Yahweh the Lord, as well as to plant the seeds of unbelief in order to establish and disproof His love and care for us His creation. But in situations like the latter, the adversary only wins when we refuse to exercise love and humane practices in the form of donations, basic help and aid to lift one another up during such trying times, by assisting others with the substance God has amply endowed us with; A work that people like Paul Newman and Andrew Carnegie did while they lived and have established through foundations to be carried out even now that they are long gone. Apart from our substance as in wealth, we can lift each other up through philanthropy and Civil rights; working and making sacrifices as ambassadors of world peace; racial equality and human rights as Dr. Martin Luther King Jr., Mr. Frederick Douglass, Dr. Kwame Nkrumah, W.E.B. DuBois, Mr. Marcus Garvey; all of blessed memory, did for our freedom, emancipation, and global well being; The same mission of goodwill is continued by Mr. Nelson Mandela and many others who strive tirelessly to this day. For God manifests through our goodness given to, and shared with others, as beings created in His image and likeness. Thus, once again we see brotherly and sisterly love taking precedence over all our good spiritual and religious habits, to further the greatness of God, as well as the well being of our fellow humans and ourselves. Our good deeds therefore, establishes the word of truth and the reality of God's existence; but the opposite establishes the devil's kingdom that is why we must strive to do good one to the other without faint.

'Negativities' in the previous paragraph, denotes the presence of destructive foreign matters and bodies that when trapped within the body system, fight to coexist with the body created in the Image and Likeness of God, which also serves as the Temple of the Holy Spirit. These negativities must thus be gotten rid of to free the body's proper functioning and progressive capabilities, in order to accelerate its adequate operation as God Almighty intended. Powers of Healing are usually present with their secondary healing partners the Archangels, who serve as the 'Spiritual Surgical Back-up Team' (SSBT), at healing crusades and also during our individual or private healing prayer and supplication sessions. When called upon as prayer tools of healing, they in turn show up by expressly propelling, aiding, and guiding the hands of, Evangelists, Ministers of Healing, Men of God, and Believers in spiritual healing, through the 'Divine System of Remission and Recovery' (DSRR), by propelling them (Ministers etc) as the 'Instruments of God' (IOG) that they scripturally are, to exude His (God's) tremendous, miraculous and insurmountable ability to furnish our bodies with 'Pure Healing and Restoration' (PHR).

The Angel known as the 'Carrion':

The Carrion is the only Angelic category or phyla with the most distinct function and purpose shared by no other Angel. Their Angelic purpose is to carry away the dark souls of the wicked and apostate to the 'holding place' after their death. They carry out this mission by positioning themselves at a fair distance, at the location where the dark soul is about to be expelled through death waiting to carry out their purpose as, the cleanup crew, or janitors of death. Carrion were created by God for no other purpose but for the protection of the kind and good souls in heaven and on earth. Like the professional cleanup crew after a bloody crime scene investigation is completed, they enforce the complete and total riddance of the sinfully dark souls of the evil, wicked and apostate, people after their death, by carrying out their complete eradication; thus making sure that their spirits or souls do not linger around after death to contaminate the living. The Carrion Angels hang around to expedite this function by taking hold of the sinful and evil soul, as soon as they take their last breath, by securing them hurriedly with divine ropes, and conveying them expressly by dragging, to the 'holding place' without delay of any kind. The Carrion performs this duty with an air of pure seriousness and divine focus; yet with a pure sense of love, for the protection and safety of the good souls living on earth and those resting in the arms of The Almighty.

They are given the same, if not a higher level of access-priority accorded to paramedics arriving on an accident scene; for when the Carrion is actively on duty, Angels of every category or phyla, retreat by clearing an express way for their hurried passage, in order to ensure the swift carrying out of its mission with the haste, seriousness and urgency it calls for. Our Guardian Angels during this time, also perform their protectorate duty by shielding us from the passing on dark soul, if we happen to be in the environment or vicinity where their deaths occurred. They do so by interweaving themselves by way of their wings, thus forming a secure and divinely impenetrable Angelic enclosure and a sort of fortress; a canopy structured in pure security built on a foundation of purity, surrounded by walls of Hevenly light, to blind the eye of the passing on dark soul. This form of protection, projected by our Guardian Angels in times like these is known as; 'Winging'. As the Carrion makes its way towards the 'holding place' with the dark soul tied up and secured, Heaven is engulfed in pure silence, to ensure and defray any negative spiritual transference of evil lurking around the dark soul, until the Carrion's mission (whisking away the dark soul in a timely and fast manner to the 'holding place',) is fully accomplished. You must realize as a Child of God that, the need for 'Standard Divine Precaution and Protocol'(SDPP) observed and carried out in the heavenly realm, when dealing with dark souls, denotes their dark arrogance and incorrigible nature which resides within them even after death; and should in no way be allowed to thrive in both realms. That is why 'Persistent Spiritual Effort' (PSE) should be exercised here on earth with all seriousness when confronted by the duty to spiritually eliminate dark forces and entities on earth, just as it (SDPP) is observed in Heaven. We have all heard of criminals going to the execution chamber with jeers and sneers on their faces, mocking authorities and family members of their victims, thus reminding us that not all can be redeemed and that even as you and I have surrendered to God and strive continuously to do good, so are others dedicated to strengthening the devil and his devices here on earth to the end. Be not deceived, evil is existent and as a child of God, denying it is very dangerous as it pleases the adversary that he has you deceived; because it strengthens his devices. And furthers his schemes.

The Carrion Angel is not dark and scary at all, as portrayed on the movie screen (see: The movie 'Ghost'. Starring Whoopie Goldberg. They are on the other hand as beautiful and comely to behold as all Angels. Their likening to the ravens black color exudes their function of securing and dragging away 'dark souls' after their deaths, and has nothing to do with their physical features, or nature. They denote the swiftness of the wind in nature. A hurried element which compliments their swiftness and precision as they carry out their task. Carrion Angels are the very embodiment of mystery, like the opal stone and may be identified by the orange tint on the tips of their beautifully strong white wings. This same orange tint is emanated on the outer fringes of their aura. My baby sister who ministers to terminally ill people in hospitals and private homes, villages and Towns in Ghana, has according to her, witnessed several patients depart this world in arrogance laced with fear and unbelief as they utter the same words; "someone with a serious look is coming for me; help! Help! I am going to be tied up. It's dark here. I am scared." She also reports that they usually let out a disturbingly sinister laughter as they give up the ghost. And yet most of them, do not relent but stick to their guns refusing to yield to the will of God no matter how much she prays with them. According to her, they all talk about having a premonition of being tied up and being surrounded by utter darkness; but we must realize that their apostate state of mind is what induces the darkness they feel as they die, for the Carrion

Angel appears to them in all beauty with tools and a serious countenance set to do business with a dark soul; hence the uttering of darkness from the lost soul. Dear reader, not all can be saved. The act of salvation goes hand in hand with total surrender drawn from a place of utmost belief that stems within humility and surrender to a higher being God. Therefore as written earlier, we must accept that there are some who will not surrender no matter how terrified they become or how closely death stares them in the face, or even on their death beds, like convicted assassins and serial killers who go to the execution chambers with a smirk and jeer on their faces; hence the function, purpose, and need for Carrion Angel created and dispatched by God. The Carrion therefore need not to be summoned, but works in tandem with the Angelic *Virtues and Angelic *Dominions of light. You will comprehend the complementary nature of their functions, duties and purposes in relation to that of the Carrion Angel as we proceed with this chapter.

How can you discern a dark soul?

As a Christian, a Child of God, and a person fashioned in the image and likeness of God, you must possess or exercise, a certain level of spiritual discernment of people, in relation to their nature and character. Here are some of the signs and character traits to watch out for or steer clear of in a person or group of people, that denotes extreme, partial and incubational stage apostate soul . I must caution you that, these people may not necessarily be found outside the protective and loving circles of family, friends and well wishers, as you may have been led to think and believe. Just keep your eyes peeled and you will find them slowly, surely, yet constantly, manifesting their incessant lust for inflicting pain and suffering on their fellow humans. This trait may be so forthcoming because, they cannot help it, as they enjoy what they do. Dark entities and souls are not the horned demonic replicas you see in movies and literary illustrations. They can be represented by and manifested in anyone who allows such negative mergence by the adversary. To be precise, they can be found among people from all walks of life. Particularly hiding under the devoted cloaks of religion and excessive spirituality. Aha you are shaking your head are you not? Your 'Divine Precautionary Duty' (DPD), is to keep your 'Spiritual Antennae' (SA) up, in order to catch negative frequency waves laden with adversities floating around you and your loved ones.

Remember that, there may be a lot of people in this world who have at a point in their lives indulged in one or two negative vices and repented of them. But, they are considered dark souls only when they indulge in these vices incessantly, reveling in and living unrepentant of them; Some go to the darker extremities of selling their very souls into carrying these vices out to an extent which renders them beyond physical and spiritual redemption. Like the selfish and corrupt leaders of resourceful countries who have plunged their people into abject poverty and want. Who through their wicked and selfish acts have acquired for them the degrading and suppressive label of 'Third world' which is not what God the Father intended for those people, but the wickedness of man has devised. When you have a relationship or encounter a dark personality, you will (believe me) live and wallow in perpetual anguish until you grab the 'Good Christian Sense'(GCS) of breaking free from their evil clutches. You must also realize that because of their dark nature, these types of people are not responsive to the Light, they do not realize, see, or feel the pain that they constantly are inflicting on others because, as they grow farther and farther away from the Light of goodness their conscience becomes seared. Therefore if you persistently and forcibly retain relationships with or keep company with them, they will end up destroying, derailing, or taking your life, in awarded exchange for a hellish trophy from the prince of the darkness of this world for whom they have been campaigning for and are in league with. Remember therefore these basic rule as you walk in Christ;

- Attain and maintain (GCS) 'good christian sense' at all times, and during every situation.
- Constantly keep your (SA) 'spiritual antennae' up in order to catch the right spiritual waves and frequencies as well as detecting adverse ones within your environment or spiritually upgrade your scriptural acumen for your own safety.

Our lesson on Angels continues with another important Angelic phyla;

The Virtues:

This category or phyla of Angels signifies peace, love, and the Holy Spirit's astute channel of instructive communication into all righteousness, as well as all things pertaining to the parental component or nature of the Godhead. Their primary purpose is to help us live our lives on earth accordingly as God intended. They are what I term, the Angelic vessels of pure admonition and reprimand; aiding in the building of good character and morals, as their primary function. They also initiate and promote changes in our lifestyle by navigating us mentally, from negative waters of decisions and foolish acts, into those of the positive. This purpose is driven primarily by way of function as previously stated. The Angel of virtues or Virtue Angel, however you may call them, is likened in nature to rivers of waters and clear babbling brooks, which signifies flexibility, reform, transparency and change. They are phosphorous in shine, as that of molten silver or mercury. This silver color is visible on their wings and gently flows to the tips where they convert into pale blue dippings that bursts into a brilliance of silver blue luminescence from the tips of their wings. This same color pattern is emanated on the outer fringes of their aura. They are the shiniest and most luminous of all the Angels. Virtues do not descend from Heaven or manifest here on earth to carry out their immaculate and sacrosanct duties. This simply means they cannot be summoned due to their purpose, functions and duties. They perform all their duties from the Heavenly realms with urgency and purity, by keeping us from straying from our God given life paths. Our disobedience usually disrupts their supervision. But they are quick to guide us back to our God driven paths of life with loving purity immersed in admonishment, thus giving us the chance to reform, repent, regret and to feel remorseful. People with dark souls like the apostate and notoriously evil, cannot respond to the Virtues because, they have utterly strayed from their God driven paths of life by adopting persistently sinful lives devoid of remorse, repentance, regret and reformation. In so doing, they have knowingly and completely given over their conscience to the searing influence of the rulers of the darkness of this world, who operate in realms that differ in purity, and that of spiritual energy, from that of the Angelic Virtues thus placing themselves on an adverse plane where they cannot be reached by the Angelic Virtues. Virtues may not be summoned and thus are not dispatched by The Father. However they may be prayed to for guidance.

The Dominions:

This Angelic phyla or category, serve their purpose to The Most High as the Heavenly record keepers. They keep records of all good deeds perpetrated by humans including thoughts and actions, by recording them on a non-deletable endless divine scroll popularly known in religious circles as, the 'Book of Life'. Which in actuality is a scroll. They serve their purpose as, guardians and enforcers of 'Divine Accuracy'(DA) by way of function, as record keepers of heaven. I call them the Divine Archivists and Records Managers of the Heavenly realms, and the Pure Publishers of the records and contents of The Book of Life. The Dominions are the busiest of Angels, the most intellectual and elite. Their very personality denotes the dignity of the cougar, exuding an air of pure intellect, divine wisdom and learning. Thus, they carry out their extensive duties tirelessly in Heaven as; Divine Librarians, Holy Information Scientists, Records Managers, and Publishers of good deeds for God, with pure accuracy and dignity by editing, processing, classifying and cataloguing appropriate human behavior for the Heavenly Libraries and Archives of Good deeds by the split second. That indeed is hard work. They are likened unto the earth because of their functional ability of instituting constantly ensured completeness in all they do, as well as the spherical wholesomeness with which their duties and purpose are rendered to God. This wholesome likening denotes their function of recording endless lines of the goodness exhibited in our very existence. Like the bloodstone, they epitomize life, which naturally flows by way of blood; the precious fluid that propels human existence, and also symbolizes goodness, health, well being and vitality; an embodiment of the nature of the records they keep. Their color tag or identification mark; a maroon tint, appears on the tips of their wings which are white like that of all Angels, and is emanated (the maroon color), on the outer fringes of their aura.

The Dominions also possess the profound ability of determining which Angelic category or phyla is most suitable for a certain or particular earthly duty or emergency that requires 'Immediate Divine Backup' (IDB). This and other required duties expected of them from God The Father, are carried out by the Dominions with pure accuracy, and distinction without the faintest hint of a flaw or inconsistency. The Dominions also furnish our Guardian Angels with every information they require pertaining to our lives, from our individual Heavenly charts and the Book of Life respectively, to the very last detail upon request. The Angelic Dominions also function as the Divine disseminators, and storehouses bursting and overflowing with the purest source of informative acquisition, by offering a complete and accurate chronological ready reference, topically or subject-wise to our Ministering Angels promptly upon inquisition. They also possess the 'Utmost Divine Power' (UDP) to expressly dispatch minions of Angels to aid and assist us in less than a twinkle of an eye, without so much of a verbal request from us through prayer, but simply by way of a casual Angelic summoning, through thought transmission and desire for 'Angelic Aid and Assistance'. (AAA) Well dear reader, you may now access your Divine triple 'A' account and take-in your extensive benefits, for it is one heck of a good contract, laced with the most incomparable services and a complete coverage immersed in ultimate efficiency and purity.

Dominions are so well endowed with the divine ability and expertise for 'Divine Espionage' (DE) dripping with high intellect, researching and excavating hidden and classified information about us that they divinely project into pure existence, for the purpose of hard evidence within their record keeping. Dominions reside in their studious realms in the Heavens, executing extensive intellectual duties, and carrying out their indispensable functions as divinely laden satellites and vehicles of high intelligence and espionage of the Godhead, by systematically and geographically tracking us down as we relocate from place to place. They also convey information about us to the Angelic council of Light (The heavenly judiciary committee) and other Angels who may essentially need them for missions, upon immediate request, with pure alertness and punctuality by way of duty. Dominions are the only Angels who possess all the details of our life's plan and span. They also function as expert advisers with readily available answers to our finances, health, relationships and investments. As authors, editors, and publishers of Heaven's core reference materials and compilers of its literary information resources pertaining to us in their entirety, their job performance is constantly washed in pure accuracy and readiness, and immersed in extreme alertness, by the constant updating of our heavenly records; thus keeping them current and in print, by the fraction of a second on a daily basis. In order to accomplish this purpose, they keep our charts close at hand at all times. Dominions are the most discreet and most reliable trustees of classified information. They exhibit their flawless nature and purpose with pure discretion and trustworthiness. The Dominions live in heaven in their multitudes. They may not be summoned, but they are the only Angelic phyla that possess the tremendous ability to divinely propel, facilitate, and effectuate, the smooth operation of all Angelic missions, errands and ministry, ranging from the expected to those of great criticality. Renaissance Artists portray them often as studious noble looking, comely Angels with scrolls and quills with searching eyes. Because they record our life records, they are the only Angels who posses the knowledge about our life span and as such know the very hour of our deaths to the split second. They are therefore, very useful to the Carrion Angel.

The only shared responsibility between the Angelic Dominions and Virtues.

Apart from the above extensive duties that the Angelic Dominions are laden with, they share a very important responsibility of a Heavenly protocol nature with the Angelic Virtues. (also a non-summoning Angelic phyla.) This duty of theirs is shared by no other Angelic phyla and is carried out with great pomp and circumstance and that is; carrying out their function as the divine welcome team that ushers in the good and kind Souls of Light, as they make their way through the 'Pearly Gates of Heaven, into the 'Divine Tunnel of Light'. (this is the same tunnel of light that people who encounter near death experiences, often describe to their families, friends and loved ones; an experience that has been misdiagnosed as stemming from clinical offsets by most medical professionals. It has therefore been labelled as a condition effectuated by adverse drug side effects which is believed to be the responsible propellant that induces such hallucination and delirium in patients; and in so doing, has led to such bizarre manifestations.) The Dominions position themselves at the end of the Tunnel of Light, while the Angelic Virtues, completely line the Tunnel; forming a gateway or aisle of Insurmountable Divine Splendor by way of the tremendous luminescence projected from the beautiful silvery shine depicted all over their wing surface, to welcome the Good and Kindly Souls of Light passing on. The Virtues line up in two rows facing each other and form an arch by joining their shiny silvery wings on top of their heads to form an arch-like passage through which the passed on soul glides to the throne of God as they are welcome by throngs of Angels and a heavenly choir with singing and rejoicing.

Please note that people who traverse the Tunnel of Light by way of near death experiences, are spiritually and lovingly transported back to the earthly realm, by the same way, but are divinely endowed with newness of strength and vitality by these two very peculiar Angelic phyla, namely; The Dominions and the Virtues, who are the only Angels divinely endowed by The Father with the ability, power and authority by way of function, and purpose to access our life's span. The Dominions just figure out which Angelic phyla is suitable for the task of taking the returned good soul the rest of the way beyond the pearly gates, and the task is done. Thus these two Angels know when to welcome you in, and when to send you back to finish the task God has laid out for you. Therefore if you have had such an experience as described above, then know that, you did not cheat death, but rather, death cheated its way into disrupting your life span chart, by trying to manipulate the expert records divinely compiled in purity and accuracy by the heavenly intellectuals and was found out, by the Winged Professors. Do not be afraid to depart this life as a Christian, for this passage is designed to spiritually transport people like you and I into a more blissful and gainful realm filled with peace beyond measure. Thus the Angelic Dominions and Virtues are the first Angels to greet the Good Souls of Light in Heaven. This really feels good to know, doesn't it? God is truly a loving Father, the Divine embodiment of loving parenthood.

The Angelic Thrones and Principalities of Light:

These Angels are the most superior; depicting the full representation of the divine maternal and paternal components of the Godhead. (see: Ps. 27: 10). They are the most elevated and most spiritual of all the Angels, and are as such endowed with the most power from God. (see also: Ezekiel 1: read the whole chapter and take note of verse 13), describing them as appearing "like coals of fire." They are both usually dispatched to minister in situations where the extremity and eminency of the danger or crisis faced with, or in progress is crucially leaning towards those of physical, emotional, and mental harm or eminent fatality.

The Angelic Thrones of Light:

They function as protectorates of children and everything that exists in natural Godliness. The Thrones of Light dutifully carry out their purposes by purely ensuring and effecting the sure propagation of fertility, excellent health, and emotional well being. They divinely respond to their dutiful purpose by responding in the darkest hour when humans have lost all hope and comfort, through 'extreme emotional exhaustion' (EEE). At this juncture of tested faith, they show up to execute their purpose by burning every negativity within sight and sound to sheer nothingness purely armed with timely focus and faultless precision. Just like the Angelic Principalities of Light, they are also statically positioned as stately sentinels situated at God's side. The Angelic Thrones of Light represent the divine maternal component of the warriors of God's army. When summoned for purpose and function driven duty, they gallantly arrive with minions of Angelic thrones on all sides brandishing flashing swords, as they fight negativities by totally banishing the forces of darkness with a pure sense of eradication. The Thrones of Light project the motherly emotions of God by fiercely and actively protecting His children(us). Their motherly tendencies are similar in likeness of devotion, affection and love, to that which exists between the baby elephant and its mother. They are by nature very refreshing, in aura, purpose, and constant by availability,(ever presence) and may be likened to the very air that we breath. The Angelic Thrones have tremendous rejuvenating and revitalizing abilities which when divinely projected, at the appropriate time, can transform ones weakness, fear and uncertainties into that of a 'Heightened Spiritual Exuberance' (HSE). They shine like gold, the precious mineral that exudes their royal and priceless duties accorded to God the Father, and also denotes the refined purity of their servitude to Him. They are identified by wings of rich purplish white; the colorful depiction of their closeness to the Divine Paragon of Royalty and Majestic Power; The Holy Lord God Almighty.

The Angelic Principalities of Light:

The Principalities of light are the Angelic representation of the Fatherly component of the Godhead. They are in charge of Continents, nations and Great cities; and as such, respond to their divine purpose as God-sent protectorates of pure religion and unadulterated spirituality. They are the Angelic escorts in charge of 'Divine Protocol' (DP) in Heaven; working hand in hand and alongside the Angelic Thrones of Light as they escort the Good and Kindly souls of light, who have passed on, into God's divine presence in Heaven, as soon as they emerge out of the 'Tunnel of Light' by taking them by the hand on both sides and forming a 'Divine Canopy' (DC) of victory by way of interlocking their enormous wings to simulate the letter 'V' above the Kind soul's head and also by engulfing him or her in a 'V' frontal clasp by way of bringing their outer wings together thus, touching beautifully at the sides and tips as they Angel-float the kind soul on a puffy cloud of glory towards God's Majestic Throne, drowned in the pure melodies, tones and vibrations of the choirs of heaven. Wow! What a just and peaceful reward for all those who have diligently sought and acquainted themselves with God. Amen. And thus the expression "gone to a better place." utilized in constancy by Christians and other religions alike as a source of hopeful yet sure word of comfort and that of 'Realistic Divine Expectation' (RDE) is truly and spiritually justified.

Because of their 'Heightened and Elevated Spiritual Status'(HESS). They possess more grace and power to deliver solace to all areas of our needs. They are as strong as fire, and endowed with great power and force that roars like an infernal blaze from within them to consume and devour manifested evil, and its tendencies, including all disrupting forces of negativities that blocks and propels adverse stumbling agents on the paths of the Children of God, as they persistently strive to live for Him. The Angelic Principalities of Light are also close to the throne of God as the Angelic Thrones of Light. (As you may have previously realized), their job description exhibits greatness in magnitude and strength, laced with high intelligence, by duty and purpose. They carry golden spears, projecting tremendous powers from within, without the need to exude or project effort and agility. The Principalities of Light move as one or in flights of twos, threes, but no more than four at a given time. And yet operate as one great force with tremendous divine ferocity. They move in smaller groups unlike other Angels, because of the greatness in magnitude of their power force. Though they may stand still, when on duty, (which usually fools the adversary,) they are able to project phenomenal energy of the highest caliber; thus underestimating their immeasurable power considering their immobile posture and fewer numbers can be very misleading; as a single Principality of Light can completely knockout trillions of darker entities or adversities onto the 'Canvas of Divine Conquest' (CDC), right within the Spiritual 'Combat Ring of Defeat', (SCRD) without physical effort, but by an inner force projected from a source of pure strength, which comprises of spiritually driven heavenly components, that serves the adversary a vanquishing platter of divine conquest, as well as spelling out to its demons, a sentence carried out by the fierce pounding of the heavenly gavel, with the pure force, strength and authority extracted from God's very own 'Divinely Refined Justice' .(DRJ)

Their primary function is to attend to God the Father, and to represent His Divine army. As dutiful as knights, they propel their divine function by making sure that, at least one of them is left at the Father's side when they are in urgent need of, on earth. They carry out their duties to God with pure devotion and unblemished loyalty. For even though God is All-Power and All-Knowledge, and sits in the heavens as King of Kings and Lord of Lords, in Divine Majesty, with the whole earth as His Footstool, all bathed in Glorious Splendor worthy of praise, worship, adoration, and utmost servitude; He has nonetheless by His Power and Lordship, appointed The principalities of Light out of all the Angelic phyla to serve His greatest purpose. Thus, whenever the Principalities of Light are Assembled, then dear reader, you must know without a doubt that God is in their midst; Divinely projecting His holy presence through His countenance of power and might too pure to behold, on account of its vast luminescence and phosphorescence, that can be completely blinding to the naked eye. Exodus (3: 2 – 6 KJV) divinely and evidently introduces us to the presence of God in the midst of the fiery assembly of an Angelic Principalities of Light as follows; "And the Angel of the Lord (Principality of Light) appeared unto him (Moses) in a flame of fire (depicting the manifestation of the power projected from within The Angelic Principality of Light when on duty for God; a function that no other Angelic Phyla possesses.) out of the midst of a bush: and he (Moses) looked and behold, the bush burned with 'FIRE', (Functional divine projection from within The Angelic Principality of Light and the bush was not consumed. And Moses said, I will now turn aside, to see this great sight, why the bush is not burnt. And when the Lord saw (authenticating my findings that, this Angelic phyla are the closest to God by function and purpose) that he turned aside to see, God called unto him out of the midst of the bush, and said, Moses, Moses. And he said, Here am I. And he said, draw nigh hither: put off thy shoes from off thy feet, for the place whereon thou standest is Holy Ground. Moreover he said, "I am the God of thy Father, the God of Abraham, The God of Isaac, and the God of Jacob. And Moses hid his face; for he was afraid to look upon God." (depicting the physical evidence of the vast luminescence and great phosphorescence in exuberance, of God's countenance, too powerful to behold; thus, completely blinding to the mortal eye.) Thus we know and as such believe that wherever the Angelic Principalities of light are gathered God is in their midst roaring with divine luminescence and brightness too vast to behold.

> " Lift up your heads
> all ye gates and be ye lifted up
> ye everlasting doors
> and the King of glory shall come in
> who is this King of glory?
> this King of glory!
> the Lord strong and mighty; exalted in battle.
> Lift up your heads
> all ye gates and be ye lifted up
> ye everlasting doors
> and the King of glory shall come in
> who is this King of glory?
> The Lord of Hosts
> He is the King of glory
> The Lord of Hosts
> He is the King of glory
> He is the King of glory
> The Lord of Hosts is the King of Glory
> He is the King of glory.
> King of Glory."

*From Handel's 'Messiah' rightly divided from the book of Psalm 24: verse 7 to 10 KJV.

Scriptural and audiovisual references supplied for Angelic research:

Ps. 34:7 (personalize and use it as your daily prayer.)
Ps. 91 (personalize and use it as your daily prayer.)
Matt. 24: 31, 25: 31, 26: 53
Mk. 1: 13, 8: 38, 12: 25
Lk. 2:13 – 15, 4: 10, 16: 22
Heb. 1: 1-14 13: 2
2Pet. 2: 11
Rev. 5: 11, 12: 7, 21: 12
Rev. 22: 5&6, 16, 20-21

Angels in movies:

- Angels in the outfield. (Starring; Danny Glover and Tony Danza.)
- Northfork; the most spiritually inspiring movie in my opinion, involving Angels. (Starring; James Woods, Nick Nolte and Mark Polish.) See if you can identify the various Angelic phyla listed below as represented in the movie, by purpose and function; and record your findings in the subsidiary pages allocated for notes in this book. They are as follows: Angelic Dominion, Cherubim, Angelic Throne and Principality of Light. This movie is spiritually deep and requires Divine and Spiritual Intellect, but the Holy Spirit will furnish and guide you into its apprehension.

Last but not the least is "The Preacher's wife" with Denzel Washington and Whitney Houston. (testifying to fact that Angels take on human form to practically feel and fit into some dire situations at hand by function and purpose)

᠁("These are my favorite but you may watch others of your choice since there are many, thank you.)

Dear reader, now that all your anxieties, questions, and uncertainties (if any) about Angels, their names, category, functions and purposes have been spiritually as well as scripturally clarified through no other source but the word of truth, rightly divided, I pray that God Himself the God of peace, within the love, wisdom and purity whence they were created, sanctify you through and through, by granting you the grace to acquire unshifting faith and belief, as you incorporate Angelic ministry into your effective prayer life, so as to enable you fulfill your spiritual quota in heaven, to be translated into victories won and goals accomplished, as you traverse this earthly realm, rightly dividing His word of truth concerning His Angels, created to serve your needs with dedication and haste in your God given life, as an heir of salvation. Amen:)

"And there were in the same country shepherds abiding in the field, keeping watch over their flock by night. And, lo, the Angel of the Lord came upon them, and the glory of the Lord shone round about them: and they were sore afraid. And the Angel said unto them, Fear not: for, behold I bring you good tidings of great joy, which shall be to all people. For unto you is born this day in the city of David a Saviour, which is Christ the Lord. And suddenly there was with the angel a multitude of the heavenly host praising God and saying, Glory to God in the highest, and on earth peace, good will toward men."

Luke 2: 8-14 (KJV.)

"… bless the Lord, ye His ANGELS that excel in strength, that do His commandments, hearkening unto the voice of His word. Bless ye the Lord, all ye His hosts; ye ministers of His, that do His pleasure. Bless the Lord, all His works in all places of His dominion: Bless the Lord, O my soul." Amen and Amen.

Psalm 103: 20–22 (KJV.)

CHAPTER FIVE:

FASTING; YOUR PRAYER TOOL TO SPIRITUAL LUCIDITY, THE ESSENTIAL LUBRICANT FOR YOUR PRAYER WHEEL.

"Fasting in our faith as Christians is by my definition, "The acquisition of spiritual elevation and the physical realization of divine performance in one's life by the deliberate yet beneficial act of the abstinence of one's body from nourishment, as well as those of physical and emotional pleasures, for the sole and divine purpose of religious cleansing, while opening the body's spiritual channels up to receive ample blessing from on high, through the propelling of one's prayers and supplication into expedited performance and manifestation by God." (ADA). It is therefore the vital tool for effective prayer that should not be overlooked and underestimated; and must be carried out on a frequent yet systematic basis. Fasting is not as difficult as you may think. It is all about focusing your need onto a higher spiritual level, in order to successfully fuel and propel its motivation. There are different ways to accomplish a fast. Ways that can be beneficial as well as suitable for all Christians, regardless of their profession, schedules and life styles. Let us begin our lesson with, the total or dry fast.

Dry or total fast:

This type of fast is accomplished by absolutely ingesting no food and water over a set period of time or number of days. You may as a beginner in the fasting arena, start a total fast on a daily basis before graduating to that of days, weeks, fortnights, and so on and so forth. You may also choose a total fast if the situation at hand or the need is urgent; which requires 'Spiritual Aggression' (SA). This may be due to the fact that, the seriousness of the situation at hand, may call for the need to institute absolute fasting in all totality, in order to attain 'Spiritual Lucidity' (SL) or transparency that in turn will propel the Hand of God into immediate and expedited operation, geared towards the ultimate goal of completely and utterly eradicating said problem. Jesus Christ was the divine pioneer of the traditional total fast, which He underwent for forty days and nights after His baptism in the Jordan River by John the Baptist, and was filled with the Holy Spirit. (Read Luke. 4: 1 & 2). Thus the traditional and ever popular forty day fast was born; a legendary act of great spiritual proportions, that has never failed to yield physically manifested, spiritual benefits and performance and has as such, aided many a Christian during trials and tribulations. You may break a total fast by gradually ingesting mild or bland fluids like clear broth, non spicy or mild soup and tepid water, then slowly but surely introduce semi solids, into your diet before graduating to regular solid foods.

The partial fast:

During this type of fast, which may last as long as the total fast, or even longer depending on the urgency and magnitude of one's individual need, a particular period of time is chosen during the day when the fast is actually put into effect. It is then broken gradually with water and mild nourishment like fruits. I know people who partially fast on a daily basis indefinitely. This promotes spiritual growth and dedication that stems from unwavering 'Spiritual Discipline' (SD). A typical example of a partial fast, is one carried out from 6a.m. until 6p.m., as a daily spiritual routine, or over a set period of time when the fast is then broken at the latter time, only to be resumed at the former time, of the next day. The partial fast attracts a lot of people who want to fast but cannot decide on how to go about it because of a health condition, work schedules, other professionally demanding reasons, social engagements, or other fast-hindering yet functionally necessary social obstacles. It is also most suitable for the highly corporate or occupationally busy Child of God, people on medications, lactating mothers, and new comers in the fasting arena. They are thus able to fast for fewer hours by choice, to suit their physical as well as spiritual capabilities, while gradually growing and graduating from the 'rookie' level of fasting, to the total fast level; or in some cases, maintaining the partial fast, routine while slowly but spiritually graduating to the total fast. There are a lot of believers who partially fast by eating fruits during the period set aside for the fast. Personally, I call that body cleansing and not fasting, because of the act of food ingestion. (see; Author's definition of fasting in paragraph one of this chapter.) I hope that Apple, the technological giant will in the very near future design a program to help busy fasting people, track their fast, just as they did with the iphone by introducing a program for busy Catholics to keep track of their sins, in order to remember them for confession. The icon is the so cute; an ornate cross, Wow! how 'cool' is that? Shall we continue our subject please; Thank you.

Sleep fasting:

This is done by sacrificing one's sleep at night, for the sole purpose of prayer and supplication. It is very effective and boosting for the worried, depressed and in agony, who are not able to sleep at night since they may be restless from worrying. Sleep fasting can be very calming and peace-giving because of the quietness and serenity the night brings. All is still at this time; and so is the fasting individual. You must realize that when you are still, spiritual reflection and divine focus is activated around you, thus propelling God's presence. For even though the body is physiologically designed to be at rest at night, when duty or circumstances call for a detour from that routine, you have to implement it no matter the cost, by doing whatever it takes to enable you gather your fair share of 'spiritual truffles.' (ST) "Be still and know that I am God." Read, (Psalm 46: 10a.). during your stillness and reflection, the Lord will definitely show up and surely redeem you from what everyone deems irredeemable. Sleep fasting projects the repressed as well as depressed soul towards the healing and recovery throne of the Almighty and also restores vitality and cheer to the hopeless and the weak. Sacrificing one's sleep for the sole purpose of prayer and spiritual reflection is as effective and spiritually yielding as other fasts and often times proves to be more potent. You may sleep fast after a meal or even without one. Which actually bears no marring effect on the 'Potential Spiritual Yield' (PSY) of the fast. You may at this time be wondering if I am in controversy, due to what you have read so far. But let me explain once again, based on my definition of 'fasting' in the first paragraph of this chapter. During this type of fast, sacrificing your sleep or time of rest, becomes your area or object of abstinence. Get it? And as such, the particular 'physical pleasure' given up for the ultimate acquisition of the need that propelled said fast, is spiritually cast in the mortar of your sleep sacrifice, which in turn propels the wheels of providence, out of the uncertain environs of dire aspiration, into those of sure manifestation for your benefit and to the glory of God.

Our Lord Jesus Christ, once again was the initiator of the sleep fast. The word of truth rightly divides this fact by telling us that, The Master took His disciples to the Garden of Gethsemane to pray all night after the last supper. He did not go to sleep that night because, He was in agony, (hence its benefit to the worried, depressed and in agony) as the son of man; and as such had the need for 'Divine Stillness and Spiritual Reflection'(DSSR), by communing with The Father, that night. The Word of truth tells us that, He prayed so intensely that night, and was sweating the likes of blood droplets onto the ground, as His agony increased. When an Angel of God appeared unto Him. (An Angelic Principality of Light) How do I know this? Because, Jesus prayed and called to God as 'Father' and as we have learned from the chapter on Angels, we know that The Angelic Principalities of light, are one of the two angelic phyla closest to the throne of God, and serve their divine purpose, ministering as the spiritual representation of the paternal embodiment of the Godhead. Thus bearing the function of executing pure Justice and instilling divine intellect in times of confusion and agony, and also projecting their tremendous strength from within, without agility, by way of divine purpose to the one in need of aid, from 'the Father'. As you may recall, the Holy Word of Truth stresses on how Jesus gained supernatural STRENGTH instantly during His time of agony, and how He prayed more earnestly, as He grew stronger after the Angelic visitation or appearance.

Please note that, even though He was in agony, even during the last supper, our Lord Jesus Christ, sleep-fasted in the Garden of Gethsemane on the night He was betrayed; a fast divinely chosen by Him, for the expedited manifestation of renewing His strength, which was fading due to the agony pertaining to what is to come, as well as to harness physical tolerance, since He was a man of flesh and blood, to enable Him face the great task ahead; being, His betrayal, arrest, trial, punishment, crucifixion, death and His ultimate resurrection. In the garden, His disciples fell asleep, even though He asked them to pray with Him. But this was not because they did not care for The Master, oh no. But because, they were troubled, confused and as such, slept 'for sorrow' as the King James Version of the Word of Truth, Rightly Divides. This particular psychological state of the disciples, actually opens our eyes to the fact that, uncertainty, leads to sorrow, which further leads to depression which shuts us down; dulling our senses, while robbing us physically of all energy, making us sleep excessively, which in turn affects our spiritual performance as well as stamina. This behavior is a true and factual medical and clinical finding, exhibited by people suffering from depression. (see: Luke 22: 39 – 45 KJV.) As a child of God, you must always prepare yourself for any type of fast by putting into consideration, your social life's schedule. Never on any occasion allow your 'Spiritual Obligation' (SO) interfere with your family life, professional, corporate and social responsibilities; but rather, let the former enhance the latter as you keep in mind, the Apostle Paul's wise instruction towards, marrying spirituality to social discipline, in order to achieve decency and order not only within the Church, but also within society, and the family. (see: 1Corinthians 14:40).

How to break a fast. (food intake after a fast.) and how to last during a fast by making good decisions. (Avoiding temptations or unwholesome diversions)

Even though the primary purpose of a fast is to induce and enhance the spiritual performance and physical realization of our prayers and supplications, which are of course the conveying vehicles of our needs and desires, it also serves as a cleansing and rejuvenating avenue for our body system. Therefore, care must be taken in the specific area of choosing the appropriate nourishment suitable enough to propel the body into alimentary normalcy, upon completion of a total fast. For example; food intake should be limited to very light and less spicy food like; chicken, fish or vegetable broth, and mild fruits (less acidic) such as; mangoes, melons, pawpaws, pears and bananas. You may also commence food intake with an initial dose of tepid water, light maize or rice porridge and organic herbal tea, to let out the air pockets trapped in the stomach due to the lack of food ingestion and the interruption or irregularity of the digestive process, depending on the type of fast you had. Appropriate fluid and food intake after a long period of total fasting, helps to prevent the onset of gastrointestinal discomfort which is usually triggered when people start ingesting food ravenously after they break total fasts. You may also choose to indulge in a fruit diet when undergoing a partial fast, or ingest meatless foods as long as you are fasting, as these foods are easier on the digestive tract. People on medication and those in delicate conditions, or the elderly and frail may stick to soup, broth and fruits during a partial fast, in order to keep their bodies in nutritional balance and of course consult their General physicians before starting any fast.

Purchasing groceries and preparing family meals during a fast, should be minimized if possible by finding alternate avenues, as this will subconsciously contaminate as well as defeat the entire abstinence process and ones spiritual focus as well. Try to do all your grocery shopping and food preparation ahead of the fast, and store them for your family if no one else is available to take up that role. Resist the temptation to taste meals cooking in the home by others during the fast, only to make up for that abstinence contamination by muttering a quick prayer, which will spiritually and realistically not bounce you back into 'spiritual focus'(SF). Accusing others like your room mate, tenants, or family members of being inconsiderate just because they happen to cook your favorite meal, should also be avoided together with the rest of the above during your fast. If the temptation arises, alternatives like a visit to the neighborhood Family Christian bookstore is always the best; where you can camp between the shelves with a spiritually enriching book, for your own edification or better still a trip to the library, a walk in the neighborhood and the beach a perfect place for reflection is also commendable. The mall is too superficial a place during this time; and there's too much food there for a person in your spiritual mindset or one trying to reach a certain spiritual height like you not to lose focus amidst the numerous wafting mouthwatering aromas; while putting into consideration shoppers walking around with yummy colossal ice cream cones, while others sink their teeth into gooey 'Cinnabon' pastry dripping with cream cheese frosting (my favorite:), or the temptation to dash over to Sainsbury's with the innocent notion of picking up an emergency item for the family, which rather finds you fighting hard to resist the temptation to quickly devour a hot and crusty meat pasty, or even worse, walking too close to the evening open market in Africa trying hopelessly to fight the urge to cheat on the fast as you are enticed by food vendors to purchase juicy mouthwatering khebabs and zesty ripe plantain chips. (Ghana has the best) These places dear reader, are just too tempting; so please stay away from them as well as supermarkets and food vending lanes and avenues. Also, when you are not so professionally engaged, during the work day, you may find a quiet place to reflect, without interruption before resuming work.

Places like lakesides, parks, and neighborhood trails, can be spiritually diverting when contamination or disruption of the abstinence during a fast is environmentally threatened. In the African countryside, meditating under a shady mango tree is the best, In Washington DC, a walk along the tidal basin amidst the famous cherry trees with a walkman, while listening to inspirational music is always a good choice; Whilst in Accra Ghana a visit to the Kwame Nkrumah Mausoleum, or a time of spiritual reflection at the Holy Trinity Cathedral (where my late sweet mother was married) on High Street, which is always open will do, or yet still a stroll around Castle drive taking in the sea breeze from the mighty Atlantic, and a stroll at Ridge Park will suffice. Always bear in mind that, prayer, reflection, focus, calmness, and serenity are key to a successful fast, and not a lengthy one filled with the opposite. Please never forget that, fasting is another way to crucify the yearnings of the flesh, when it is carried out in all truth, humility and 'spiritual discipline' (SD), for believe me, when that flesh is fully crucified, there will be no room for sightings of 'golden arches' on the horizon because, your focused and disciplined mind, will be resting on nothing else, but the utter Godly performance and great physical manifestation of the need that initially propelled the fast.

How to spiritually prepare yourself for a fast.

Before commencing a fast, the first thought that should engage your mind is Spiritual 'cleansing'; that is to purify by getting rid of contaminants and matters of obstruction within the body. In this case you have to search every nook, cranny and crevice of your soul, and as such your mind, for every negativity that is hidden within. These negativities may be social; like indifference with others, and wrongful acts that ought to be put right. All these and others should be appropriately resolved, by way of confession, correction, amendment of character, and adequate compensation where necessary. The aggregate of such cleansing must surely be carried out without pride, arrogance and defensiveness; for it is by way of shedding the latter that your very being will be ready for that 'Spiritual Elevation' (SE), which can only be manifested when you have lost that weight of unconfessed sins and matters not rectified, after which you must go to God with a prayer of forgiveness, in total repentance. Once again, the word of God admonishes us that, "if we say that we have no sin, we deceive ourselves and the truth is not in us; and that if we confess our sins He is faithful and just to forgive us our sins, and to cleanse us from all unrighteousness." (see: 1John 1: 8&9KJV) You as a fasting Christian must constantly but spiritually bear in mind that, every aspect of your spiritual life should be in total balance by applying this scripture to ensure the swift and sure transportation of your requests and supplications to the prayer halls of heaven.

Unbelief is also another stumbling block that steadily, but surely in a very obstructive way, infiltrates stains of negativity into your fast, thus preventing and of course obstructing the free flow of your supplications to the throne of God. In view of these facts, you must disengage your conscience from even the slightest possibility of entertaining thoughts of unbelief, as well as making a conscious effort to free your body in its entirety from all forms of perversions and adverse entanglements, in order to rightly present yourself in pureness of spirit as one who is traversing the river of God's blessed abundance, while waiting in complete faith for the sure expectation of being transported aboard His divine vessel of beneficence, across the prosperous oceans overflowing abundantly with greater manifestations, and that of the undisputed evidence of His goodness in your life. (wow! this is by far my longest sentences aha!) "Blessed are the pure in heart, for they shall see God." (see: Matthew 5: 8KJV.) The ability to see God in this biblical passage is not the visual perception of what the scriptural text literarily denotes, alone; but the divine manifestation of God's blessing in your life as revealed by His goodness towards you, by way of prosperity, reversal of adversities, and a significant shift in the level and fulfillment of peace in all areas of your life. As a Child of God, employed in the corporate circles, (since most of you are) you must take spiritual caution, by making sure that your corporate responsibilities do not conflict with your fast (spiritual duty.) Thus before setting time for the fast, try as much as possible to get rid of any overdue and outstanding workload, to ensure a less stressful environment during the fast. Also try to keep a solemn demeanor and try as much as possible to proportion your focus on God, with that of your work by keeping both duties in perfect balance. Never on any occasion and for any reason neglect your corporate duties due to the fast; as this will spark the element of chastisement from the Lord of the fast in your direction, for the simple act of failing to Rightly Divide His Word of Truth which teaches that, "The laborer is worthy of his hire" (see Luke 10: 7b) as this scripture though usually applied to favor the hired most times was written to cut both ways by its right division within the substance of truth from whence it was devised. In a nutshell, you must learn to always keep both work and fast in appropriate balance and be sure to grasp whenever possible, little free periods during the work day to meditate or read the word of God. You may also, utilize mental prayer as you go about your daily routine and duties, while keeping in mind that as a child of God, in a world that is going through a lot of changes spiritually (most of which may be counter biblical or adversely religious and so confusing), one must learn to grow alongside those changes without being affected by them; a state of mind that can only be achieved by allowing one's faith to malleably tread a sound scriptural path alongside them by the astute application of good Christian sensibilities, and not being reformed by them (the changes and new doctrines) as you Christ-walk in this world of adversities, going about your earthly duties and responsibilities.

As the world advances daily in all social aspects, religion is most affected and Christians must not find themselves being forcibly compelled to tag along with it, but must rather assume a defensive spiritual posture of self preservation, or be thrown unguardedly into a challenging situation, where as adherents committed to rightly divide the word of truth, are left with the desperate choice of conforming to the pressures of these rapid changes. If we mean to withstand the pressure, then we must quickly shift gears of faith, belief and hope onto a well balanced and scripturally upgraded hard-drive, in order to strategically texturize our religion, by systematically excavating the fossils of resilience embedded within the divine layers of the word of truth, and utilize them to encrust our doctrine from Genesis to Revelation; thereby shielding it from adulteration. Our daily lives as Christians of this century must in no way reflect the tell tale signs of having to succumb to the pressures of this world, but rather be texturized with ingredients extracted from core scriptural sources and resources to incorporate therein, so as to deflect temptations and weakness we may be confronted with, as we journey in this world. Fulfilling our duties therefore as children of God, means upholding and defending our faith non violently, while firmly administering adequately amplified versions of balanced Christian teachings into our scriptural curriculum, in order to obliterate forces that mean to plunge us into obscurity and decadence. This is the only way we can adequately function prayerfully within the required divine standards of our Faith, in God and belief in Jesus Christ His begotten Son; but we do not have to do this unadvisedly, for the Holy spirit is provided by the ever outstretched hand of providence of Jehovah-Jireh, to instruct us unto all righteousness.

We are all aware of the fact that, the world has experienced a drastic technological transformation. So also have we; as well as the adversary with whom we wrestle daily. For his attacks are becoming more complex, changing by leaps and bounds alongside the world; and that is the more reason why we as Christians of the new millennium, some of whom are stuck in the analogue era of spiritual defense, must shed all traces of spiritual dormancy, and rise with haste to update our spiritual defense strategies by applying adequate scriptural techniques. For when the new millennium ushered us into this profound technologically advanced era, so were the principalities and powers of the darkness of this world. Believe it or not they have conformed and upgraded their strategies of spiritual attacks digitally, while we as Christians sit and wonder why our prayers are not being answered. I know why. Because as ambassadors of Christ and heirs of salvation, we have failed to represent God's word of truth wholesomely, by the sheer lack of 'good christian sense' (GCS) which constitutes divine wisdom given freely from God when asked for; which when appropriately applied scripturally, propels the upgrading of our spiritual hard drives; A move in the winning direction for our Faith, which entails the prompt cessation of incessant scriptural stagnancy induced by the continuous lack of divine acumen, that in actuality is fueled by the persistent lack of in-depth bible study, extensive scriptural researching, teaching, absorption, retention and utilization, even though we live lives that readily show off our cloaks of regular church attendance, and other ritualized services in the Fold, devoid of practical scriptural substance and elements of spiritual sustenance, we can overturn our shortcomings by putting on the whole armor of God, while shedding these pretentious cloaks in order to gain the boldness to recover our lost footing on the global religious platform. A move that is sure to swiftly surge us into higher voltage of unprecedented spiritual advancement that will definitely shock the adversary into retreating, as it confidently propels us into a realm of rare spirituality that supersedes that of the rapidly changing world; thus making us divinely and scripturally qualified upholders and defenders of our Faith, while we reap outstanding prayer outcomes as we faithfully await the brightness of Christ's coming. Amen.

How fasting expedites your prayer into effectiveness:

When you fast, you basically drain your body entirely of all sensation; thus crucifying your mortal self, which is 'the flesh' against all pleasurable sensation. In so doing, your spirit-man is quickened and made lighter for the penetration of the positive feedback of the requests you made of God during the fast, by way of prayers and supplication.

Physically, you become lighter, lucid and 'transparent', thus enabling God to touch you within, while reaching through your lucid self to transform your needs into direct accomplishments; because your crucified and cleansed self, becomes more conducive to His pure nature, it assumes the image of His likeness within you; And as such, grants Him pure access to your lucid self, to perform wonders and inject miracles of restoration and recovery into your contorted life without delay. Based on the above findings, I can theoretically as well as theologically profess that;

"Fasting is the divine twin to the baptism of the Holy Spirit. The latter (the Holy Spirit) grants you access to speak mysteries directly unto God, bypassing every human reasoning, and that of the unholy forces of the adversary as well; while the former (fasting) rids your spiritual life of hovering adversities and interfering forces, while at the same time granting God direct access to your prayers as He transforms your needs to those of victorious accomplishments and miraculous manifestations surpassing all human analogy and understanding without delay." (ANQ)

The timeless spiritual and physical benefits derived from fasting:

(1) Fasting restores your spiritual vitality.

(2) It injects supernatural praying capabilities and performance into your body system.

(3) Fasting transports you to immeasurable spiritual heights.

(4) It rids your life and surroundings of negativities, by totally weakening, crippling and eradicating their rejuvenating sources and capabilities.

(5) Fasting purifies your body, thus granting God the Father direct access to work on you as well as your needs.

(6) It grants you expedited access to your life's benefits from God, by acting as the catalyst that physically propels your forthcoming breakthroughs into total manifestation.

(7) Fasting cleanses your body physically, and mentally of adverse contaminants, while clinically boosting your health and immune system.

(8) It also reawakens your neurons intellectually, by way of freeing them from toxic blockages that cause hormonal stagnation and physiological imbalances thus, rejuvenating the divine wisdom given to you from God, for the uninterrupted absorption of His word of truth in your life.

(9) Fasting projects your prayers into a more serious, urgent, and determined light before God's throne.

(10) Fasting injects efficiency and effectiveness into your prayers

(11) It facilitates the remission and total eradication of chronic and incurable maladies and acts as a solution path to divers irreconcilable life issues.

(12) Fasting induces the sure and effective propagation of complete and utter focus within your prayer requests, by utterly cloaking them with precision.

When fasting does not get rid of a negative situation after a considerable period of time, we must let go and allow God's will to be done about that particular circumstance because, the Almighty knows what is best for us.

Thus, in this case complete cessation of that prayer request must be put into effect, by the faithful act of acceptance and belief that, it is a sure and divine path to a new and fruitful beginning, as God who is forever almighty and omniscient sees spiritually and physically fit for the life He has endowed you. Trust me by the very testimony of this written work. For I too have been there, tossed in billows of difficulties and at said time lost it all, in the eyes of the adversary and my peers; losing all my friends like chaff in the wind simply because I had nought; to the point that not one living soul except my close family visited me nor lent their support or condolences when my parents passed away exactly one year after the other. Thus, I wasted years and precious time looking outside of myself for the recovery of my assets and dignity while wondering why me, over and over again. Yet in Christ, I had long won simply because, I lived and died not, and as such my benefits were preserved; hidden within myself in Christ, and not in the degrading and insulting circumstances I found myself in. The Word of truth which never lies, continued unfailingly to make those losses even more fruitful a turn in my life, for my spiritual well being and physical benefit. For at the set time, through those adversities, I went back to retrieve my true self as it had always been gifted unto me since I was born by my creator on high. I had spent half my life being what I was not, and as such no one really knew the real me. A natural writer schooled in heaven long before I was born to Allen and Grace (of blessed memory) in Sub-saharan Africa, by the Angelic Dominions; the winged Professors. This very work you enjoy is testimony enough; for all along my breakthrough was hidden within me; the temple of the Holy Ghost, by the grace of God Almighty whom I profess and uplift in praise and adoration as Lord of this very literary work. Amen.

Jeremiah 29: 11-13NIV makes this clear; "For I know the plans I have for you declares the Lord, plans to make you prosper not to harm you, plans to give you hope and a future. Then you will call upon me, and come and pray to me and I will listen to you, and you will seek me, and find me, when you seek me with all your heart." Yes dear reader in the Lord, you will find Him with all the answers you need, to effectuate that closure you so desperately yearn for, when you held the fast; but take care not to contaminate your fast, because it always leads to a contorted response. Therefore, let your fast be true; for all true fasts yield truthful and fruitful outcomes blessed from the Father above.

Negativities that can hinder your fast and render it non-effective:

(1)   Lack of repentance, character reform, and unconfessed sins or shortcomings.

(1)   Harboring of resentment in the heart, and in the mind thus creating a well of bitterness.

(2)   A wandering and a spiritually unfocused mind lurking in a body that is in the process of a fast.

(3)   Distraction caused by the mind's inability to crucify the flesh. As in food cravings, heightened sexual desires, and the excessive and incessant projection of profanities by way of negative verbal rapport projected by instincts and actions.

(4)   Irreconcilable social differences.

(5)   Excessive public display and boastful acts of broadcasting the fast to all and sundry. (just like the Pharisees and the Sadducees.) Refrain from that by not "wearing the fast" (AOQ) in public or elsewhere, but rather internalizing it; and it will be counted unto your for righteousness.

(6)   The emission of a 'holier than thou attitude' towards others who are not fasting, or towards other Christians, in general.

(7)   Spiritual imbalance perpetuated by the conscious and constant projection of all forms of lies and deception, during the fast.

(8)   Inconsistencies in abstinence during the fast; (sneaking food) thus exhibiting the lack of 'spiritual discipline' (SD)

(9)   Fasting for the wrong reasons; as in fasting for revenge, for a prayer request already answered by the Father that does not meet with your approval, or was far from your expectation due to a set mind. I term such a fast, 'the self-gratification fast", or "The obstinate fast" .

Alertness during your fast should be paramount. Be on the lookout for negative aggression from the adversary by way of upsetting the normalcy of your environment and social life during the fast. These must definitely be overlooked as they are projected to distract your 'spiritual focus.'(SF) These distractions serve the same purpose as going through painful and time consuming physical therapy after bodily injury in order to re-mobilize the body once again. Always remember that, the grace of God is sufficient for you; for His power is made perfect in your weakness; therefore you must never keep your weakness hidden, but bring them boldly before God, and

He will perfect them, so that the power of Christ may continuously dwell in you, and never depart from you. (see: 2Corinthians.12: 9 &10) For at all times, God's power is made perfect in your weakness, therefore when you are weak, then are you strengthened. This scriptural passage depicts the reversal of what is physically deemed normal. Note that during your fast, physiologically you are weakened, but spiritually, you attain tremendous strength from being rendered lucid and divinely elevated towards the heavenly halls of supplications by the Father above.

Remember that the physical weakness of your body during the fast is just the superficial manifestation of the state of your mortal body, when the theory of mind over matter is in reverse, but not in effect as it should be, with the spirit of God controlling the mind to the point of achieving the appropriate spiritual height or elevation to carry out the fast into total completion. Yes! For as your fast progresses, and your mind becomes spiritually saturated with the ultimate goal of touching the Divine, reaching the ultimate, and achieving the absolute, your physical weakness becomes utterly insignificant as your spiritually elevated and saturated mind has no place to process or respond to its physiological manifestations of hunger and apparent weakness of the flesh relayed to your neurons for processing for the body to physically carry out. As such, your mind thus adjusts neurologically to this new physiological state of your body, rendering the adverse effects projected by the absence of nourishment, and other pleasures of the body, non-effective to your physical bodily function and day to day activities. But you as a Child of God must never forget the blessed assurance that the word of truth denotes. For, the Holy Spirit is quickened into greater expedition, and performance in its duties of counseling, and also towards ensuring a victorious and perfect end to your prayer requests, by the 'Divine acceleration'(DA) of it's conviction, depending on the truthfulness, seriousness and pureness of your fast.

The Holy Spirit is not the only divine component of the Godhead that benefits you during a pure and truly balanced fast. Your channels of blessing abiding in the Most High God Jehovah-Jireh the God of Providence and the only true source of accomplishment, are flung open, as you are granted multiple spiritual visas to access the areas of your life restricted and thus contaminated by negativities and adversities, as well as those areas of your life that hold the highly sensitive plans and blue prints of your prospective, and progressive accomplishments. Known in Christian circles as 'breakthroughs'. Thus, fasting the true and pure way, activates the electro-spiritual neon sign on the doors to your dreams and aspirations into

127

blinking 'access granted.' It also propels your prayer requests that land in the heavenly in-tray before God to be expressly processed and transferred to the out-tray within seconds with the highest priority. It places the stamp of approval on the expectant envelopes of your prayer requests and supplications; thus, allowing God to bless you beyond measure. Dear reader, if you ever find yourself too weak physically to fast, focus and surrender your mind in its entirety on the restorative attributes of God by, "mind and thought fasting". You can successfully attain the same or if not, more spiritual height, by exercising this divine process in your sick bed, or wherever you find yourself incapacitated. Remember that, no matter your physical condition, the 'Lord of the fast' has a way out for your spiritual edification because His generosity, in all areas of your life and that of your spiritual growth is limitless, and extensive enough to provide you with a fast that is adequate and suitable for any condition you may find yourself in and under any circumstance.

Therefore if you find yourself too sick to fast, but feel the need for 'intensive spiritual intervention'(ISI) for your present condition, simply propel your mind in its entirety by way of complete surrender, by focusing on the healing and divine restorative attributes of God. Fast in mind and in thought and in spirit, even in your sick bed; this process of fasting unites the three above named components of your body into a spiritually charged medium that can propel your needs to the throne of the Almighty without interruption, for an express reversal of that physical state or condition. Remember that, even though humanly speaking, the sick bed is very unpleasant a place for all who find themselves there, it can still be very beneficial a place of stillness, as well as a place of spiritual reflection, and also that of strength building by way of spiritual growth, that can obviously and without doubt propel one towards the throne of God and right into His comforting arms of love, restoration and healing. Because when a Child of God is propelled spiritually into the comforting arms of God the Father in times of physical weakness or dire need, the appropriate spiritual component in Charge of comforting issues known as the Holy Spirit, assumes office and commences auto-spiritual function on the one in need, by instilling calm through the eradication of stress and pain, while at the same time, infusing wisdom and instruction to the Child of God, together with the Angelic Principalities and thrones of light, (the spiritual representation of God the Father's parental nature of pure love, pure protection and pure devotion.) in order to ensure utter perfection during the healing process. You must also realize that, it is only when a person is totally physically incapable of all the other types of fasting, and has to resort to sleep fasting, and mind fasting, that The Father dispatches the appropriate Angelic phyla to strengthen and to 'power boost' that individual spiritually; like the Angel that appeared to Our Lord Jesus Christ in the garden of Gethsemane, to strengthen Him for the task ahead of Him. Another instance that propels Angelic 'power boost' is by the total yielding of ones mind to things spiritual pertaining to the particular Angelic function and purpose of which one has need of. This process serves as a source of atmospheric fuel for Angelic manifestation, and ministration. Thus have we all learned by this revelation that, there is a fast available for all physical situations. But how often must we fast?

I would say, as often as you nourish your body with food and nutritional substitutes like vitamins and minerals; and as often as you purge your body system for regularity, to ensure adequacy of bodily function and physiological balance, so often should you fast. When you lose regularity in your bowels, you feel inadequate, stuffed and backed-up, cranky, bloated and even look unpleasant and unsightly. Thus, when your body is not in spiritual balance it feels chocked and clogged with impurities that fuel stagnation and putridity, like a babbling brook clogged by rubbish and overgrown water hyacinths and reeds, rendering it stagnant. For when water is unable to flow naturally as it should, it stinks. As Christians, we must cultivate the habit of purging our bodies, spiritually, by fasting to make way for the free flow of God's Divine plan of victory for our Christian lives to be realized by way of manifestation. If there is one other thing that fasting can do for you as a Child of God that I have failed to mention in the list of benefits, it is the boldness, and resistance it exudes from your person, by endowing you with the one and only 'Gigantic Spiritual Air' (GSA); A divinely propelled and instilled attitude of balanced spiritual grandeur which in turn propels you to the utmost spiritual heights of accomplishments. Our Lord Jesus Christ, after He was baptized in the river Jordan, fasted forty days and forty nights, after which upon realizing His apparent state of physical weakness, at the time, the adversary, (devil) came to tempt him, forgetting that Jesus' outward state of weakness due to lack of nourishment was not really a translation of His inner self which by then was not only divinely strengthened, but scripturally elevated into a holy state of G.S.A., backed by purity and perfection from heaven.

During the time of temptation, as you may remember, the adversary sought to derail The Master by accurately quoting scripture from both the old and new testament, twisting the truth with his lies; but Christ was spiritually prepared, bathed in boldness and resistance with the Gigantic Spiritual Status He had acquired (GSA) after the fast. Yes! Our Lord's mind and as such His neurons were fully charged scripturally and spiritually, for He boldly and reversibly quoted the appropriate scripture to resist the adversary as often as the adversary counter-quoted scripture upon scripture, until he fled from 'The Master.' Observe how Our Lord Jesus Christ carried out His spiritual resistance with precision, accuracy and brevity, as He boldly uttered reverse scriptural proclamations with authoritative emphasis and aggression, obliterating the adversary's counter scriptural quotations. Note how appropriately they coordinated in text scripturally, and as such voiding the devil's pronouncements while reestablishing their real meaning, as well as reemphasizing the true purpose of the scriptural texts the devil twistingly used; The Master utilized divine acumen (DA) making His proclamations fit perfectly like the right puzzle pieces do when placed in the coordinating spaces allocated on the puzzle board. Thus God's strength was made perfect in Christ through the word of truth, as the devil sought to prey on His weakened physiological state of hunger, shaking the adversary off completely as He walked away in triumph after slaying the devil by rightly dividing the word of truth; after which Angels came and ministered unto Him. (see: Matthew 4: 1-11); (see also: James 4: 7). Christ himself demonstrated by example the practical importance and indispensability of scripture study and memorizing, and I sincerely hope that as you continue reading this guide, you will grasp my reason for repetitively stressing its importance in the preceding pages of this book. "Resist the devil and he will flee from you" says the word of truth. Learn to apply the word of truth like mortar to the bricks of your mortal resistance as a Christian, and your wall of fortification will hold together; it will act as your permanent protection and shield, by ensuring you a firm footing in life, keeping you from fainting and collapsing during rough times. Not only should you stay alert after the fast, but do so during your fast; as the adversary will try to confuse you with specks of doubt and traces of wavering in the spirit, to distort the flow of the spirit of God within the fast. But if you boldly use your weapon of resistance (the word of truth,) and execute it with precision and accuracy,(by rightly dividing it) you will find yourself spiritually home-free as well as scripturally settled within yourself; yet divinely hid with Christ in God.

Fasting also makes you shine with righteousness. It projects the light of purity, on your countenance like a headlamp on the forehead of a miner, that lights his way out of the dark passages and tunnels of the mine when he loses his way. When righteousness fills you up, you are automatically, spiritually, encompassed and armed with divine boldness, to battle and face any foe and adversary. "the righteous are bold as a lion" (please research and record the source of this scripture together with the text in the subsidiary pages of your guide to effective prayer under 'notes'. This will serve as your first scriptural credential research assignment after having been spiritually as well as scripturally spoon-fed for the literary time of five chapters, which I can assure you as a writer is no joke.) can you imagine the negativities you will be vanquishing around you when you step out daily into the world roaring out there in the spirit like a lion, with a noble mane of righteousness flowing atop your head and down your back in scriptural stresses? Or as a lioness, drooling with 'Spiritual Intellect,' (SI) when you make scriptural research and its practical application a vital part of your life? Remember that righteousness is a virtue awarded by God unto us when we surrender all our yearnings and desires to Him in Faith believing before the fact, like our Father Abraham, who after being promised a son, was strong in faith, hoping against hope, and giving no consideration to his aged physiological state, nor that of his wife Sarah, who was spent in years and past childbearing, staggered not at God's promise through unbelief, but was strong in faith giving glory to God; rejoicing within the full persuasion of utter surrender and as such securing the divine blessings poured unto those who have not seen and yet believe, within which his very attitude and style of absorption and processing of the promise of God to make him a father of many nations earned him an imputable crown of righteousness, which as the word of truth rightly divides, is not limited to him alone but for us also if only we would believe wholly and not partially or when we please, on Him who raised Christ Jesus from the dead, the same shall be imputed unto us. For righteousness does not operate on its own unless married to its two other components namely, joy and peace. All three together are cloaked in the joyous realm of the incomparable wisdom of the Holy Spirit, the divine counselor and comforter. As you come to the end of this chapter, please take time to reflect on the wonderful feeling of peace, solace and serenity, derived from the wisdom you have acquired through this chapter; please apply boldness and set down your prayer load of conscientious self denial, as you boldly and joyfully walk away into a life filled with promises, in the subsequent pages. I pray that you and yours will be strengthened in Him as you choose to glorify the Lord by fasting in truth. Psalm 37: 5 assures you as an heir of salvation thus; "Commit

thy way unto the Lord; trust also in Him; and He shall bring it to pass."
Amen.

Scriptural references on fasting:

1Samuel. 7:6, 31:13
2Samuel. 1:12, 12:16, 21, 22, 23.
Isaiah. 58: 3-6.
1Kings. 21: 9,12, 27.
1Chronicles. 10:12.
2Chronicles. 20: 3.
Ezra. 8: 21-23.
Esther. 4: 3 &16. 9: 31&32
Psalms. 35: 13, 69: 10-13, 109: 24-31
Jeremiah. 14: 10 -12, 36: 5&6.
Daniel. 9: 3.
Joel. 1: 14, 2: 12, 2:15.
Judges. 20: 26
Matthew. 4: 2, 6: 16-18, 9: 14-15.
Acts. 13: 2-3

"May God himself the God of peace sanctify you through and through.
May your whole spirit soul and body, be kept blameless, at the coming of
our Lord Jesus Christ. Faithful is He that calleth you, who also will do
it"

(1Thessalonians. 5: 23-24 NIV &KJV)

Chapter six

How long can one pray for a request or a need? Is there such a thing as a time to stop praying, when circumstances do not change?

The word of God teaches us in the book of Thessalonians to pray without ceasing (see: 1Thessalonians 5:17.) This is because, God is aware of the trials we are daily faced with in the world as His Children. Circumstances that are triggered by adverse experiences, reveal to us the unpredictability of life; thus making the act or process of praying ceaselessly automatic in ones Christian life, even without literarily pausing to reflect on this verse. But this scriptural text does not necessarily mean praying visibly every minute of the day. It simply means allowing God to lead you spiritually as you make your way physically through this life. I can assure you by way of experience that, when you allow God's leadership in your life, you tend to constantly pray to Him at random for guidance in all areas of your life's decisions because, He becomes part of the steady but effective stream that propels your decision making channels. For believe me by giving God precedence and total control over your life, you end up with no other choice of communicating with Him but through prayer. Also dear reader, as often as you see the need to seek His face by way of counsel and advice before making decisions and taking steps, you are left constantly with the sole option of prayer and nothing else. Thus, maintaining a close and personal relationship with God is totally impotent without incessant prayer.

You must also realize that going about your daily business and life's routines without the outward signs of prayerfulness does not make one out to be a Christian who is not ceaselessly praying. Why? Because, prayer can be verbalized, as well as utilized in the mental capacity, to a venue of more or even greater spiritual heights of effectiveness. Daily prayer is the fuse box that controls and balances the currents that spiritually projects our lives into motion, without fear of overload and apparent collapse. Prayer is also the most potent spiritually infused antioxidant in all religion and Christianity is notably graded thanks be to God, within this list I am sure. The Bible is laden with divers instructions and directives on how to pray effectively. It teaches us about the futility of praying amiss, that is the unconscious use of vain repetitions, as that propagates the seed of doubt and wavering which in turn diverts our requests and supplication away from the throne of God. The Bible teaches us that our Father God knows what we need before we ask him. But the question always arises even among Christians and non-believers alike; if so then why pray? Let me free your mind from this persistent tentacle of doubtful and controversial inquisition; you see, when you go to God in prayer for requests already known to Him, He feels known to you by way of the depth of your faith and height of reverence you attach to His capabilities, to His performance power, and by your personal acknowledgment of His divine character, by that simple act of prayer laced with faith. God realizes that despite your knowledge of His omniscience and great power of providence as Jehovah-Jireh, you still realize as well as respect the need to intimately connect with him through the bond of prayer, as a child does to a parent or guardian, by asking before taking the chocolate chip cookie out of that jar while knowing inwardly that they could grab one without asking since it's been made available for their snacking needs anyway. In that instance, the parent feels appreciated, needed, respected and acknowledged. The bonds of family and love are thus tightened by that simple gesture. Another instance is with sheep grazing in an open meadow and yet, decide to stay close to the shepherd's nook still knowing that no matter how far they wander, the shepherd is constantly keeping watch over them, to rescue them from danger. You must realize that praying to God for a need that He already is obviously aware of is a form of spiritual courtesy and Christian ethic (if I may term it so) that should always be enforced by every Child of

God, as they are effectively steered, by the Holy Spirit towards the practical highway of victorious Christian living.

But regrettably, many a Christian have fallen into the abyss of praying over situations that do not conform to the will of God, because of their own selfish and obstinate desires, by misconstruing and manipulating God's final answer to their particular request or situation, in order to make it seem like a partial answer to a prayer request that is on its way to completion and fruition. Thus they spend time fasting and praying for that situation by surreptitiously relying on certain scriptures, in order to fan their desires into a falsified spiritual acceptance and thereby distorting God's Divine function as omniscient. Therefore as Christians we must always bear in mind that, aside of God's directive role in our lives as the creator of the universe, and the author and finisher of our faith, we were at the juncture of creation equipped with a body made in His own image and likeness; He made us wise by endowing us with the ability to balance our prayers in a total spiritual equation, considering the need, the purpose of the need, and its positive effect on our lives. Yet, our human instincts and willpower, triggered by our fervent desires, coupled with the beneficial and anticipated end to our situation, blinds our spiritual sight and clogs our ears from hearing the still small voice of God the Father. Yes! Because oftentimes, we desire the roaring of the fire, the turbulence of the storm in the wind, and the surprise prophesy accompanied by spiritual hip hopping through the isles while overlooking the divine signal itself. Please bear in mind dear reader is that, God's mind is not to be known of humans; for He is the Divine embodiment of pure discretion, righteous in word, and in deed and truth. Let us start our prayer core lesson by observing and analyzing this very common situation; The prayer of a person in a tumultuous marital situation. It relates to a wife's incessant prayer to God for peace and stability, in her marriage.

Now shall we analyze the matrimonial equation, to this situation, from the very beginning; after years of marital turbulence, salvaged periodically by counseling, teaching and direction by the church family and leadership, coupled with series of domestic intervention by the appropriate authorities, the following discoveries were made and found out to be the underlying current of instability and destruction that is and has been eating away at the core of the marital relationship and thereby, found to be the impediment spiritually blocking the prayer channels open by the praying wife in that relationship and household respectively. In this case, the destructive content contained facts about the husband's incorrigible personality of uncontrolled violence and abuse, his financial irresponsibility as a father, a husband and a Head. How long dear reader in Christ should a woman caught in such a dilemma, but totally immersed in the fear of God (which is of course the beginning of wisdom) who is also in total servitude and dedication to her family, keep praying for a breakthrough under these circumstances? And how long should she dedicate her prayer time to such an unchanging situation regarding her spouse? How can one save another if they don't want to be saved? And how long and how much more should those innocent children endure psychological and physical turmoil in that household just because separation or eminent divorce is being avoided for spiritual reasons. Is it worth the mental agony? And does the Father approve of such suffering for a child who loves him and is living within His precepts? Scripture warns us about God's hatred for divorce; but what do we do when the heart and mind of someone who once loved God has drifted from his path so far that they are speedily traveling above and beyond the legal speed limits of regulated Christian living and almost at the point of skidding onto the highway of the apostate?

The only solution to this problem that has span for years, is to rightly divide the word of truth regarding this situation before the vulnerable people involved, are plunged into irreparable hurt or get immersed into irretrievable dungeons of fatalities. As Children of God, we must draw the line between the "waiting on the Lord period," and the "walking in His promises and expectations by faith period." By using this formula, that really and truly worked for me, I confess; the Child of God in trouble frees themselves, together with their vulnerable loved ones, from psychological scars of dysfunction for a better life abundant in God's grace that is of course sufficient for His Children; and potent in perfect power during their time of weakness and vulnerability. The equipment needed for the accurate preparation of this formula is the daring ability to venture into the depths of the appropriate scriptural text to free one's self from that bondage, by the application of 'spiritual wisdom' (SW) and exhibition of 'expert divine acumen' (EDA). "My people perish for lack of knowledge." (Proverbs. 29:18) says the word of God. What will you do as the head Minister of her church family, when one of the sheep entrusted to you by The Master is fallen into a muddy pit of such depth, together with its young ones? Would you continue calling her to the prayer line for hands to be laid on her time after time, hoping for a change without the proper application of the word of truth in regards to her needs as head of the fold?

This woman may even be at risk for a fatality considering her spouse's undisciplined and violent temper. You do not know what spousal abuse is until you have lived with a person who portrays a different manner to outsiders with calculated wit, immersed in extreme generosity and kindness to people outside the relationship, (a psycho outfitted as a human) while you live in fear want and nervousness like an abused pet, treading on eggshells every minute you spend with them. In this case no one believes you and as such you are very alone but for the love of God. As a child of God, you must weigh the gravity and assess the lifespan of the adverse circumstances entailed within the problem and those surrounding it; and at the same time realizing that, Christians are not exempt from trials and tribulations, because they come to test our spiritual grounding, while others show up to remind us of ill-considered choices and imbalances in our life's decisions; while some adversities crop up to forewarn us of the eminent or sure end to certain situations that have been eating us up for decades; thus robbing us of our victories in life as Christians. Do not misconstrue my words because, some situations do change, but only when the perpetrator allows God to take charge by stepping down the ladder of sin and self absorption. Yes! circumstances may change miraculously by persistent and effective prayer, but not without the spiritual participation, complete surrender or yielding on the part of the perpetrator to the operative authority of the Godhead by way of total regret and pure repentance. Others with similar cases on the other hand, are beyond redemption, for they exhibit total disregard to spiritual authority, without fear, because Godly reverence is totally absent in their lives entirely and as such with the church family. Thus after continuous spiritual instruction and assistance over a period of time without change, such a person should be released from the counsel of the brethren which in spiritual practicality declares him an unbeliever from that moment onwards. After such a declaration, the lost soul is thus left without the spiritual coverings that once guaranteed his pure security and spiritual providence to live outside the protective realms of the Most High God of virtues, for the conscientious lack of spiritual discipline. They may wittingly change church families but that is for the world to acknowledge but in the sight of God they are lost.

The woman in question ought to have stopped praying about this situation in the former direction, but should be praying about her new condition and state of affairs by modifying her prayers and thus redirecting them towards the new life she has been endowed with together with her children if any, in Christ. which without a doubt is automatically covered and practically immersed in His love and constant devotion as authenticated by The word of truth in (Isaiah. 54: 5 KJV.) "For thy maker is thine Husband; The Lord of Hosts is His name: and thy redeemer the Holy one of Israel; the God of the whole earth shall He be called." What a blessed assurance for this woman who is faced with a new beginning which as you can testify, dear reader in Christ is filled with divine promises, pressed down, shaken together and running over. The Church family or the Body of Christ must then assume the total and indubitable task of full time ministration of long term resettlement and recovery both spiritually, physically and psychologically. Remember dear reader that, this is not a loss at all but is in spiritual actuality, gain as projected in Christ, through newness of life overflowing with God's providence and all sufficiency. Every Christian must live with the reality that, among us walks people with seared consciences, living beyond the Grace of God, wicked sin loving souls who have sold themselves into utter obeisance to the prince of the darkness of this world, just as you and I have also given our lives entirely to be used of God. By these preceding paragraphs you may have realized that I did opt for total separation for the woman in turmoil, which I believe to be biblically approved by the word of God, as well as it being spiritually and divinely justified by the righteous mercies of Jehovah-Tsidqenu, coupled by the authority vested in the church at large, for severance in cases like these, based on pure judgment and the apparent disclosure of the unsalvageable nature of the situation, and also its foreseeable end which may turn tragic if not thus salvaged.

No person on this earth has the power to change the other character-wise, only God has that authority and power; and He alone can reach the unreachable and cause them to hearken to the voice of His word of truth and of life. God affirms this in His holy word; "My sheep hear my voice, and I know them, and they follow me. And I give them eternal life and they shall never perish, neither shall anyone snatch them out of my hand." (see: John10: 27&28 NKJ) Now if you find yourself in such a predicament, like the woman in prayer, who had to go through severance in order to receive and attain her full measure and stature in life by way of victorious Christian living, you must rid yourself of all guilt and look to the almighty in hope. You must also realize that, your spouse, has been snatched out of God's hand and as such yours, not because of your mistakes but because he (your spouse) hearkened to the voice of treason and not of reason, by allowing himself to be fed from the contaminated trough of the shepherd of adversities, who through treacherous vices was able to override his spiritual reasoning and responsibility to God the Father Almighty and to you his family. Yes! The great deceiver of all time got to him because, he joined or allowed himself to be a part of that sinful sheepfold, through his continuous response to the evil shepherd's persistent call, and also by seeking and finally finding false security, and assurance in the deceptive nook of the devil's crooked staff.

"Behold I stand at the door, and knock: if any man hear my voice and open the door, I will come to him, and will sup with him, and he with me. To him that overcometh will I grant to sit with me in my throne, even as I also overcame, and I am set down with my father in His throne. He that hath an ear, let him hear what the spirit saith unto the churches." (see; Revelation. 3: 20-22 KJV.) This scripture opens our eyes to the fact that, God knows that, not everyone and or situation will bow or submit to His divine authority, as long as the seared conscience of man and his unbendable will is in full gear on the apostate highway. Some prayers may yield 'negative' answers; bearing results or outcomes that are contrary to what we expect from the Father Almighty. But as Children of God and diligent seekers of Him, we must be divinely rest in the assurance that, those answers that do not please us or fall outside our circles of expectation, are always lined with the protective substance composed of a positively blessed and expectant end. As a Christian you may live your full life span and yet leave some of your life's issues not overcome as seen in the public eye and in social circles. Like a life of childlessness, spinsterhood and a history of divorce in your past. But that is not a stain or weakness, nor is it to be viewed or weighed against you spiritually. For it is not a triggering cause for deduction when the overall tally of your victorious Christian life is analyzed spiritually and physically. God hates a considerable number of vices and has spoken against divorce in the word of truth; in fact it is the only thing that he hates that is not a vice but a situation induced condition. I think God hates the divorce which severs our love and commitment to him, and not the divorce involving mortals. That is why He will not allow you to perish (man or woman) in a destructive situation, or in a marriage that is by all indications only partially and not wholly existing in Him. No! the word of God instructs us that the two shall be one. Therefore if the two are existing as two separate individuals then there must be an infection of instability spreading at the juncture or point of fusion that is preventing this unity; and if this infection is left untreated, it will spread to the other parts of the relationship; become gangrened, sever and ultimately maim the relationship. This happens if during treatment, it does not respond to the antidote of spiritual and moral rectitude, propelled by incessant transgression and disruption of spiritual instruction poisonously projected by adverse distractions and diversion which can only be salvaged where necessary by immediate and absolute severance or amputation of said relationship, to restore and preserve what is left of the participants.

These instances, explanations and teaching now gives you the insight, and wisdom to accept that, cessation of prayer about a particular need, should only be effectuated when there is a clear indication of an adverse turn in the particular situation that called for the prayer in the first place, manifesting itself as an unteachable spirit, a situation that keeps getting worse and dangerously fatal to the parties involved after persistent counseling (both spiritual and professional) and 'intensive verbal spiritual intervention' (IVSI) and of course prayer, due to lack of spiritual discipline, lack of repentance, a hardened heart, and sometimes a sure intervention of said situation by way of prophetic uttering, miraculous manifestations, coupled with the constant stagnancy of certain situations. As a Christian in such a predicament you have to loose your prayer covering over that situation by reversing your prayer not in the persistent direction of an attempt to forcibly overcome the helpless situation (not hopeless,) but in order to accurately navigate the sails of your praying vessel through the billows of bleakness perpetuated by critical bystanders, as you set sail armed with an anchor fashioned from insurmountable faith and hope, within the teaching confines of The Holy Ghost; the counselor and instructor at the helm, to guide you against the adverse tides and winds of opposition and resistance, towards a greater expectancy in The Lord God Almighty, giving glory to Him as you ought to do in all things and at all times.

If on the other hand, your prayer is answered to your hearts content and as such falls within your original expectation, give thanks and glory to God, and continue praying for His guidance so that the rectified situation will flourish into uninterrupted realization as it travels towards its goal of fruition. Either way, I see the response to both prayers (expected and unexpected) as rightly answered, in the way that the omniscient God sees fit for the divine penetration of His beneficence into the praying person's life, by way of adequately rendering the appropriate outcome to prayers, based on His spiritually sketched blueprint or plan for the life of the one who prayed for that particular request. Therefore acknowledge the pure fact that, there is no cessation in prayer, and no cut-off time either; but rather a time of modification and shifting of prayer gears towards the appropriate direction depending on circumstances, because prayer is the spiritual embodiment of our existence in the Christian faith, as well as the bonding substance that propels our relationship with God the Father, God the Son and God the Holy Spirit into proper balance to ensure and secure its divine amalgamation. However, you may as a Child of God, always make room for 'prayer pause', to create room for the shifting of spiritual gears, and to effect changes for reflection and redirection of the motive, need and the goal of your prayer. But only when God sees it fit to steer you towards a different direction due to the stagnancy of the situation or its unresponsiveness. Therefore make prayer on-going in your life as a Child of God; form and propagate that 'spiritual habit' (SH) because, there's always the need for direction from The Author and Finisher of our faith. Also remember that in Christ there is no such thing as a hopeless situation, it is always a matter of helplessness, grafted and nursed by the persistent lack of 'spiritual sight' (SS) and 'divine acumen'(DA) the two key standpoints that steers the Child of God towards the rightful division of God's word of truth. However when praying for a person who is consciously and persistently leading a life of extreme incorrigibleness and exhibiting signs of 'constant spiritual rebellion'(CSR) laced with a seared conscience, (due to a deadened Christ conscience,) which leads to the absence of the Holy Spirit, caused by the presence of the evil or adverse spirit, and the perpetuation of abject cruelty, and wickedness, you must decide once and for all to totally turn it over to God, while believing that no matter what the outcome, He will bring that situation to an expected end by His chosen mode and means.

In other prayer situations, that are so problematically acute and complicated, you must learn to allow your faith in prayer as a spiritual communication channel to God, supersede its regular degree in substance, where your level of hope is concerned, by completely and utterly accelerating it onto a higher level of dedication and utter dependency on God's word as you transform your belief in His word, into a divine fixation encrusted in trust of the highest caliber; an obsession of a spiritual caliber if I may term it so. At such a high degree of hopefulness of a heart fixed in faith and trusting in God, faith will then melt into oceans of high expectations and then gently break waves onto the bright and expectant shores of divine manifestations, laden with pure and perfect accomplishments. Oftentimes faith has always played a big role in prayer; and has constantly been mentioned and affiliated with things spiritual supplication-wise. But what exactly is faith? And what role does it play in our prayers as adherents of the word of truth? "The Holy word teaches us that faith is the substance of things hoped for, the evidence of things not seen." (your next scriptural assignment dear reader, is to locate this scripture and record your finding with your notes in the subsidiary pages of this guide, Amen.) this verse of scripture denotes faith as "The sole spiritual receptacle; the very embodiment of the divine constituents, that impels one's hope into realization, accomplishment and manifestation." (AOQ) our Father Abraham did not waver at the promises of God through unbelief, but was strong in faith, giving glory to God, while waiting in blessed expectation for the fulfillment of God's promises concerning His life.

The Bible states that "Abraham staggered not at the promises of God through unbelief ..." (read; Romans. 4: 20) He also hoped against hope in order to precipitate his expectations into being. (Verse.18) And as he hoped, the Bible states, he made sure that he exhibited no weakness in the arena of his faith in God by, ignoring the adverse circumstances around him like, his age at the time of promise, the physiological balance of his body or even that of his wife Sarah who was clinically long past the age of reproduction. But instead what did Father Abraham do? He shifted his prayer gears fully into the divine height of steadfast and constant persuasion, whilst believing that what God had promised him will be projected into realization, to the glory and honor of His name. And God increased Abraham's spiritual credibility by awarding him with a higher credit score of righteousness. Beloved reader in Christ, you too can receive the same gift by living your Christian life in practicality of spirit; by faith and not by sight, like our Father Abraham, 'The Father of Faith.' who without a shred of doubt, plunged into the rivers of faith, completely believing in God's divine capability to fulfill His promises as, The Lord Jehovah-Yahweh; keeper of covenants. "Keep and live by the spiritual wisdom and dedication that holds fast the root of faith in the soil of greater expectations; for then and only then will you find the comfort to rest assuredly in the hope that, you too can and are able to receive of God as Father Abraham and other faithfuls in the days of yore did." (ANQ) Learn to depend solely on God's counsel and providence; keep your feet grounded in His word as you live for Him in faith through Christ Jesus; "And the God of all grace who called you to His eternal glory in Christ, after you have suffered a little while, will Himself restore you and make you strong firm and steadfast. To Him be the power, and glory forever Amen." (read 1Peter 5:10 & 11NIV)

When you are plagued by doubt as you wait on God in prayerful anticipation, pray with the following scripture. Also try to memorize it and mentally affirm it when you find yourself in a less conducive environment.

"I wait for the Lord, my soul waits and in His word I do hope. My soul waits for the Lord more than those who watch for the morning." (read: Psalm 130: 5-6 NKJ.); remember His word of truth in (Romans 5:5) "For hope does not disappoint because the Love of God has been shed abroad in our hearts by the Holy Spirit given unto us." (read; Psalm 33: 11-12KJV) "The counsel of the Lord standeth forever, the thoughts of His heart to all generations. Blessed is the nation whose God is the Lord; and the people He hath chosen for His own inheritance." Write (Isaiah 60: 20 KJV.) on the tablets of your heart. "Thy sun shall no more go Down; neither shall thy moon withdraw itself: for the Lord shall be thine everlasting light and the days of thy mourning shall be ended." Beloved reader, when the answer to your prayer takes a difficult turn as seen through the carnal eye, you are by the manifest power of God in Christ, closer to the shores of abundance and goodness, as long as your heart steadfastly beats with a steady rhythm of trust for He who holds the future and all it contains.

Ephesians 1: 12, ; 1: 5&6 RSV. Reiterates on the sure rewards of hoping in God. "We who first hoped in Christ, have been destined and appointed to live for the praise His glory. He destined us in love to be His sons through Jesus Christ according to the purpose of His will, to the praise of His glorious Grace, which He freely bestowed on us, in the beloved." I love this scripture; don't you? Sometimes scripture has to be rightly divided with the sword of divine acumen thus; by letting a latter verse from the same chapter compliment the former into greater understanding in order to edify the heirs of salvation hallelujah! Can you feel the intensity of the vibrant hope and promise it emits into your life as you digest it word by word? There is no other joy that supersedes that which the word of God delivers, be it that of reprimand, of encouragement and hope, of instruction, and of guidance, of healing and of all other areas of life that requires His divine wisdom to keep us in spiritual and physical balance. The Father promises in (Joshua.1: 5b); (retreat to Verse 5a.) "As I am with Moses, so will I be with thee: I will not fail thee, nor forsake thee. There shall shall not any man be able to stand before thee all the days of thy life:" (KJV.) Here's another great scripture; why don't you try memorizing it for the sake of spiritual edification. "Remember your word to your servant, upon which you have caused to hope. This is my comfort and my affliction for your word has given me life. I rise before the dawning of the morning, and cry for help I hope in your word." What an effective tool of hopeful reassurance in God this scripture projects. Find it in the book of Psalms119: 49 – 50 & 147 NKJ. It is one of several scriptures that vividly displays the therapeutic nature of God as depicted in his word. Here is another scripture from (1Thessalonians 4:13 – 14&18 NKJ.) I term it the 'Hospice scripture.' Another scripture recorded by inspiration of God, for the therapeutic benefit of the terminally ill, and the spiritual uplifting with hope, their families and loved ones, who in spite of what lies ahead must believe that God is ever present with them, always caring and constantly showering them with His love through His word that promises them a blessed end in Him regardless of the terminal condition of their loved one. We must as Children of God learn to accept death as a new beginning and a time of planting of the remains of loved ones and friends, for the carrying out of the spiritual process of divine transformation of the dead in Christ. May you be comforted by these words of truth, beloved reader if you find yourself traversing the river of grief and that of loss. "I do not want you to be ignorant brethren concerning those who have fallen asleep, lest you sorrow as others who have no hope. For if we believe that Jesus died and rose again, even so God will bring with Him those who sleep in Jesus, therefore comfort one another with these words." What perfect love The Father has for us who live in him. For look at the canopies of scriptural provision He has furnished, and stored up for our every need and at all times. Philip, Craig and Dean, rightly divide the word of truth in their song 'crucified with Christ'; and it has for years ministered to the grieving and bereaved, and even to the passing on soul; a profound prayer tool laden with Divine words of comfort, reassurance, and hope. As I mentioned earlier in this book, you must as a Christian cultivate the habit of constituting the appropriate Christian music that reflects and ministers to your need, into your prayer and also into your daily life situations; only then will you reap its full benefit by the realization of its indispensability as a vital prayer tool. Yes! You must make it's acquisition, collection, lyrical and melodic study a part of your spiritual resource for the adequate carrying out of your scriptural and spiritual research.

"For to me to live is Christ, and to die is gain." Philippians 1: 21 KJV.

"I will glory in the power of the cross. The things I thought were gain, I count as loss. And with His suffering I identify. And by His resurrection power I'm alive. For I am crucified with Christ and yet I live. Not I but Christ that lives within me; His cross will never ask for more than I can give. There's no greater sacrifice. For I am crucified with Christ and yet I live. For to me to live is Christ, and to die is truly gain..." By Philip, Craig and Dean anointed music ministers. An authentic sample of the word of truth rightly divided by way of song ministration. God bless them, Amen.

As you can tell beloved reader, ours is not a hopeless situation at all. For even if we find ourselves in a terminal situation, or lose our marital status, and even when we are forsaken and betrayed, left in shame and in want, stripped of all human dignity, we are destined to overcome, because victory is a sure goal in all crisis if only we would learn to pray effectively. For in so doing, the magnificence and benevolence of Him who has enlisted us into battles, predestined for sure victories in life and even in death, will show up to deliver us with His mighty hand. Amen. How good it is to be called into such hope and understanding, through Christ Jesus our Lord and Savior who teaches us to give thanks in all things and at all times; for even in the midst of the most turbulent storms, our gratitude and reliance on God's sure performance must and will enrich as we voyage into calmer waters of peace and tranquility. Let us therefore, dearly beloved, rid ourselves of unnecessary fears of what the future holds, but rather affirm our belief in faith and hope in our Father God who is ever ready to endow us with beauty for ashes, strengthening us when we are afraid, and who also bestows us with contentment and comfort when we are in deep sorrow, while bathing us in His calming waters of serenity, when we find ourselves in desperation. Yes! He is the rock of ages, constantly cleft to shield and to protect us from adversities, and uncertainties.

As Christians, we must hold secure the constancy and stability of our faith under all circumstances. I can assure you that the most difficult to digest and accept prayer outcome, is the one prayer response amongst a million that holds the ticket to the best seat at the ballpark of incomparable and insurmountable success, and yields the greatest outcome for our future well being. We must also refrain from the incessant habit of blaming the 'devil' for things that do not sit well in our lives, or are imbalanced around us, simply because we refuse to tackle or straighten out, or are not bold enough to stand up to the despicable truths revealed to us by God about our lives. The Father chastens us because He loves us and longs for us to live in victory and triumph. Therefore if we desire to experience the full measure of His love, then the exhibition of 'extreme spiritual discipline'(ESD) by way of 'spiritually driven self preservation' (SDSP) must be fervently observed by us through the constant act of filling our bodies and minds with good thoughts and motives as we live in a world in which we are a part of, but are not partakers of; because when our bodies are left hollow, due to the absence of prayer and fervent Bible study, coupled with true fellowship, the fetid and incessant indulgence in negativities and vices will seep in and clog up our spiritual air waves thereby disrupting the modulation of our frequencies. And by so doing, distort our divine transmission thus, rendering the receptive signals of our full benefits from God utterly unreachable.

Beloved reader in Christ, always keep your entire being balanced in the Lord as fervently as you can; leave no room whatsoever for the incubation of any scheming device of the adversary; and by your great endeavor, experience the hand of God on your life in its entirety. Because you child of God, are the very representation of His image and likeness and should strive to live it here on earth, no matter the obstacles; for if you fall due to trespasses, the Lord God who is faithful in love and gracious in mercy, will continually lift you up and uphold you in His right hand. Ephesians 2:8 KJV instructs us thus; "For by grace are ye saved through faith; and that not of ourselves: it is the gift of God: Not of works. Lest any man should boast." And if your obstacles come from the conscious obstruction of others, the Lord will fight for you and hold your peace. We are all aware of the spiritual wickedness in high and low places of the Pharisees and Sadducees of our century; (especially those of us who are of non-caucasian descent and have suffered at their hands through slavery and segregation which is still in force today under other guises) For they adorn themselves with big Bibles tirelessly dispersing seeds of religious extremism, feigning to love God more than all else, by boasting about their good deeds; counting them in full public view as they judge and dissect others, questioning their religious footing in the faith as if they are more righteous in the eyes of God; condemning others while exalting themselves under cloaks of division, hatred, racism, and discrediting those whom God have called into His eternal glory in Christ. For they please God not; by their so called good deeds. because in their hearts they despise His very creation, by continuously setting themselves on earth as superior creations of God; belittling and suppressing other Children of God through His very word by uttering blasphemies; thus dismissing the very omniscient and omnipotent power of God as Yahweh and Jehovah; the creator of all; The Lord. Be strong even in your oppression child of God; for the Lord has already spewed them from His mouth. "What? know ye not that your body is the temple of the Holy Ghost which is in you, which ye have of

God, and ye are not your own?" (1Corinthian 6: 19 KJV.) Please memorize (1Peter. 5:8) "Be sober, be vigilant; because your adversary the devil, as a roaring lion, walketh about, seeking whom he may devour:" Knowing all this, and having been forewarned by the Father above, should we not as Children of God, set our spiritual goals towards the tireless and endless indulgence in fervent but persistent prayer as long as we live, and under any circumstance we find ourselves in, while asking The Father to endow us with His divine guidance and wisdom, as the vulnerable sheep grazing faithfully but hopefully, on the tufts of His word of truth within the holy confines of His divine verdant pastures which nourishes us continually with His abundant love and providence?

"Grace be to you and peace from God the Father, and from our Lord Jesus Christ, who gave Himself for our sins, that He might deliver us from the adversities of this world, according to the will of God and our Father: To whom be glory for ever and ever. A-men."
(Author with Galatians 1: 3-5 KJV)

Chapter seven

The benefits of praying to God for spiritual guidance.

As soldiers of Christ, marching on in a world filled with spiritual and physical warfare, we must strategically plan our lines of defense with great divine precision to enable us hit the divers targets of adversities directed at us, at the focal point of total and absolute destruction. Therefore, if our goal in this battle is to successfully procure a plausible standpoint as defenders of the Christian faith, then we must adopt the spiritually induced standard protocol procedure of asking for guidance, before setting out to make decisions and plans concerning our lives. By so doing we are clearly and accurately able to select the precise location to set up our spiritual camps, as well as making room to accord ourselves complete overview of our shortcomings and setbacks, on the battlefields of life. The word of God is laden with rich scriptural texts and verses, depicting God's ample guiding nature. David the Psalmist, cultivated the good habit of depending on God for guidance, in every aspect of his decision making; he talked to The Father, unfailingly, and did so in utter constancy, while sincerely and repetitively exalting Him as his sole source of divine dependence. You see, David knew God by His attributes, and used them synonymously to his benefit as he built a long lasting and fruitful relationship with God The Father; whom also he invoked continuously as Jehovah-Raah; the good shepherd.

"Show me your way o Lord. teach me your paths guide me in your truth and teach me, for you are my God my savior, my hope is in you all day long:Teach me thy way, O Lord, and lead me in a plain path, because of mine enemies. Teach me your way, O Lord and I will walk in your truth, give me an undivided heart, that I may fear your name. Shew me a token for good; that they which hate me may see it, and be ashamed: because thou, Lord, hast holpen me, and comforted me" (Psalm 25: 4 – 5NIV; 27: 11KJV 86: 11 NIV & 17KJV) beloved reader in Christ, when you give God the forefront position as General, overseer, and commander in chief, of your life and its battles, victory will certainly follow in order of eminency and perpetually. You must also realize that, your ultimate attainment or the possibility of you ever walking into your grand blessings depicted by the total estimate and depth of your victorious Christian life, rests solely on how accessibly yielding you are to God's guidance. Therefore, the overall percentage of your yield and surrender to His will, should supersede every tendency of haughtiness in you in order to produce ample surplus, of steadfastness, when married to the height of your faith, hope and trust in Him, while proportionately overlapping the stumbling blocks of negative tendencies like fears and uncertainties that crop up to distract your spiritual focus. (please take time to read the story of Job) Yes! Child of God, You will certainly run into trials, but when your life in Christ meets the above spiritual aggregate, then will you be rest assured of the fact that your divine armor did withstand the rigidities of adverse pressure, and that you have successfully attained the honorable status of complete dependency on God. Psalm 32: 8 NIV. authenticates God's hand of guidance on His children. "I will instruct you and teach you in the way you should go; I will counsel you and watch over you."What more can we ask for when we have the assurance and reassurance of a God who exudes a nature of divine truth and faithfulness in His promises to us. "For God is not a man that He should lie,…hath He said, and shall He not do it? Or hath He spoken, and shall He not make it good?(Numbers 23: 19 KJV.)

Humility is also an important virtue that steers us towards the desire to be guided by God. It is also the tarmac dear reader, on which your utter submission to God's authority takes flight. (Proverbs 16: 18) strongly admonishes the spirit of pride. "Pride leads to destruction and a haughty spirit before a fall." Therefore lay aside all aspects of pride and arrogance in your life; so as to allow the effective operation of the Holy Spirit, which in turn will fill you with wisdom, as it instructs you into all righteousness. Traces of pride and arrogance in a God fearing person, retrogresses the performance function of the Holy Spirit; thus, triggering with rapidity the adverse incubation of highly destructive elements of decay, that may spread to distort progress in our lives. Let us read; (Psalm 25: 8,9, 12 – 14 NIV.) "Good and upright is the Lord therefore, He instructs sinners in His ways. He guides the humble in what is right and teaches them His Way. Who then is the man that fears the Lord. He will instruct Him in the way chosen for him, he will spend his days in prosperity and his descendants will inherit the land, the Lord confides in those who fear Him. He makes His covenant known to them." Our blessed assurance in God is evidently without a doubt incapsulated in divine favor within the walls of grace, as long as we maintain our spiritual aggregate of abject dependency on God, at the right gradient. "Lead me O Lord in your righteousness, because of my enemies, make straight your way before me." (Psalm 5: 8 NIV.) "For surely o Lord you bless the righteous; you surround them with your favor as with a shield." (Verse 12) So you see, you are untouchable by adversities, as long as you remain within the protective realm of God's favor, which is doubtlessly the sure and purest source of your inheritance. For though adversities may visit you, they will not pitch heir tent with or around you.

If there ever was a man who faithfully exhibited and elevated, his love, devotion, and dependency on God through fervent prayer; that man was David and no other. He could communicate with God in creative diction which though profoundly poetic, was fully laden with rare spiritual precision, appropriately embedded within the soundly balanced consistency of choice verbal expressions, set within a surrendering sea of billowing need conveying literary components, scripturally suited for the right division of the Father's guiding word of truth. When theologically analyzed, one can deduce the pure fact that, David's scriptural records, truly reveals an uninterrupted spiritually induced prayer sequence that increasingly glowed like a shimmering sunset on a wide river and continuously flowed within his Psalms, depicting him as a man whose very life was driven by nothing else but that of a natural dependency on God; a lifestyle which also throws him as well, into the spotlight of prayerful humility. In fact David's profound spirituality, was so deeply rooted within the confines of God's guidance that, it irresistibly echoed total surrender throughout his scriptural texts, which ended up being literarily projected, superiorly in the graded heights of scriptural eloquence, throughout his Psalms, where I personally gained and grew my prayer skills and wings respectively. David lived for God; and kept in touch with Him, through prayer, supplication and thanksgiving, while unfailingly and tirelessly, expressing his love for Him; and God returned that love to David in countless folds, as frequently as David endeavored to reach Him, by the sheer willing of his life's decisions to His divine leadership, and guidance prayerfully.

Yet as much as God loved and protected David, so did He not spare him by way of chastisement and reprimand. For this applies to us too. God chastened David as much as needed and necessary, but was able to spare him during some grave instances of transgression, by awarding him the utmost clemency of 'divine immunity' (DI) because of the loving relationship that existed between them. Such benefits we must remember, are also ours to bathe in as well. God covered those grievous sins with love and buried them in the sea of forgetfulness, but David lived to bear the consequences, which were designed by God in a manner that would not destroy David, but build him up in spirit, as well as aiding him in the attainment of prospective moral superiority, through obedience, without destroying their loving relationship; just as it applies to us His children today. He continued to live as a man who could talk to The Father with ease at all times, yet his words of supplication never fell short of the right consistency of utter devotion and pure reverence to God, as he kept his communication with God spiritually accurate, but also within the right limits, of verbal proportions that depicted a total submission to the will of God. We as adherents of God's word of truth, must like David, maintain a well versed status within the zealous utilization of effective prayer tools. In fact he applied them so well during prayer and supplication that they actually expanded spiritually in faith, leavening scripturally in hope, while decreasing in fear and doubt by density, and as such prayerfully paving the way for its express transformation and ultimate transcending to the bubbling and uninterrupted sparkling miraculous heights of 'Spiritual Effervescence' (SE) past the prayer halls of heaven, directly to the throne of God for expedited attention. Thus like David, we must cultivate the spiritual habit to always consult God for counsel with accuracy, humility, and an unpretentious display of honesty and scriptural precision, while exhibiting with calculated yet sincere indication, a reverent and profitable spiritual mélange of praise, worship, confession, and thanksgiving, grounded in hope, faith and total dependency; keeping in mind to incorporate that 'good spiritual habit', (GSH) which became the basic fundamental format set within accurate spiritual proportions, that he David repetitively utilized for the effective disbursement of his prayers, which were without a doubt always spiritually whipped to the right consistency of holiness, fortified and comprehensively conveyed in fitness for swift divine absorption, and spiritual effectuation at the Mighty throne of God. This dear reader in Christ was his portion, but has now by the grace and mercies of God been translated unto our platters of supplication, uttered in faith, garnished with belief for in its sure outcome, lies our portion forever, as victorious Christians.

As Christians, we must adapt the spiritual habit of incorporating praise, worship, thanksgiving, hope, faith, and confession into our prayers, to render them fit and suitable for 'divine transit' (DT). Our prayers though constantly offered, must be methodical and meaningful to us, but free from vain repetition, in order to be heard of God, who promises in His word to always guide us and satisfy our needs, to the extent of strengthening our sun scorched bodies, and rejuvenating them into the likeness of well watered gardens and springs whose waters never fail. (Isaiah 58: 11.) Being expectant vessels, as well as praying receptacles, it is incumbent upon us to know that, the spiritual guidance of God, which is one of our vital victorious Christian living ingredients, will always be a priced commodity, as it cuts across every need we encounter regardless of the urgency and magnitude within which it presents itself. As a true Child of God; "you must never allow yourself to be drowned by crippling circumstances; but rather, cripple those circumstances by, drowning them within the divinely propelled spiritual force extracted from the strength you have attained through the fervent study, accurate scriptural application, and utilization of the word of God; for God within you is the perfect guide because, He is also the light of the world. "in the beginning was the word...in Him was life and the life was the light of men. The light shineth in the darkness and the darkness comprehended it not." (John. 1: 1-5 KJV.) therefore if God is the source of your very life then why shouldn't you entrust Him with the navigating task of illuminating your life's radar for the detection of adversities and stumbling blocks, before you pick latitudes and longitudes of long and short term decisions. If you are truly living by faith and not by sight, then you can be sure that the Light of the world being the propeller of that faith in you, should also be the sole outfitter and guide to your life. He is the divine paragon of all leadership, because it is only by way of His light that all adversities and powers of darkness are vanquished, an essential act which makes way for prayers to be heard and answered.

God is able to guide you out of that sordid situation which renders you so desperate and triggers thoughts of self-destruction, and self-harm constantly racing through your mind. These thoughts could occur consciously and subconsciously; periodically or constantly. At this juncture,

I believe that some of my readers will be wondering how such a situation would plague a Child of God but it does more often than you can ever imagine; and do you know why? Because, no matter your spiritual ripening or age in the faith, as long as you exist and function in a world in which you are a physically a part of but are not in tune with, in spiritual practicality, which is controlled by the adversary who believes it to be his jurisdiction, then you must work hard to protect the integrity of your faith by steering clear of his lures, trappings through the adverse projection of false modesty, which ultimately progresses into self degradation and shame. Remember beloved reader that, the adversary is no respecter of persons. Was he not bold enough to tempt the Master? And do you think he will resist from ever toying with your mind after such a bold display of irreverence and dismissal of his devices from you, by accepting Christ? You must realize that the adversary only needs a tiny fraction and exhibition of helplessness from you to arm him with an excuse to move in with you in thought, by filling that helpless area of your thoughts with total hopelessness, that will definitely end up triggering the adverse thoughts and actions mentioned previously. But guess what? You have a weapon of resistance, just like Christ had and utilized to its full potential, after His forty day fast, as well as in the garden of Gethsemane, before His betrayal, arrest and crucifixion as recorded in the word of truth, rightly divided with the sword of justice and of righteousness.

No matter how difficult your situation, rearrange your thinking faculties in a spiritual manner and take a step of faith and watch the Holy Spirit take over your weakness and frailty by way of its quickening nature. And as (Zechariah 4:6b KJV)) reveals to us, "not by might nor by power, but by my spirit says the Lord of hosts." Yes, you can by yourself do nothing without the intervention of the Holy Spirit, which in turn takes you into the spiritual realm of God's guidance; a destination that boasts of 100% full protectorate coverage over your life. Dear reader in Christ, let the Lord be your guide, as you are schooled in the ethics of spiritual guidance and total dependence on God by the Holy Spirit. You must also know as a true adherent of the Christian Faith that, surrendering to the Father's guidance, is actually an act of surrender to the power of the Holy Trinity, which is virtually carried out by way of abject humility, and the total subjection to the triple embodiment of their Holy authority, with equanimity.

(Psalm 27: 11-14 NIV.) assures us; "Teach me thy way o Lord, lead me in a straight path because of my oppressors. Do not turn me over to the desire of my foes, for false witnesses rise up against me breathing out violence. I am still confident of this, I will see the goodness of the Lord, in the Land of the living." "The word of God as we know, was recorded by spiritual inspiration for our own good purpose and greater benefit. And is to date still reigning at the forefront of all literary materials as the only printed word that spans across all subject areas from the arts to the sciences. It is also driven by the utmost divine power within a holy capability that severs and divides, uproots, and propagates, multiplies and deducts, while subjecting the powers of darkness, together with their vices and adversities, into the perfect but volatile equation of the totally vanquished, by its divine luminescence." (ANQ) Our other duty as children of God is to focus our strength as we hope and wait on the Lord, to fight for us, as well as hold our peace. Doing so in stillness of spirit and thought, by looking to God and to His strength as we seek His face daily. (Please refer to Psalm 31: 24; & Exodus 14: 14; and please read 1Chronicle 16: 11). Our guidance, once again, is physically present in God's word by prophetic scriptural manifestation. "It is God who makes my way perfect and arms me with strength; as for God, His way is perfect, the word of the lord is flawless. He is a shield for all who take refuge in him." (please read Psalm 18: 32; and retreat to verse 30. NIV.)

Trials and tribulations, build character and maturity in us through the word of God; acting as a buffer on our armor by shielding it from wear and tear, and ultimate damage perpetuated by adversities that we encounter on the battlefields of our lives. But thanks be to God for His leadership and guidance, that balances us into the perfect posture of goodness and uprightness; that protects and restrains us from bending over in shame and disappointment, and from walking around lopsided, with the burden of negativities on our backs. Thanks be to God for His continuous guidance despite our shortcomings; for endowing us with the freedom of accepting and receiving His guidance together with the divine package of guilt erasure, and lifting the burdens we have been carrying around due to the lack of 'spiritual guidance'. (SG). (please find the scriptural text for the following quotation and record them in the subsidiary pages reserved for notes in your book, thank you.:) "For if the Son sets you free, you will be free indeed." "It is for freedom that Christ has set us free, stand firm then, and do not let yourself be burdened again by the yoke of slavery." (The bondage of bitterness, guilt, and that of an accusing memory of a past incidence in your life, or an accident that happened in your family, that you feel responsible for, and have not forgiven yourself of, even though others have. What about the bondage of guilt by severe criticism inflicted on you by other Christians who judge circumstances involving you partially without even according you the benefit of the doubt by hearing your side of things?) Dear brothers, sisters and elders in Christ; your foundation of peace in all such situations, is once again rightly divided in the word of truth as follows: "Forget the former things do not dwell on the past, see I am doing a new thing. Now it springs forth do you not perceive it, I am making a way in the desert and streams in the wastelands. (the wastelands of negativities that have been washed by the divine streams of God's guiding light and encouraging love.) I even I am he who blots out your transgressions for my own sake and remember your sin no more." (Isaiah 43: 18, 19&25. NIV.)

The benefits derived from a life guided by God.
(1) All your steps are ordered by the Lord because He delights in you.
(1) You are blessed with prosperity.
(2) The same measure of blessing and even more is handed down to your descendants.
(3) Your reverence and fear of the Lord is rewarded with greatness of stature.
(4) God reveals your future to you by directing you as you correct your mistakes and make amends in humility; An act which frees you to embrace a richer and fuller life in God on earth and hereafter.
(5) Your thoughts are exempt from the negative effects of wrongful accusation and judgment.
(6) God confides in you by making known His covenant to you.
(7) Your life is free from the haunting thoughts of regret.
(8) Your heart becomes lighter and your overall countenance exudes peace.
(9) God's favor surrounds you perpetually.
(10) You are continuously led in God's righteousness.
(11) God teaches you His ways.
(12) The everlasting mercies of God surround you.
(13) You are not easily manipulated by sin and adverse temptations.
(14) You are exceptionally and physically illuminated with blessings from God. (divine glow of blessings.)
(16) You attain the benefits of great peace.
(17) Your stumbling blocks crumble into nothingness before you.
(18) Your expectations are continuously focused on God, and not on mankind.

155

(19) Your future is guaranteed with hope.

(20) Your needs are satisfied entirely.

(21) You gain a continuous flow of strength from within.

(22) Failure is forever absent in your life because, weakness is wrestled down before it sprouts roots, as God guides you into progress and ultimate victory.

(23) You are blessed with a full life span which pertains not to how long you live, but how well you live doing the will of God for the greater good of humanity. (This verse was written to honor the great and blessed memory of Dr. Martin Luther King Jr. whose life span, though cut short by the plotting of mortals, is eternally reestablished through the changes we experience globally, pertaining to racial injustice; for we know and believe that he is divinely secured within the secret place of the Most High, where he abides under the shadow of the Almighty, amidst the heavenly melodies of the angels, in Christ's bosom. Amen.)

(24) Your future is secured in God.

(25) God's perfect plan for your entire life unfolds before your very eyes.

(26) God becomes your refuge, your shield and your fortress in the midst of all adversities.

(27) You constantly exude perfection in every venture you undertake.

(28) God guides you with his truth by teaching you to make the right decisions in life.

Bible study on God's guidance;

Psalms1: 1-3) (5: 1 – 3, 8, & 12) (18: 2-6 30 & 32) (25: 4 – 5) (27: 11 – 14) (32: 8) (86: 11&17) and (119: 29-34, 102, 105, 109, 111-112, 132-135,165-170)

Isaiah 30: 21) (58: 11)

Jeremiah. 29: 11 – 13.

Hymns are the oldest and greatest prayer tools, because they teach spiritual eloquence through inspiration. But they seem lost within the rapidly growing contemporary Christian music. I grew up singing Hymns at St. Paul's Anglican Church in the Town of La where I attended primary school and also where my mother taught for decades. And have never forgotten it. Dear reader re-visit the inspirational world of hymns and utilize them daily for divine enrichment. Here are two of them.

Guide me O thou great redeemer
Pilgrim through this barren land
I am weak. But thou art mighty
Hold me with thy powerful hand
Bread of heaven, bread of heaven
Feed me till I want no more
Feed me till I want no more.

Lead me Lord
Lead me in thy righteousness
Make thy way straight before my face
For it is thou Lord, thou Lord only
That makest me dwell in safety.
For it is thou Lord, thou Lord only
That makest me dwell in safety. A-men.

CHAPTER EIGHT:

SEEKING ENCOURAGEMENT FROM GOD'S WORD.

The responsive outcome to some of our prayer requests, demand grace and encouragement from God, to render them feasible for our digestion and absorption. Once again, God's Holy word becomes the only plausible and reliable source for such help. We should not in times like these be frightened or nervous to go on with our regular life schedule or feel embarrassed when our human emotions come gushing out in torrents of disappointment and uncertainty. God in all His divine wisdom, knowledge and power knows what is best for us; as the author and finisher of our faith, He cannot let our anticipated desires and aspirations as humans hold down the perfect and expected end He has in store for us. This end though spiritually perfect, as we can recall from the previous chapter, may be revealed diversely through answered prayer, and viewed as negative or affirmative, by the carnal eye. Our duty therefore as children of God, is to adjust our lives, with the sure and perfect encouragement from the Father. This is usually to many a Christian not easy to accomplish when their hearts are set on a different prayer outcome. Yes, I must admit in all sincerity and practicality as a Christian that, spiritual progressive steps geared towards victory in regards to an expected end in The Lord is not easily initiated under such circumstances. A clear example is that of a person given the 'green light' to undertake a particular or certain venture by God while the other, is clearly restrained from even venturing or attempting to initiate the same request by God, because of reasons best known to Him (omniscient God.) But regardless of the degree in variation of these two situations, both persons, still require spiritual assistance by way of divine encouragement to forge ahead, armed with divine encouragement in pursuance of The Father's plan and purpose for them.

Let us consider as well as study this classic situation of waiting on the Lord for His response to a prayer need. Do we as children of God sit and worry with anxiety, wondering about the possible outcome of our prayer request? Or do we rest assured in the Lord, and wait patiently for Him to manifest His perfect will for our lives. The word of God teaches us to invest quality time earnestly, waiting on the Lord in all modesty and spirituality. "Delight thyself also in the Lord, and He will give you the desires of your Heart." (Read,Psalms 37: 4, 5 &7 KJV.) This waiting period must be solely spent on the reflection as well as in the study of God's word for scriptural edification and strengthening with a total air of gladness and not of fear, anxiety and nervous anticipation. As humans we are prone to the spirit of uncertainty. But God has originally endowed us with a spirit of love, of power and of a sound mind as well. Yes, all these benefits are ready for us to reap in abundance; but we must learn to commit our plans trustingly, to the Father of providence. Verse 5 of psalm 37 teaches us the one and only way to receive from God. " Commit thy way unto the Lord; trust also in Him; and He shall bring it to pass," This is so true in all types of relationships as well as that which involves God and man. For: "Pure commitment is the sole incubating agent, needed for the sure propagation and the positive manifestation of a wholesome life together with the blessings it brings" (ANQ) Our Father God, is the only spiritual embodiment of goodness who hears the ardent cries and desires of the afflicted, and in turn encourages them, with His word of truth and of healing. The Lord God is also as the Bible reveals to us, closest to the broken in heart, and crushed in the spirit. It (the Bible) goes on to reiterate the divine fact that; "A righteous man, may have many troubles, but the Lord delivers Him from them all. (Psalm 34: 17 – 19NIV.) David, being a devout man of God who exercised unwaveringly his faith in Him, found it spiritually necessary to reassure himself when he was troubled, by self-searching and self-interrogating his soul, while at the same time, therapeutically reassuring and re-stabilizing himself with the truthful evidence of God's omnipresent nature as; Jehovah-Shamah; our God who is 'there' for us in every situation we encounter. David felt a twinge of humanly induced helplessness, but found solace in his knowledge of God by stature, function and purpose; He called upon God by name, but did so appropriately in order to properly fuel and charge the synonym of God he invoked, into expedited divine action and greatness of power for the express eradication of the adverse situation he found himself in at the time. By taking this sport of action, David did null as well as voided, the last eight letters in the word that projected his emotional state which was 'helplessness.'

In (Psalm 42: 11NIV.) David presents to God, a prayer of self-inquisition as follows; "Why are you downcast o my soul, why so disturbed within me? Put your hope in God. For I will yet praise Him my Savior and my God." With this prayer, David positively and precisely, with accuracy of verbal spiritual rapport, injected the spirit of encouragement into his depressed soul, in the form of hopeful supplication. He firmly, though difficult as it seemed at the time, considering his emotional state, literarily summoned faith and courage. He firmly yet emotionally reprimanded his saddened and melancholy soul into a state of hopefulness, that in turn reflected on his physical person. He also went on supplication-wise, to clearly demarcate the well-known human tendency that is given to extreme vulnerability in his state at the time, by exposing his human susceptibility to depression, pain, disappointment, loss and the fear of change as well as that of loneliness. David addressed his soul; (also known as the spirit; the unseen part the human being that coexists with the flesh; by functioning as the sole source of the vital essence of life, through the channels of physiological benefits; which at the time or juncture of death, being the precise moment of the complete and total cessation of breath, is released from the bodily receptacle, and thus assumes, its original indiscernible form.) which at that time was physically projecting its emotions onto the flesh, to snap out of its depressive state, by summoning it into focusing on God, on whom he (David), totally depended. Take note of David's description of God in that scriptural text; "My savior (The Christ) and my God, (The Father Almighty)." and yes this was the old testament when the word had not yet been made flesh to dwell amongst humans. I stress on this because, many a Christian have proclaimed themselves new testament Christians not for the sake of the gift of salvation alone but within the irresolute mindedness of not wanting anything to do with the old testament. To them say I this; The Bible cannot be studied and embraced in the Christian faith partially but wholesomely. The old testament compliments the new and the new is dysfunctional without the old; being that, the possibility of rightly dividing the word of truth is made ineffective, and any attempt made at salvaging it without the fusion of it's two vital components which are like the dicotyledon hidden within the seed waiting to unfold after germination; they simply cannot propel life without the other's input. Therefore I implore such Christians to take heed in their scriptural judgement while they classify the word of truth like a monocotyledon seed with a single leaf; which is a very sinful notion indeed. Well, this is scripturally induced agricultural science for your reading pleasure. Hope you are having lots of divine fun; please pass it on; will ya thank you.:)

Beloved reader, this divine attestation as you can acknowledge is the scriptural proclamation of a man who lived before Christ, but confessed His (Christ's) coexistence with the Father. Thus David reaffirms the authenticity of the new testament scripture "...He was in the beginning with God..." and "I and my Father are one." I hope you do realize (if you are one of those Christians who adamantly refuse to associate themselves studiously, with the Old Testament, by narrow-mindedly living in false spiritual practicality as squarely pruned 'New Testament Christians') that your Christian life is incomplete and off balance if you are not dually rooted in the scriptures as, the old testament embodies the new and vice versa. If such is your attitude in the Church of The Almighty, then may I humbly ask that you reconsider this decision, while you correct your spiritual posture immediately before scriptural lopsidedness and lack of divine uprightness sets in to contaminate your life and faith in Christ who was there with the Father from the very beginning; "And God said, let us make man in our own image, after our likeness:..." "And the Lord God said, behold, the man is become as one of us, to know good and evil:.." (your assignment is to find the previous scriptures in the Old Testament of the Bible and record them with your notes, in the subsidiary pages, thank you.) May we continue please.

Spiritual encouragement is found lacking in your life when adversities and negativities that plague you emotionally, are morbidly and physically projected on your person. Thus when goodness overtakes you in life, your spirit is elevated and gladdened. This reflects on your person, as it physically plays out by way of glows, smiles, and even exhibits itself as excellent health and sound complexion. But in times of extreme adversities, your spirit is weighed down by an anchor of depression, regret, loss and other negative vices. All these adverse emotions, gush out of your system portraying acute sullenness in your life and appearance. Your friends, neighbors and coworkers may notice this and pass remarks of concern.

Your outward pleasantries are muted. Your beauty fades, taking with it all your physical attributes and radiance. This is a form of reality, which can hit anyone in life. Yes, even Christians. But once again, the word of God encourages His children during difficult situations and circumstances in (Psalm 37: 23 - 25 KJV); "The steps of a good man are ordered by the Lord: and He delighteth in his way. Though he fall, he shall not be utterly cast down: for the Lord upholdeth him with His hand. I have been young, and now am old; yet have I not seen the righteous forsaken, nor his seed begging for bread."

I have personally experienced the spiritual difficulty of waiting on the Lord under the most trying and difficult circumstances. I can also stake my very existence as a fully functioning human being on my commitment, trust and rest assuredness in God. I am however, very blessed to share my experience with you in these pages, as I relate to you, God's faithfulness and of His truth, that He kept in word and in covenant within my life continuously and accordingly as I journeyed through the valley of acute adversities and trials, and also about my discovery of true fellowship in Him by way of divine encouragement, that led me onto the healing paths of inspiration and restoration, through the power of His living word of truth. As an individual, a woman, and a Child of God, I have endured more than my fair share of negative setbacks in life, which in turn rendered me very spiritually fatigued. This state of extreme tiredness was not due to work. It was a condition that plagued me internally as in soul and in body. Yes, I was perfectly functioning professionally, in the job arena but was humanly just in plain physiological existence. This simply meant that my spirit was gradually withering within me not because I was brokenhearted, but because I was extremely humiliated by the adversity; and needed quickening by something very pure and faultless enough to revive it gradually on a systematic basis first, and finally permanently. I was lead through fervent prayer to a clear and present source of revival, and found the strength to go on, professionally as well as humanly. At that point the positive spirit exuded by my interaction with my clients daily, brought me sustenance of great restorative depth. I found myself rising earlier than usual, and looking forward to my workday, and anticipating the weeks to come with greater expectation. You see, the Lord pointed out an avenue of therapeutic relief for me right under my very nose. He used my occupation at the time to occupy my mental faculties positively and contentedly in order to accord me, physiological excellence, and psychological well being.

My first introduction to pain, hatred and strife in life, commenced in the second year of my marriage. You see, I lived in a state of ignorance, which later graduated into self-judgment. For years, I suffered as God gradually revealed to me the impediment; I was never in denial at anytime during this crisis; but rather in shock because abuse had never been part of my life as a child or adult. I grew up in a very large family (multi) with very loving parents, who were unique in very special ways thus, I count myself very blessed. My parents joined in wedlock bringing in children from their first marriages, yet our home was nonetheless very loving and highly interactive. My Papa a very studious man, was an ordained Methodist Priest, who later plunged into politics and Government to become The first Priest to win a constituency in Ghanaian political history; but was best known as the First Minister of Defense and Minister resident in Guinea in the first republic. My Mama was an Educator; a Senior superintendent in the Ghana education Service. I had elder siblings; our home was busy, noisy and fun. Neither I nor my siblings witnessed our Mama or Papa argue or raise their voices in anger around us. My parents Allen and Gee loved and cared for all of us as one family, and it was the most fun as well as nurturing house hold ever to grow up in for us. Therefore when I think of my years growing up, I realize how innocent and happily my parents strived to create the perfect environment for us as children, despite their previous relationships that failed. If there ever was any indication of domestic abuse or the like, then they must have been very good at concealing it from curious, inquisitive and smart children like us. I remember asking my Mama a few years before she passed away if they ever had quarrels. "We are human aren't we? Yes we have our moments, but you must understand that we do it diplomatically, because we believe it should have no bearing on you. Usually when we send you off to the cinema, we deal with issues; but your father has never lifted a hand in abuse towards me, never."

The material point is that, there was a lot of us and we were everywhere around the house that is why there is no way that secret behaviors and temperaments could be concealed or harbored by them. We got into everything. Unlike most children of our ethnicity, we were raised to be very vocal and expressive in opinions and ideas around our parents. We engaged in family debates with our Papa, my Big Brother Sam won a lot of them. He was also the closest to me, taking care of me, babysitting me and even dressing me up for church. I was a very happy child. There were books everywhere, and the atmosphere was very academically charged; I remember stumbling upon books written about Andrew Carnegie, and

Dr. Martin Luther King when I was barely six years old. Like all families, and parents, we had our setbacks and challenges, which were eventually overcome or dealt with. We also had divers forms of recreation, and were also disciplined, not abused by our Mama and Papa, in fairness of love and affection. And so I believe that you will agree with me when I affirm that, one's childhood experiences and memories, are vividly and candidly displayed no matter how much they are concealed, by the character and behavior projected in one's life; just like a quilt on display for all to see. Character cannot be hidden and behavior cannot be concealed by any means; as the popular African proverb goes; "Character is like pregnancy; give it ample time; nourish it and it will pop out for all to see." I also firmly believe that, what you have inside, is what you project outwardly to people you meet and encounter in relationships be it personal or professional. This hard fact awakened in me the reason I was experiencing so much pain in my relationship. There was no form or type of abuse and humiliation that a woman could suffer in a relationship that I did not experience.

When things got out of hand, I wondered at first what I had done wrong. I think I did not want divorce on my life's resume, so I fought with the arm of flesh to keep my marriage going, even when love and affection for my spouse at the time had completely deserted me. My ego or rather my pride sought and secured a way for me to preserve my dignity, status, and self image more than thinking about my well being. I was also very wrong by taking that step due to said pride; because for the longest time which was, after a year and a half of the marriage I was not even in love. I was only functioning as a wife, and doing what my Pastor at the time, and elders who counseled me from a cultural perspective wrongly, which was chuck full of traditional concepts that were twisted to favor one and not the other and as such, repressed the female and kept the male misbehaving, together with biblical theories and strategies which never dissolved into the perfect solution of scriptural advice rightly divided concerning the situation. A considerable number of people in the Fold, that I was acquainted with, revealed their true nature through betrayal, lined with extreme cruelty of a magnitude that can throw one into the abyss of self-destruction. A vast amount of these betrayal were shockingly perpetrated on my person by people and 'friends' who played key roles in our wedding as well as others who walked into my home on a frequent basis without ceremony; knowing that they will be automatically received with of course a wholesome meal, (which was common fare in my home coupled with warm hospitality of other dimensions.) As a wife, I was very matronly and an expert hostess like my mother, and grandmother before me and as such, entertained a lot. Being a very excellent cook and homemaker, with a brain of course, I believed strongly that I was an ideal woman possessing most qualities that made strong unions, so I just could not grasp the notion of accepting the deteriorating magnitude of the situation at the core to realize that, I was suffering because I had to be discarded for someone else, chosen by a man of God who was the other woman's Pastor while we were still married. Wow! Imagine my shock when the Pastor called me to tell me that my marriage was over. These were his exact words; "Look here stupid, the man does not want you; can't you get it into your thick head?" So you can tell how betrayed I felt in realizing that those whom I trusted, as friends even in the Lord were not real with me or with the Lord. A year later, they dedicated a baby daughter, officiated by the same Pastor, God-Fathered by our best man, and God mothered by the Mother of the groom, which was attended by a great number of our special guests when we were married; exactly a year after I had lost mine through a miscarriage. But it is well with my soul because, this is not a publicity stunt but a testimony of praise and adoration to God even though many have pressured me over the years to sell my story as a script to African filmmakers.

My adverse experience could only be likened by severity and horror as a scene from a vampire movie in which one innocently runs to their loved ones for help, but finds them all transformed into the very monster they were running from. That sort of experience can easily drive you insane. But not me. Yes, I was shaken and kicked around, but not trampled on to the ultimate degree of losing my self respect and dignity. At a point, my perpetrators resorted to the continuous habit of character assassination, Legal summons were served to me from the other woman by sheriffs, my answering machine was filled with alternative messages of insults from my spouse's sister and the other woman while I was being persistently victimized by my spouse. At the time, even as a child of God, I realized why people in situations like mine just lose it all and go on killing rampages; but I had Jesus in my heart and God in my corner; and besides I ain't dying crying or going to jail for no man; Oh no! my Grandma will rise from the grave and knock me unconscious for destroying a good female family trend and I had ambitions in life to pursue; so I said, "forget these people." Even though the constant mélange of searing heat from the marital pressure cooker, almost shattered my strong spirited personality The inadequacies that ensued; some of which are too explicitly gross for the subject and content of this book, commenced a series of unsightly visible displays on my person; my beautiful bouncy curly hair was falling out in clustered strands, by the fistful. Within months, I was almost thin haired and subsequently bald. I lost weight and my skin lost its natural glow. But in the darkness of the situation the light of God illuminated my faculties to the divine truth that, even though my parents were miles away and the head perpetrator had cunningly and manipulatively blinded everyone around us with his satan-endowed slickness of tongue and false sultry demeanor, God almighty was with me, and was on my side, and had seen right through the lies and deceit. Yes, God the Father provided a shoulder of rest for me to lean on, and gave me encouragement, comfort and divine defense.

He lifted up my head, as His divine glory overshadowed my calamities and vanquished them. I in turn sought fervent encouragement from His word of truth and lived to testify of His beneficence I continue to embrace to this day, within his arms of deliverance. Beloved reader, if you have tasted of His providence like I have, through His Holy word, you will realize that deriving and seeking encouragement from God's word is handed out in a dual-package of friendship and companionship. God's words from the following scriptures comforted as well as encouraged me. (Psalm 62: 1-2, 5-8 11 -12. KJV.) "Truly my soul waiteth upon God: from Him cometh my salvation. He only is my rock and my salvation. He is my defense; I shall not be greatly moved." This simply means that as children of God, we are allowed to feel hurt, depressed, rejected, scorned, et cetera; but are not allowed to sink into their depressive abyss by allowing those negativities or vices to completely drown us; of course they will move us periodically, or constantly, but not a lot more than we can bear, and certainly not GREATLY, when we resort to the Words of The Divine Master for encouragement and strength. "My soul wait thou upon God; for my expectation is from Him. He only is my rock and my salvation: He is my defense; I shall not be moved. In God is my salvation and my glory; the rock of my strength, and my refuge is in God. In God is my salvation and my glory: the rock of my strength, and my refuge is in God. Trust in him at all times; ye people, pour out your heart before him: God is a refuge for us. God has spoken once; twice have I heard this; that power belongeth unto God. Also unto thee, O Lord, belongeth mercy: For thou renderest to every man according to his work."

When adversities of this magnitude spawn around you, your only retreat is to hide in Christ, and heed the Holy Spirit, as you call upon God for back-up. This spiritual concept that I adopted as an 'immediate spiritual maneuver' (ISM) flung me to wholly and completely pledge myself into 'total Godly reliance'(TGR), which was the sure and only way to sign up for 'spiritual therapy' (ST). I researched, studied and memorized scripture, just like we memorized complete textbooks in Ghanaian schools. This process referred to as 'cramming' by students in my native country Ghana, entailed the following; 'chewing' which is reading and memorizing a particular subject area or a several from a whole textbook; 'pouring' that is the ability to write down all the essential points and facts on that particular subject, at the time of testing; and 'passing and forgetting'; which is the ability to make the highest grade or good grade when the test results are posted, and the subsequent act of temporarily disregarding that particular subject area as long as you made the grade. This style of learning that I acquired in school, came in very handy because I had the experience and the discipline to render it scripturally as well as spiritually feasible. For at that time, I was able to utilize it for my spiritual benefit and to procure my scriptural credentials. Yes, I was going to engage in 'cramming' but must do so with precision and retention for my 'lifelong spiritual benefit.' (LSB)

I also took the following social step of shutting down all outlets of baseless and certain spun gender suppressing traditional marital conventions, that I was being badgered with, by select religious leaders, acquaintances, marital friends who had initially been my bosom friends, who had shifted alliance, to honor and uphold the perpetrator not because he was in the right, but because of his gender (a very backward notion indeed); and others who were friends of the head perpetrator, including men of the collar in name but not in deed, by refusing and rejecting all invitations to their backward and male chauvinistic interviews, meetings and gatherings overflowing with illogical gender repressive brainwash. Please do not misconstrue my words, I love my people and my culture which is full of great attributes but some of them need reform as far as my gender is concerned. The good news was that my parents and extended family at the time offered me full support and my 'Mama dearest' of blessed memory was dispatched by my late 'Papa most loving' to live with me and offer moral support as well as resident advice to both I and my abuser in an effort of to instill positiveness and not division and partiality, even when she knew that it was over because that is how things were handled by Christians and people of good stock. I then invented a strategic spiritual plan with which I sought the helpful hand of He who sees and knows all things, to permanently eradicate my suffering, sleeping in my mother's arms every night while she offered me comfort. This was also my time for 'spiritual excavation' (SE) geared towards 'spiritual recovery'(SR). After this line of therapy I picked up the handset of self acceptance and dialed JESUS, by the empowerment of the Holy Spirit, who then tapped on God's shoulder, and that was how I officially got into therapy.

This really relieved my suffering since growing up with a father who was a former Statesman in the intelligence arena, I had somewhat become a 'coded' personality by upbringing, as i was not raised to broadcast my private issues and as such had kept things under wrap and was forced to divulge them when they had festered in the worst way. I must also admit that my pride and arrogance were awakened regarding the whole issue and I felt humiliated by this man that treated me like he [picked me on a rubbish dump. Never on any occasion did I feel broken hearted or find myself in emotional suspense; my whole issue was due to the lack of respect for me, my family and the marriage even though we were all aware it was on its last limb, and the continuous degradation and humiliation I suffered unjustly at the hand of not only this man towards whom if I was to apply certain formulas of society and breeding, should never have had the chance to look me in the eye or would not dare set foot where I trod, but the other woman as well; for had I not paved the way for him, with the lack of judgement and Godly guidance, I wouldn't find myself in a such a mess. But that is in the past. During my sessions, which typically lasted within the time-wise period of twenty-four hours, seven days a week and three hundred and sixty five days a year, I drowned myself within things scripturally spiritual, which comprised of ardent Bible study, church fellowship, fervent and ceaseless prayer attitude, coupled with the constant and dedicated Godly Pastoral duty exhibited through the injection of personal Christian ministry, of Forgiveness, healing, recovery and self–rejuvenation by my family friends Pastor and Mrs. Mahama Yoda. (God bless them for their tireless efforts and for not giving in to the deceit and lies of the enemy.) I also sought audio counsel from Christian radio stations including after hours ministry. Thus byundergoing all the above, I was able to strengthen my relationship with God and reposition my footing in Him. The intensity of our relationship(God and I) through dedicated scriptural study, rightly divided supplication and thanksgiving, kept me alive and nurtured me spiritually. During sleepless nights, which was rampant (before my Mama dearest came to live with me) because I missed my parents, who loved me tremendously especially my late Papa, to whom I was very close and the only man who ever loved me completely,

I researched into the word of God, and read a bundle of scriptural core reference materials and commentaries. I also acquired theological expertise from my Papa while I also upgraded my praying techniques, to enable me confuse the adversary who was then thickly on my trails in destructive mode seeking my very life.

One of my favorite Christian radio programs was Focus on the family; recommended by my good friend Maria, which is spearheaded by the Scriptural psychological expertise of the acclaimed Doctor. The daytime and late night discussions and teachings were very beneficial and very potent with helpful hints and advice for victorious Christian living during dire setbacks and adversities. The following scriptures inspired my courage and offered me divine therapeutic help as they comforted my body, heart and soul. "For the Lord loveth judgment and forsaketh not His saints; They are preserved for ever: I have seen the wicked in great power, and spreading himself like a green bay tree. Yet he passed away, and lo, he was not: yea I sought him, but he could not be found. Mark the perfect man, and behold the upright for the end of that man is peace. But the transgressors shall be destroyed together: the end of the wicked shall be cut off. But the salvation of the righteous is of the lord: He is their strength in the time of trouble. And the Lord shall help them, and deliver them; He shall deliver them from the wicked, and save them, because they trust in Him." (please research the source and record it with your notes in the subsidiary pages, thank you.)

This scripture breaks encouragement down into trust and hope. Here the Father offers us great promises, regardless of the magnitude of our oppression. As you read this chapter, remember that, your absolute trust in God's word is your sole weapon of freedom from the bondage that besieges you. (Psalm 8: 9 & 10 KJV.)reassures you and I as we rely on God's hand to deliver us; " The Lord will be a refuge for the oppressed, a refuge in times of trouble. And they that know thy name will put their trust in thee: For thou Lord, hast not forsaken them that seek thee." Yes, beloved reader, my experiences and divine visitation from God will seem baseless if I do not let others benefit from them by doing exactly what verse 11 of Psalm 9 says; "sing praises to the Lord, which dwelleth in Zion: declare among the people His doings." There are so many ways that you can exalt the Lord, and proclaim His greatness, in gratitude of heart from a person who has tasted, witnessed and experienced within great adversity, his deep love and beneficence. You may choose to sing unto Him in Psalms and hymns and spiritual songs. I do that on a regular basis in plenty or in want; but for this instance, I choose to testify; not orally but literarily. " O God my Father everlasting, who bestows upon me benefits beyond measure; I proclaim the greatness of your love, of your blessings and of your insurmountable grace and mercy on my life. Yes! Father, I reveal my experiences to the world together with the depth of love and intimacy of the relationship I shared and still have with you to be publicized for the spiritual encouragement and scriptural benefit of my readers; and also for the world to know that you are still in business and in control of the whole universe as Lord of all. A-men."(AOP) I realized after a period of extensive scriptural research that I had accrued a considerable amount of spiritual research materials and gathered a substantial load of findings from my excavating ventures. Therefore in fullness of equipage, I boldly gathered all the negativities that were plaguing my life, and handed them over to the heavenly laboratory for refining, where the Master Himself together with the Angelic hosts distilled those negative vices of trials and tribulations. Yes! I stood and watched in prayer as those adversities made their way clearly transformed into positive expectations, through the divine sterile system of deliverance, and finally dropping as blessings into the flask of hope where they were elevated into sure accomplishments. That is when I knew for good that God never fails His own, as long as you and I put our implicit trust in Him.

Yes the lord gave me of the distilled and divinely purified concoction of encouragement and restoration to drink into newness of life. As the popular saying goes; "Seeing is believing." But in God, "Not seeing, but exhibiting dutiful trust laced with unshakeable faith, and hoping against hope for a sure outcome is believing." (AOQ) " for blessed are they that have not seen, and yet believed" (John. 20: 29.KJV.) Beloved reader my testimony is yours to decipher. It is in your hands to measure by its weight in divine authenticity, and by way of my sure existence as a Child of God who still stands well aligned in the faith, regardless of adversities. For "though the mountains be shaken and hills be removed, God's unfailing love for me will not be shaken; nor will His covenant of peace be removed, (from my life). Says the Lord who hath compassion on me." Isaiah 54:10. (personalized scripture)

So you see, your need and desperate cry for encouragement in this world of adversities and negativities, of trials and tribulations, can only be channeled through one who has walked miles and miles in your shoes, the Lord Christ Jesus, the redeemer of us all. And in actuality; as in establishing living facts and proof of God's mighty hand still at work today, you need real life pioneers and warriors of Christ; 'spiritually elevated role models' (SERM) to inject you by sight and verbally or literarily by testimony, set within unshakeable faith, as they testify of their experiences. I do hope since I am not a celebrated Minister on earth but surely one recognized in heaven by the Father God Almighty, that I too can be counted worthy of such a calling, so that by God's power working within me, a spark of hope and encouragement may be ignited into the adversities that plague you, for tiny as it may seem, that spark is sizable enough to vanquish all adversity in your life. Shall we read Psalm 27: 11-14 KJV. "Teach me thy way o Lord, and lead me in a plain path, because of my enemies. Deliver me not over unto the will of my enemies: for false witnesses are risen against me, such as breath out cruelty. I had fainted, unless I had believed to see the goodness of the Lord in the land of the living. Wait, on the Lord: and He shall strengthen thine heart: wait, I say, on the Lord."

Shall we infuse the following scripture with the previous to ensure an added depth of encouragement; in order to prevent the infiltration of hopelessness from murdering the vitality of our courage? Psalm, 28: 6&7 KJV; "Blessed be the Lord, because He hath heard the voice of my supplications. The Lord is my strength and my shield; my heart trusted in Him, and I am helped: Therefore my heart greatly rejoiceth; and with my song will I praise Him." Let us add considerable depth to our faith with Psalm, 36: 10&11KJV; "O continue thy loving kindness unto them that know thee; and thy righteousness to the upright in heart. Let not the foot of pride come against me, and let not the hand of the wicked remove me." What tremendous encouragement will fill your heart, soul and body when you ceaselessly pray with these scriptures and others alike, seeking the Father's encouragement and comfort, through His sure and ultimate therapeutic rightly divided word of truth within which, He portrays Himself as the friend of the friendless and constant companion to the poor and needy. One of my favorite scriptures for help, encouragement and assistance is found in the book of Psalms, chapter 3 "Lord how are they increased that trouble me! Many are they that rise up against me. Many there be which say of my soul, there is no help for him in God. But thou, O Lord, art a shield for me; my glory, and the lifter up of my head. I cried unto the Lord with my voice, and He heard me out of His holy hill. I laid me down and slept; I awakened; for the Lord sustained me. I will not be afraid of ten thousand of people, that have set themselves against me round about. Arise, O Lord; save me, O my God: for thou hast smitten all mine enemies upon the cheek bone; thou hast broken the teeth of the ungodly.

Salvation belongeth unto the Lord: thy blessing is upon thy people." God made all these proclamations manifest in the life of David, His servant. For God is faithful to the end, the ancient of days, He is El-Shaddai; constant and unchanging. Why not put your trust in Him, with faith that has transcended hope to an insurmountable height that defies common sense and human reasoning. "My yoke is easy and my burden is light;" says the Lord who encourages you from within. Would you please find this scripture and record it in your notes section please? GREAT!!!

A lot of times, when our perpetrators or the adversities that plague us, seem to be gaining grounds, our faith is rigidly put to the test, and our pedestal of hope wobbles at the base, but with courage from God's word, and strong belief in His faithfulness and love, we can re-stabilize our hope, as we root ourselves in God's promises which are constantly Yea and Amen. I recall my perpetrator's exact words at a time during the marital crisis when every thing was perfectly going his way yet driven on the tracks of adversity, while I even though I was the one constantly perpetrated by him, and still steadfastly walking in the precepts of God the Father and doing what was right morally, found myself continuously in the gapping jaws of condemnation, tribal persecution and adversity by him and his cohorts. But did I lean against the ropes of unbelief, or throw in the towel of righteousness, to seek the arm of flesh even though I could subdue him in a lot more ways than the physical; if you know what I mean. No I did not. I summoned encouragement from the word of God and faced the adversary in faith refreshed with hopeful obedience, as I made my way painfully (due to lack of divine guidance when I chose him as a spouse yet God was still with me; amen?) up towards the pinnacle of divine expectations; there I flung myself into 'spiritual combat' (SC) with the adversary, as I bounced courageously on the canvas of great expectations, shod with divine feet of boldness that exhibited the foot-works of a child of God about to claim the victory, as I prepared for the final show down with the adversary, fully persuaded that, what God had promise me, would be brought into existence through my ultimate winning performance, in the conquering ring of the believing-just and victorious. (note that, you may be just in your circumstance but, righteousness devoid of Christ-like principles embossed within scriptural verity has no spiritual depth and scripturally valueless for it is the breeding ground for countless ill circumstances) Therefore having been fueled spiritually to vanquish and prevail, I unbalanced the enemy with a divinely projected left hook, followed by series of simultaneous combinations, and a final upper-cut dislocating his treacherous jaw thus, ridding him of all speech as I knocked the adversary out on the divine canvas of defeat; and God received the glory. Amen.

Note my grammatical use of the phrase, 'the marital crisis." This is because, it was a crisis perpetrated on me, by a person who enjoyed it to the fullest and of course found it fun and exciting. Why? Because of the role he breathlessly played as head perpetrator of all the negativities through his indulgence, insinuation, participation and ardent devotion to the propagation of said negativities.) his words to me were as follows "if you are really praying to God, why is He not taking sides with you? Why has he allowed all our friends to take sides with me even the ones you introduced into this relationship huh?" this is just one out of several instances, but in defense to these adversities, I answered him thus; "because they were never my friends in the first place, but go ahead and justify your deeds; and I promise you this: that you shall never encounter a woman of my standard, breeding and spiritual girth ever in your life again. I haven't lost anything; you have therefore depart from me satan." But he came back stronger with more vile words and it reminded me of Christ's experience with the devil after His 40day fast. Ha! My Lord had long walked in those shoes before I did. Hallelujah! So I took the scriptural route to silence this evil person forever.

I had learned from Christ that, under such interrogatories, a carnal verbal retort never worked for self-defense. I know and have experienced this for a fact, because I kept loosing my spiritual stand, for failing to adequately utilize the word of truth towards my self-defense. Yes, dear reader in Christ; I lost that sequence because, as a child of God, I realized that one cannot get into mortal verbal combat with a person expressly endowed with the deceptive forked tongue of adversity speaking blasphemy and lies, and taking the righteousness of the righteous from them. Oh no! Not when that vessel is contaminated and is fashioned to twist the truth into lies; a system propelled by the adversary's demonically installed neurological chip, fully loaded and functioning as a constant updated archive of answers to every question put to those who serve his purpose. This works to their advantage because, it impressively clouds the third party's judgment, (if they are not grounded in the word as most shallow and biased people in the Fold are) but positively contributes literarily nothing to resolve the issue at hand and as such, favoring the negative party since, at that material moment the father of lies takes over the body system completely thus, using them to his adverse advantage while putting the child of God into a shameful position. This discovery of immeasurable spiritual heights kept me on my guard. For as the adversary relentlessly and persistently used that person who was then closest to me (not without their yielding of course) to distort my footing in God, I learned from experience not to apply the foolish and thoughtless verbal avenues retrieved from my storehouse of carnal intellect and eloquence again; but applied 'divine strategy'(DS), and spiritual intellect wherein lay my treasure of scriptural eloquence endowed by 'The Most High God'(TMHG), through His word of truth which I had then rightly divided for said purpose and need.

Our Lord and Savior Jesus the Christ being the divine originator and pioneer of said strategy, applied a similar divine strategy scripturally, when the devil tempted Him in the wilderness after His forty day fast. He thereafter set the spiritual stage for the sure utilization of aggressive, but accurate scriptural proclamations under divers situations, but took time to categorize His scriptural selection, by the balancing of its contents in relation to the adverse subject matter contained within the attack at hand, to enable Him expressly as well as accurately, and selectively, re-quote the precise scripture punctually and rightly divided, and literarily served it purposely and prospectively by function, in order to obliterate the specific outcome the adversary meant to achieve, while outsmarting the father of lies and confusion. Married couples and people in serious relationships must realize that, the minute physical abuse, deception and lies creep into these unions, the red flag of trouble flies full mast. This signifies the presence of adversity and evil because the Holy spirit then departs the vessel perpetrating the lies since it cannot dwell in a body tainted by the characteristics of it's enemy the evil spirit. Thus one takes leave as the other takes residence; And the more agitated and serious your marital problems become, and the higher they escalate, can be spiritually tallied to the density and strength of the adversary's hold on the life of the tainted vessel within; and I do not mean to scare you, but this is the time when being a realistic personality is both spiritually as well as physically beneficial and I thank God that He created me to be a firm realist.

My realism is so profound and practical, it could not be misconstrued as a learned trait, but it is in truth, one endowed by 'the Father above'(TFA) which causes me to quickly ascertain situations, find ways of saving myself and moving on without lingering. Thus I have known who I am since I caught my first glimpse of the the world when I was but a babe swinging under the west African coconut trees. Dear reader, please never forget to seek the counsel of God and ask for guidance in all that you do; do not enter into any relationship unadvisedly or unguarded scripturally and spiritually; never succumb to pressure or think you can change someone; oh no! do not make that mistake. For the first time your partner physically or verbally abuses you, or lies to you is when you must get out and cancel that wedding, or give back that engagement ring. You can say all you want about forgiveness and tolerance but you cannot pour fluids into full vessels; Do not risk it for you may not be fortunate, to live with a constant backache like me, but may lose your life over a worthless creature. Yes, I wrote 'creature' because by then that person would have transcended the realms of civil human tendencies; hence the word. Shall we please continue our lesson? Thank you.

Well after that verbal swing at God Himself, by the perpetrator jeering at me because my spirituality was not rewarded by God, and humans, like his adversity had been enthroned by mortals, which was nothing short of mocking, I proceeded aggressively in prayer, that was to date my most spirit-filled prayer time of all; for the spirit of God consumed me totally and my prayer came from a place within that I could not place. I realized then that, I was 'wailing' as my brother Noel often described deep prayer to us, when we were children. My belly ached not with pain, but with scriptural agony, devotion and spiritual passion of the greatest heights. I prayed with understanding, and yet I never uttered a slip of tongue. For as my prayer progressed it shifted from the English language to my own ethnic dialect; and my lips were not mine anymore but the Lord's. I finally fell to the floor exhausted but relieved and at that time the adversary jumped on the phone and called his mistress on speakerphone just to sway my spiritual stance to derail me as they both condemned me as a lunatic 'bordamfo' was the word they used from the twi dialect, jeering and gloating... "Father forgive them for they know not against whom they wrestle ha!" But what a brilliant lunatic I turned out to be. " for I was then a lunatic by circumstance due to an unfortunate marriage, and lack of Godly obedience, but never one by birth and the poor fool knows that right well Hallelujah!!! "The heart of man is wicked above all things who can know it..." (please research the source of this scripture and record it in the notes section of your comprehensive guide to prayer. Thank you.) Before he could harness another load of adverse rubbish, I charged with greater spiritual prowess not to argue back and forth with a creature of darkness which he was, but to accomplish a daring feat in the name of God; for you see this creature possessed a complexity in character by way of extreme abusive behavior that was dark and utterly deceptive and conniving enough to derail men of God who attempted to counsel us during the crisis.

On behalf of all abused sisters, I humbly ask our African Pastors to take extra time to listen to daughters who bring their domestic crisis before them, especially those living abroad; for being outside their element and facing such demise can destroy them or end in fatality. I plead on behalf of women of my descent struggling with gender suppression and abuse in their relationships to know that it is not okay when he slaps you and slams you around like a piece of furniture, or calls you names; stop stirring that pot of 'eba and bitterleaf soup'; put down that 'fufu' pestle, leave the rice cooker alone, stop peeling plantains, and chopping spinach, turn off the burner under that 'palmnut soup' and get help by any means necessary; don't ever be afraid or embarrassed girls, rise and take charge, for your sake and that of your family and loved ones. The key expression in this instance that I charge you never to forget is "it is not okay." I therefore sincerely hope our Men of God will respond to my plea for I know that there are a lot of good and upright African Pastors out there; who are more than willing to offer these daughters of Africa the adequate spiritual as well as the physical assistance, they require in all totality because, even though I escaped mine with lifelong injuries, the ripple effect projected by the lack of proper ministry and care from my Church-home at the time, continued into all areas of my life. Everything I tried to do out of hard work, goodness and sincerity turned to mush while some of them projected me wrongly in the social light just because, I was left alone to untangle myself for years from the residual struggles the situation emitted, which were manifested in their negative multitudes. Amen? I hear you sisters, stop hiding your bruised bodies under colorful ethnic attires, and your hair loss under elegant head gears. I know your pain and as such empower you to act on the scriptural stage with a contrite heart in all boldness and spirituality. You deserve better; for your price is far above rubies, Amen. (Our lesson continues please.)

The following scripture took care of the adversary's sacrilegious pronouncement. When he said blatantly to me the following; "...look here crazy woman, I am sick and tired of hearing you pray in this house okay; trust me if you do not stop praying and repeating those verses, I will have to shut you up for good before you think about another one." Ha what nerves huh? But this man whom most think they know better take it from me, I knew more than his own parents did, for I was married to him; I must tell you that he was so utterly endowed with the artful dodging tactics of the prince of darkness himself that even a lot of well meaning Pastors were spiritually eluded; losing their very hard earned 'Godly Light of Divine

Perception' which I call the (GLDP). When dealing with a forked tongue like this sort, one must take precaution against any slight chance of the minutest display of spiritual instability, wobble, and imbalance which might not necessarily mean backsliding behavior but simply an exhibition of fear, uncertainty, loss of scriptural grasp and eloquence. (Psalm 31:18) (Isaiah 5:18-21, 23 &24 KJV was my fortress and stay, while my mouth spewed out the non-carnal weapons of warfare which were indeed mighty through God, as they pulled down the strongholds of the syndicate that badgered my life. The head of the perpetrator was crushed with the word disassembling the entire faction in Jesus' name. Now dearest reader infuse the following scripture into the temple of the Holy spirit and let it settle with the foundation for all time. Amen? Here we go.

"Let the lying lips be put to silence; which speak grievous things proudly and contemptuously against the righteous." "Woe unto them that draw iniquity with cords of vanity, and sin as it were a cart rope: that say, let us hasten his work, that we may see it: and let the counsel of the Holy One of Israel draw nigh and come, that we may see it: Woe unto them that call evil good and good evil, that put bitter for sweet and sweet for bitter! Which justify the wicked for reward, and take the righteousness of the righteous from him! Therefore as the fire devoureth the stubble, and the flame consumeth the chaff, so their root shall be as rotteness, and their blossom shall go up as dust: because they have cast away the law of the Lord of Hosts and despised the word of the Holy One of Israel." Amen? Just typing this scripture set me trotting and bouncing in the spirit because, it echoed in wholesome completeness, my entire demise and called to avenge my cause; for I know in truth that when all the members of that syndicate who humiliated me beyond measure, throwing themselves in the most unfathomably wicked way into my marriage and thus turning a civil occurrence into that of torture and near fatality without cause, read or hear this, they will know that the Law and the Prophets are come to adjudicate them. Yes! How often we forget that this same God that we worship bringeth low and lifted up; blesses and curses; maketh rich and maketh poor; He is Almighty; a God of truth without iniquity; just and right is He. A-men.

As I finished my aggressive proclamation, at the time, I fell to the floor exhausted and drained; I felt pain in my abdominal cavity, the likes of which one experiences a day or two after commencing abdominal crunches. I then realized I had been wailing spiritually. Later as I narrated this experience to my brother Noel, he explained to me that, the anger that I felt on God's behalf when the forked one spoke against Him, was at that actual moment imputed unto me for righteousness, which then further propelled me into accomplishing that spiritual feat of 'scriptural self defense' (SSD) utilizing what I loved, believed and leaned on which was of course the Word of Truth. Wow! How 'kool' was that! I later realized that, I was bathed in God's divine anointing, which in turn helped me divulge in perfection His studied Word as He propelled me into spiritual action in boldness and accuracy that displaced the lies of the adversary as I threw him down on his back. Only God knows what I have encountered and the consequences I had to pay.

As you may have experienced through my testimony dear reader, this book is not a publicity stunt, but a truthful account of the experiences of a child of God, who though no different from you by way of adversities experienced, has indeed tasted and seen the goodness of the Lord even from the land of adversities and certain death right into the land of the living, and is therefore extending a hand of encouragement to you in print after a lengthy period of scriptural research, and the painstaking task dedicated to the appropriation of scripture related to the subject of prayer, as well as the abject belief in it's potency, so that you too will be blessed, as you draw water from His divine wells of encouragement. The purpose of this literary testimony and teaching guide pertaining to attaining and maintaining the knowledge of the true essence of the word of truth's utmost spiritual capacity to deliver on a deadline together with the adequate consistency of divinely acquired hopeful expectation for the sure presentation of non-amiss supplication effectively before God, was fully devised to steer you closer to the hem of Christ's garment. (Ha! Long sentence) But it is entirely up to you dear reader, as a well grounded, Bible studying, living, breathing and believing child of God, to find as well as define your grasp, by scripturally as well as spiritually determining at what gradient you are fully prepared to perch your belief and faith in the power of His word, in order to initiate that divine touch of it's hem by 'faith propelled self motivation' (FPSM), in order to re-claim newness and wholesomeness of life in Him. "For only with the right portion of the substance of things you prayerfully hope for, and the precise and credible amount weighed within measures of ultimate expectancy, of the evidence of things unforeseen and unknown by you, while on the other hand observed, and known of the Father on high, as that faith which is no larger than a mustard seed, is all it takes to ignite the tiny spark of divine expectancy steadily growing within you, into the blazing fiery glory of His sovereign divine ability to physically make manifest, in order to burn those crumbling cinders of bleak desperation and disappointments plaguing your life, into ashes of nothingness, as He lifting you up with vibrant joy, reveals to you a future of abundant joy, by the outpouring of divine brightness projected from His very holy luminescence." (ANQ).

Dear reader, I must caution you by way of experience to never fail or hesitate to call God for divine direction, in every decision you make, no matter how great or insignificant they may be, and even when the evidence of false positive rears it's head to pronounce said decision as likely to succeed. You must also never proceed with important matters as well as delicate decisions without calling on God for 'explicit divine approval and direction' (EDAD); because when matters fly off handle due to ill-considered and disobedient decisions on your path, leaving you without adequate spiritual as well as physical strength, you are bound to sink due to the deficiency, rendering you as a child of God who has not reached his or her full potential in the arena of spiritual excavation wherein lies the tools of self preparedness, towards the spiritual task ahead of you. Believe it or not many a Child of God have sunk under despair and ultimate self-destruction due to the imbalance displayed in tallied atrocity weight compounding their physical endurance, and thereby choking their very spiritual depth. Thus can we deduce that when we take matters into our own hands by leaning entirely on the arm of flesh, we definitely set ourselves upon the tedious path for a virtual recall, or a prospective total impound; And yet despite our disobedience and blatant lack of 'spiritual judgement',(SJ) God's loving arms are still constantly wide open to receive and pull us out of our demise, as long as we grant Him access by way of repentance from a contrite and broken heart. (Read Isaiah 5:25). "Because like a shepherd guides his flock with love, tenderness and devotion, so does our Father God in heaven above, the Good Shepherd (Jehovah-Raah) lead us in pastures green where grassy meadows of encouragement and edible scriptural foliage laden with eternal spiritual nourishment filled with divine counsel thrive." (AOQ) He will never reject us whatever the transgression, but accord us divine clemency even when we are denied one on this earth, but receive us with sweet reproof, at the nick of time, within the nook of His staff. How 'kool' is that? That even the condemned may yet be redeemed by love unfailing when repentant hands are stretched out to the Master from a contrite heart, Amen.

"Our Father God loves and cares for us, and constantly as Jehovah Elshaddai, desires our happiness because it is He who has secured it by striking a high bargain thousands of years ago, laden with great love and sacrifice. But we must prove ourselves worthy and deserving of that love and mercy, through genuine repentance, by completely and utterly surrendering to His divine purpose of encouragement, and to that of His supreme leadership and guidance in our lives, by following the true and divine way laid down in His word of truth, through practical christianity embroiled in ardent bible study and fellowship, in order to claim its full warranty, together with the benefits of His divine encouragement in its entirety, exclusive of any form of adversely incurred deductibles." (ANQ) Get it? :))))

The benefits of relying on God for encouragement:

1. You are secured under God's protection.
2. God becomes your refuge and fortress.
3. You put your trust in God and not man.
4. You receive divine comfort during crisis.
5. God is attentive to your cries for help and responds with utmost urgency.
6. The more broken in spirit your demise renders you, the wider His hands are stretched out to sooth you.
7. The Lord saves your soul, and erases all harmful scars, and imprints of adversities you encounter.
8. He delivers you from all your troubles.
9. Your hope and strength in God is rejuvenated into steadfastness of mind and of the spirit.
10. The Lord awards you with incomprehensible strength and endurance.
11. He crowns you with righteousness.
12. Your hope in God is transformed into persuasion and utmost manifestation.
13. God's great faithfulness is awarded you, and is daily renewed for your spiritual vitality.
14. God relieves you of all burdens.
15. Your needs are met without question.
16. God reveals to you the secrets of contentment in every dire situation you find yourself and equips you with grace, tact

and precision as you hold your head up in confidence. (been there:)

17. Your physical capabilities as well as abilities become endless because they are propelled by the hand of God.
18. The Lord grants you sleep at night because you are His beloved.
19. He takes away your fears and anxieties by endowing you daily with newness of joy, through His great faithfulness.
20. God bathes you with great peace, as you look up to Him for counsel and direction via His word of truth.

Bible study on encouragement.

Psalm 10: 17 &18) (34: 18-20 & 22) (59: 16-17) (91: 1-2.)
Matthew 11: 28-30
Philippians 4: 12-13
2Timothy 4: 7, retreat to (verse 6) then skip to (verse 8)
2Thessalonians 1: 11 &12

Largo from "Xerxes"
By the illustrious: George Frederick Handel.

Holy, most Holy art thou
Lord God Almighty
Holy a'rt thou, Holy a'rt thou
Lord God Almighty, which w'ert and a'rt and are to come.
Holy a'rt thou, Holy a'rt thou
Lord God Almighty
Glory and Majesty, in heaven a'rt thine
Earth lowly bending, Swells the full harmony
Blessings and Glory to the lamb, Forever more
For Worthy, Worthy a'rt thou
Let all Nations and Kindreds and Peoples
Give thanks to thee forever more.
A-men.

Chapter nine

Acquiring divine healing through obedience and faith in the word of God.

Beloved reader, as we get closer to the end of our literary journey through the word of God, I am certain that you have gathered a substantial amount of spiritual riches by way of the Holy Scriptures. But before then, shall we continue to replenish our scriptural coffers once again as we focus on the potency of the divine healing capabilities derived from the word of God by following this procedure? I promise you that it will be a fun-filled scriptural instruction laden with wholesome spiritual samplings devoid of the traditional boring stuff. It will be one heck of a 'kool' flight into rejuvenation and restoration. On this note dear reader, let's hit the tarmac. First, you must extend your spiritual antennae, then check-in all luggage containing adversities and negativities that may induce spiritual stagnation during the divine process of healing such as; disappointments, regrets, bitterness, resentment, unforgiven offenses, self directed anger, and even anger directed at God. You may now proceed across the hall of departure from your lifelong saddled burdens, onto the gateway to divine healing together with your scriptural boarding pass in all solemnity of spirit, and make your way through the tunnel of self-searching, into the spiritual flyer to locate your seat of blessed assurance; but before you get seated, remember first and foremost to toss your carry-on luggage containing hidden negativities and prayer hindering vices which you may knowingly or unknowingly have clung to over time with genuine surrender into the overhead compartment. After completing the above spiritual steps, you may now settle into your seat, buckle up and attend to the following flight instructions from your ministering flight crew. See, that was not so difficult was it? thank you.:)

I (the Author), will serve as ministering attendant to some of your spiritual needs and inquisitions that categorically fall within my literary, yet spiritually endowed capabilities. Also operating on the controls in the cockpit by the power and divinely endowed intellect of the Holy Spirit with the superb gift of expert flight mobility, balance and safety, is our dependable and experienced pilot, Captain Grace, carrying out her aviation duties constantly and persistently focused on God the Father. Here she is on the P.A. System. "Ladies and gentlemen in Christ, this is your pilot Captain Grace extending a warm welcome to you aboard this remarkable flight. In a few minutes, we will be taking off for good from the land of trials and tribulations, across the sea of forgetfulness as we make our way to the beautiful City of Victory-ville in the Land of Conquest. Please follow all the necessary spiritual guidelines as instructed by the ministering flight crew and attendant on duty for the Lord. If you encounter any unsettling doubts as this spiritual journey gradually unfolds, you may request for express spiritual counsel by simply pushing the overhead button for omniscient assistance, and spiritual guidance, and divine assurance will be wholesomely fed to you by the ministering attendant. Also provided on-call for immediate spiritual convenience, are Guardian and Ministering Angels, who will be gliding in and out of the passenger cabin to assist you by showering you with Angelic services of pure aid and intervention, with divine perfection as sanctioned by God the Father. Please I must caution you to not look back after we cross the sea of forgetfulness or your journey will be in vain. Enjoy your flight in Jesus' name, Amen." Beloved reader, it should take us about the time it personally takes you to read this chapter, and the next, to arrive at our divine destination. I am very certain that by then, you will be fully and wholly restored in mind, soul and body, by God's unfailing arm of utter redemption.

Let us commence our lesson by first and foremost making this proclamation from God's living word, by reciting the following scripture in truth seven times with boldness, as well as in faith laced with unshakeable expectation; the number seven symbolizing, "the divine numerical code denoting the most amplified and full throttled power driven performance of God's ultimate prowess for the reversal and restoration of lost causes." Think about every adversity in your life about which you desire divine refurbishment, and infuse that yearning into your aggressive proclamation of God's Holy word of healing and restoration, from the very depths of your heart. Please turn your Bibles to the book of Psalms Chapter 107 verse 20. I am writing from the New King James Version: "He sent His word and healed them, and delivered them from their destructions." Please personalize this scripture as you proclaim it in faith thus: " He sent His word and healed me, and delivered me from my destructions." How about that for a blessed assurance of healing from the Father Himself huh?:) (Try to keep it in memory for future reference, or record it under 'healing' or this chapter's heading in the subsidiary pages allocated for 'notes', of your book.) Also proclaim it as you extend your thoughts in prayer for others hurting in Haiti and all over the world, especially the surviving victims of natural disasters, and most prayerfully for the people of Japan who have suffered more than they can physically endure; For the starving peoples of East Africa and war torn Darfur, including the sick and dying worldwide; Father rain manna of healing upon them and grant them divine shelter in the midst of all their troubles. Let us also remember, all the bold African nations reaching out for self-government and a taste at democracy, as they reel and squirm under the thumb of despotic leaders, Lord deliver them one and all from their adversities, and install on their behalf, divine recuperative strongholds to help them build firm foundations for a peaceful and prosperous future in the lands you have bestowed them. Surely we must remember our brethren, sisters, elderly and children of Grace Church New Zealand still struggling from their crisis; Father restore unto them a sense of calm within the joy of your salvation; for nothing is too difficult for thee. Dispatch to thy children in Grace Church minions of angels to rejuvenate , assist, aid and heal every aspect of their lives; and may you visit their very lives individually as Jehovah Repheka to bless them with your divine providence, so that they may once more find their footing on earth, as well as in you. Amen.

"Great Physician of yore, let your divine healing fires of rejuvenation, recovery and restoration, globally cleanse and purify all obstructing negativities plaguing the lives of these children of yours, and subside their pain, afflictions, traumas and all negativities that have come to plague them. We also remember the infirm and dying; Father in heaven, hear my humble prayer. Do not look upon my mortal shortcomings and turn your face away from me, for thou art merciful in deed and gracious in truth; let your love and tender mercies rest over me as I intercede on behalf of my fellow humans; Lord, take your word of truth that lives within me, and convert it into a river of hope and love. Let it flow through this affirmation to all who have been touched by said negativities. Father I humbly ask that you take this book, and let it divinely speak with unfathomable transformation power to touch and heal nations and peoples; that they might know you; The one true God and receive life eternal through Jesus Christ whom thou did send. Therefore, Let the God who answereth by fire, show up to redeem His people, and relieve their suffering in the name of the Father, and of the Son, and of the Holy Spirit A-men."(AOP)

Let us at this time, begin the core lesson of our journey's purpose which is; Divine healing. But what exactly is divine healing? I will define it as: "The positive outcome and visible proof of a complete physiological regression, tied to the total cessation and utter eradication of a source or cause of an unhealthy condition, malady, affliction, or pathological imbalance in an individual, or individuals, propagated within absolute spiritual means, primarily rooted and procured solely and dependently through fervent prayers and supplications uttered by a person or persons propelled by unshakeable belief, while substantially driven by persuasive faith drawn with cords of hope, in the one true God alone." (ADA) Dear reader, you have to realize that this type of healing is fruitless without the breathless encapsulation of raw persuasion, utter surrender, and total dependency on the divine healing power of God. Therefore, one can deduce the pure fact that, this melange of unequivocal spiritual standards, becomes the necessary prerequisite that ultimately progresses supernaturally into the vivid incarnation, of the desired prayer outcome, which of course is navigated into the divine waters of evident spiritual performance, and thereafter docked with the anchor of hope assuredly, at the divine harbor of miracles, where the total flawless and divine manifestation of the expedited and permanent reversal of said condition is candidly displayed, to the glory of God., A-men.

As you may have noticed, I referred sickness at large to the word 'malady'. But take care not to confine yourself dear reader, to the area of regular or common physical impairments as you digest that paragraph; this is because, towards the end of my definition, I deliberately utilized another noun to enable me clarify, demarcate, as well as grammatically qualify the complete definitive attribute of the subject in question; As such, I resolved to sum up my definition, using the word 'condition' a noun. My sole reason for taking this literary route was to widen the scope of the process of divine healing beyond the regular physiological boarders of the reader's mind, while keeping in spiritual focus, that vulnerable part of the body system, repetitively prone to divers hindrances of doubt and unbelief, that in turn considerably impedes balanced spiritual growth within the critical spiritual arena of faith and belief in check; So as to keep title and divine purpose of this book continuously radiating within it's contents, by the right division of the word of truth. Beloved reader, there is no condition too difficult or complex for the Lord God to vanquish in the healing arena, including those pertaining to other areas of your life that need His mending touch of 'pure divine rectification.' (PDR)

Shall we then proceed with our next scriptural proclamation from Isaiah 53: 4 & 5 (NIV). 'Surely He took up our infirmities and carried our sorrows, yet we considered Him smitten by God, smitten by Him and afflicted. For He was bruised for OUR TRANSGRESSION, He was CRUSHED FOR OUR INIQUITIES, the punishment that brought us peace was upon Him; BY HIS WOUNDS WE ARE HEALED." Let us digest this scriptural passage as our 'spiritual snack'(SS); the divine alternative to the ever popular traditional peanut and apple juice refreshment that has for decades secured the post of foremost alimentary snack choice for air travel, as we continue this journey to Victory-ville. Beloved reader, and partaker of this spiritual voyage, in a few minutes, Ministering Angels will be distributing pillows stuffed with the downright comforting and healing word of God, to facilitate your rest assuredness in Him, as found in Psalm16: 8&9(NIV). "I have set the Lord always before me because He is in my right hand, I will not be shaken, therefore my heart is blessed and my tongue rejoices, my body also rest secure." And Psalm 37:7a (KJV). "Rest in the Lord and wait patiently for Him;"

We are all aware that in spite of all the standard equipage utilized by people worldwide for the physical act of being at rest, the pillow plays one of the most vital roles, since it serves the purpose of offering adequate support for the neck and head which in turn functions to propel the entire body into the peaceful process of slumber. Thus, sleep and rest are unachievable without the complete participation of the head; for the head as we know, is supported by the neck which also is attached to the torso. But our focus at the moment is on the head which comprises of the eyes, ears, nose, and mouth on the exterior taking care of our visual, auditory and oral sensory responses. It also serves as the encasing receptacle in which that vital neurological substance known as the brain is accommodated, triggered, and propelled into functional mode, which is then physically carried out electronically by the body system through neurological transmission. It is therefore a very vital part of the human anatomy, giving its characteristics, functions, and purposes. Upon such was the ever popular lexicon "rest your head" introduced into the world of grammar and linguistics; for when our bodies are at rest, our entire immune system and our very physiology undergoes a replenishing surge, emitting revitalizing waves of considerable amounts, which in turn are transformed into renewed strength and energy. At times, lingering aches and pain in our bodies, diminish altogether. But to achieve a good rest, one needs a pillow that contains the right stuffing for adequate neck support, as well as comfort, which is very essential to the entire sleeping process; because the neck not only supports the head, but also serves characteristically as the upward extension of the vertebrae; (the spine) which functions essentially as the vital propellant of our entire mobility system. A very important part of the human anatomy; (a word, which also serves a similar function in book publication "the spine" ; the most important feature of a book is a prominent and study spine, since it holds all the pages together; for without it, there cannot be a book. one of the first things I learned in Library school) Thus, we realize that, the neck's proper alignment contributes greatly to comfortable rest, and a well aligned sleep posture.

As children of God, we can only grow in faith by spending quality time with Him, by way of His word of truth, for the sake of our individual spiritual edification, as well as that of our physical well being, while we reap, process, and absorb 'scriptural nourishment' (SN) into our body system for the appropriate divine processing of the healing we seek. Our duty therefore as adherents of the word of truth is to commit ourselves entirely to tireless Bible study, genuine Christian fellowship, and fervent prayer. Our Bible study must be systematically categorized, to reflect our needs, topically, and subject-wise from the general to the very specific. Therefore, if a child of God desires divine healing, then he or she must scripturally endeavor to do so methodically, in order to spiritually as well as substantially excavate the word of truth scripturally, and nourishingly, by digging into the selected verses laden with the right components that reflect God's power of divine healing for their long-term spiritual retention and absorption, through faith, belief, and hopeful surrender. Then and only then, can they stuff their pillows with the divine essence of healing power, they have gathered scripturally. These scriptures of healing, will in turn serve as the tools of prayer that will in Godly time, convey them assuredly to the restful realms of total healing, which first takes place within them, and is later outwardly projected as the ultimate visible manifestation of great physical and mental health, vitality, and well being, to the glory of God. A-men.

Let us read Proverbs (17: 22) (18:14), "A joyful heart is good medicine. But a broken spirit dries up the bones. The spirit of a man will endure his sickness but a broken spirit who can bear." (NAS) As we have previously learned, our outward appearances reflect the depth and gravity of our internal balance and stability. Which simply means that, the acuteness of our inner afflictions, displayed physiologically and pathologically on our persons, are the sole culprits that propagate and propel our spirits onto the weary and destructive paths of brokenness. But to prevent the latter from occurring, we must enthusiastically apply as well as ingest our scriptural antidote, within the insurmountable dosages of extensive 'Divine intellect' (DI) accorded us by the Holy Spirit, panned from the bountiful depths of scriptural streams laden with the word of truth, while declaring our unshakeable belief shamelessly secured within the hopeful boundaries of faith, anchored in hope, to save our vulnerable bodies from the crumbling side effects of utter physiological deterioration. The adversary, as you may be aware of dear reader, is joyful when we are cast down in the spirit by divers affliction, crisis, trials and tribulation. The Holy Spirit on the other hand is rendered dormant; but not without divine sustenance, just inactive due to our lopsided spiritual posture within which it cannot perform, even though it is inwardly churning and perfecting it's potency in order to erupt as soon as we regain our full spiritually responsive Christian posture, to perform mightily by instructing us into all righteousness; For as a dormant volcano sits still outwardly, but inwardly churns with lava and molten magma waiting for it's geologically appropriate day for erupting, so does the Holy spirit self-revives as soon as we reposition our Christian faith within the confines of persuasion, faith, hope and belief, its instructive work to perform. For, it is 'grieved' because we are seized and held with unbelief, as we sink deeper and deeper into the dismal abyss of helplessness, which in turn breeds hopelessness, and graduates into depression and sadly for others end in self-destruction, as a result of said adverse condition (physical, mental, and emotional) which is of course very unchristian, as it is propelled by our cessation to trust God, a sin against the Trinity according to our doctrine. "For when lack of trust is awarded a substantially fertile breeding ground, belief is rendered dormant and faith is obliterated as it flees on the wings of hope." (ANQ)

Therefore as believers, let us adopt the undying attitude of surrendering our life's issues in all totality to God for divine rejuvenation, reconstruction and restoration; for He is Jehovah-Repheka the great physician of yore; the Divine paragon of healing, readily administering remedies through His holy word of truth, which though described by many as a mere historical book laden with unfounded religious and theological philosophies, has always been to us Believers, a life source as well as a powerful force to be reckoned with in all things pertaining to goodness, soundness and balance. For to us, it is a living word, that self-replenishes when believed in, and delivers sure results when put to the test; overruling the adversary's objection to the divine availability, possibility, and reality of spiritual healing, while outliving as well as remedying all situations of intense adversity and its mutilating effect on our vulnerable persons. The word of truth is also therapeutic to the core. In that, it functions by directly and specifically deleting all the deep rooted areas of fears and uncertainties in our lives, by infusing replenishing fluids of aspiration into us, which in turn is established into our body systems, as streams of spiritual foundations resting on the solid rock of boldness and power, that in turn drives our very will to faithfully forge ahead in life as 'Victorious Christians' (VC). It is also divinely pre-programmed with the certain supernatural ability to deliver results to its adherents on a deadline, due to its unmatchable capability to summon complete healing at will, with love-laden constancy embedded within restorative spiritual devices, divinely structured to administer as well as deliver flawlessly on a functional and purposeful basis for the Children of God. At this juncture I deem it appropriate to sum up this entire paragraph with the following notable quote: "The healing word of God projects divine performance in all constancy, to those who tirelessly believe in its endless capabilities." (ANQ).

As Christians we sometimes if not most times, tend to be careless with our faith in God; which is a divine state and condition of mind that guarantees our hopeful future. Yet, we religiously without question wake up daily and jump into vehicles that we trust will take us from point 'A' to 'B', knowing subconsciously that no matter how well they are maintained, or how comprehensive and voluminously they are insured, these glossy and flashy contraptions may well serve as ultimate death traps by our doing or another's someday. Nevertheless, we deposit ourselves into them constantly, and tend to them lovingly, by servicing, washing and detailing them with pure dedication, believing that they will serve us by taking us to our various destinations. Perhaps for once, we could channel the same, if not a fraction of that level of trust towards the living

God and His word of truth, by relying fully and wholly on Him for the definitive and precise healing of our minds and bodies. Beloved reader in Christ, please do not lose focus as we are still in flight towards our healing destination. On that note, may I please remind you never to hesitate to use the overhead button for spiritual assistance anytime; Also for your spiritual informative purpose, all fruit beverages on this flight will be served in the following rejuvenating one hundred percent flavors namely: forgiveness, hope, guidance, encouragement, and prosperity. You may savor all flavors by themselves or request a punch mixture of which ever serves your rejuvenating purpose by combining flavors as needed; for example you may order the encouragement and guidance punch which has a very popular reputation as a scripturally potent pre-rejuvenation liquid boost. You may also make your choice depending on the gravity and range of your adversities and needs.

All beverages will be mixed and served to you from the concentrates of each named flavor, and not from the instantly acquired freshly squeezed bases that constitute a more desirable choice by carnal nutritional standards, as it is not compatible and effective for 'appropriate spiritual absorption'(ASA) in terms of the spiritual nourishment we seek during this journey, pertaining to ensuring our scriptural stability through its potent reliability. For you see the stability and reliability of a thing, can only be established when tested and tried to ensure its tireless capability to keep from spoilage or better still, from getting corrupted by outside elements, even during the worst turmoil; and as our purpose for embarking on this journey is because, we have for years and decades clung to the Bible, which is a book not just written today, but inspirationally directed by God centuries ago; which has aged and spiritually weathered negativity storms, remaining yet stronger at the spine, after enduring trials, disputes, controversies, and anarchy, while it continually thrives and withstands all adversities as the rightly divided word of truth, we must ingest fluids that can withstand spoilage and adverse conformity. As such, choosing the concentrates of these beverages, offer you and I not only a higher level of a potent spiritual base, but at the same time reflects the density and impermeability of God's word boldly displaying its ability to withstand adulteration, as it takes over your system entirely to commence the process of Divine healing. Your duty therefore as a child of God, is to slowly sip your 'spiritual beverage'(SB) once served, at slow but constant intervals, allowing it to gently work its way into your body system while disarming the adversities plaguing it, in order to adequately perform its sure restorative function.

'Ding dong'! Here is an announcement from our Pilot Captain Grace. "dear brothers and sisters in Christ, we will be landing in an hour and a half at Healinshire airport in the city of Victoryville . Your ministering flight attendant will occupy you in the meantime with scriptural lessons on the Grace of God, for the remainder of the flight; be blessed with God's sufficiency." "Over to you Attendant." "Thank you Captain." Please turn your Bibles to 2 Corinthians12: 9. This scriptural verse is the 'Pilot's special' on our spiritual menu; which turns out to be the first divine meal to be tackled on our spiritual journey. Let us read together; "My grace is sufficient for thee: for my strength is made perfect in weakness. Most gladly therefore will I rather glory in my infirmities, that the power of Christ may rest upon me."(KJV) Now that our spiritual meal is served within our conscience, shall we by way of reflection, prayerfully chew on this great promise and assurance, to ensure it's proper digestion and absorption for us to achieve spiritual upheaval in our Christian lives, so oft plagued with stagnation. Beloved reader, I am sure that you are aware that life is filled with divers pressure; some individuals respond to the adversities it inflicts by temporarily bending under them, then eventually bouncing up again, while others get physically and mentally broken under it since they only possess the carnal knowledge and tools needed to materially escape its grip without the appropriate spiritual source and expertise required to wrangle it down into submission and ultimate conquest. But as Believers, we ofttimes forget that, at the precise venue and time of Christ-acceptance, were we primarily adorned with this spiritual weapon, 'the divine source', together with the Holy spirit that serves as the 'divine intellectual medium' (DIM), positioned to instruct, as well as teach us the academics cum geology of rightly dividing God's word of truth.

Thus have we deduced by our lessons so far that, the people who know their God by divine capability, function and purpose, fueled by self-persuasive belief, are never adversely affected by pressure of any form or kind to the point of self-distraction and destruction, keep their hearts fixed and trusting in Him by established faith washed in the maintaining waters of shiftless focus. They do not shudder at the amount of aggression exhibited and portrayed by adverse pressure, or even the situation at hand as they "walk by faith and not by sight;" (Read 2 Corinthians 5: 7 KJV) yet humanly speaking, they may be a little shaken at times; yes! But that is a very natural mortal reaction devoid of one's spiritual age, and scriptural height. For they are nonetheless divinely endowed with the swift tendency to bounce back into full focus and appropriate Christian posture to await greater exploits with strength from God, by way of His holy word of truth. So you see dear reader, "when you find yourself under a lot of pressure from adversities, then must you supersize your trust in the word of truth believing that, being edified by spiritual strength as well as being led into great restorative accomplishments during times of pressure, are yours for the taking as long as your seedlings of belief and faith in God's divine capabilities, are firmly transplanted into unwavering scriptural soils richly situated within the faith substantiated depths of your hopeful heart. Amen." (ANQ)

Even under severe pressure, the word of God reassures us of His tremendous ability to furnish our needs entirely; and healing is not exempt. In 2 Corinthians 9: 8 (NIV), the literary evidence of this promise is made clear. " God is able to make all grace abound to you, so that in all things and at all times, having all that you need you will abound in every good work." Amen. Our second meal choice is a divinely selected recipe served as the 'richness in Christ by His grace platter'. This scriptural meal is exceptionally good for the emotional healing and well being of one's mental faculties when devastated through impoverishment; Very common in Africa my Continent of Birth, and home of my brave ancestors. Which reminds me to share this with you; I remember this about my late Mama dearest, who was always worried and genuinely concerned about images of hungry African Children displayed in the media, not because she only disliked it, but stressed on how those children not only suffered from hunger, but sleep deprivation; a condition that no one even thinks about when they see those images; but this great Lady who mothered me did. Making me realize at a tender age, how blessed I was not only to have three square meals a day with treats, but also the ability to acquire a good night's sleep. Right from childhood, I realized that my mother's main concern was that her children do not go hungry; it was a thing she feared above all things and worked hard in life to make sure we never encountered it; She told me that it was one thing that drove fear within her especially after the 1966 coup d'etat in Ghana when my Papa was placed in protective custody; because being in protective custody in Africa is not the same as being there in a developed country. It meant starvation and maltreatment and torture under a sound roof surrounded by the 'adverse military'. She told me about how my late father was starved there and how she wittingly devised a culinary tactic of blending high protein beans and pulses into thermal canisters and sneaking them to my father in custody because she was afraid he might die of starvation there due to his natural lanky frame. Poverty gives birth to hunger and starvation; but oppression is the worse culprit she said. She was a very special person, an Angel living amongst humans, for she did all she could not only to offer care and sustenance to her own, but to those of others as well, who found themselves in her life. Because, she despised poverty, she tried her best by helping people she encountered in life steer clear of it, by devising strategies for other mothers to adequately stretch their budgets, by improvising within their surroundings, as well as steering them towards God's divine arm of providence through the word of truth. She was the only Mother in the world, who served her children and guests warm store bought cookies straight from the oven, when she ran out of homemade ones; I mean who can top that? Let us continue our trip:) Please read (2 Corinthians 8:9 NIV). "For you know the grace of our Lord Jesus Christ, that though He was rich yet for your sake He became poor that you, through His poverty might become rich." Here the Bible is referring not only to self-sufficiency and provision, but also to richness of mind, body and soul, also known as 'spiritual soundness' that propels Godly providence and not the carnal riches derived from large bank accounts, stocks, bonds, portfolios and assets drawn from corruption, greed and exploitation. Our Lord Jesus Christ, being as wise as the Father (GOD), offered freely to us the richness of all riches itself, expensively acquired through the means of great sacrifice by way of His sacred blood. Yes! 'sacred' because precious blood is acquired all over the world through kind and compassionate donors; however, sacred blood is only attainable through the Master Jesus the Christ. Amen?

Let us therefore ascribe greatness and acclaim the love of Christ Jesus, whose blood became the authentic source of our purchasing, derived from a supreme source. This extensive and intensive investment deal of great sacrificial depth, gotten at high spiritual expense that the Lord struck two thousand years ago, became the ultimate divine sacrifice of all times and has since been non-contending and unequivocal in the religious world. Thus it became the ultimate most talked about sacrifice signed and sealed in His very sacred essence of life symbolizing, 'spiritual currency' (SC) that has since been appreciating as it replenishes and multiplies in value both in heaven and on earth, thus making evident and authentically permanent our 'victorious Christian Benefits' (VCB).

Our third meal on the scriptural menu is the 'flight cabin Minister's special' and I am honored to be the first inspirational writer to introduce this scriptural healing source into the Christian literary media as the 'no condemnation combo'. This particular meal has served many a Christian and will continue to serve more as it contains the utmost 'indispensable spiritual groundbreaking tool' (ISGT). A very welcoming non-judgmental scriptural source and an embracing literary spiritual asset from the holy scriptures, that has for centuries facilitated the conversion of many into the Christian faith. " There is therefore now no condemnation to them which are in Christ Jesus, who walk not after the flesh, but after the spirit. For the law of the spirit of life in Christ Jesus hath made me free from the law of sin and death." Romans 8:1to 2 (KJV). Dearest reader, when God heals your situation, every haunting memory and bothering scar, in forms of self-criticism, accusation, past mistakes, slander, judgment and all of your personal shortcomings become irrelevant. Yes! Those evidences of regret and loss as well as those of adverse spiritual credibility planted by the devil and his agents to discredit as well as dislocate your footing in Christ Jesus, will be annulled and plunged into the void, to enable the express projection of God's paramount supremacy in your life to project light onto the whitewashed wall where your life's testimonies are exhibited to His glory. Dear Victory bound passengers, this is no time for sleep, for the adversary never slumbers nor sleeps; but is always wide awake cooking up schemes of adversity, while constantly negotiating the trenches and sewers of our minds and bodies, where most of our mortal weakness linger. Therefore dear reader in Christ, stay awake and alert, as we come closer to our journey's end, in the final chapter. A-men.

Benefits derived from the healing promises found in God's word of truth.

1. Your heart is constantly overjoyed with great expectations.
2. Your spirit is exempt from brokenness.
3. Your prayer life is effortlessly driven by ernest zeal.
4. Your susceptibility to fall into a sin driven lifestyle is transformed into that of divine control and abstinence, as you are driven effortlessly into a life of righteousness.
5. The Lord longs to hear from you.
6. God's response to your healing requests become eminent as they are made evident for all to see.
7. God's unchanging nature and characteristic as Jehovah El-shaddai 'The Almighty' is revealed unto you.

8. God cleanses you from within with His word of truth.
9. You are not totally moved and shaken by crisis and adversity, because He arms you with hope impregnated with strength.
10. Your heart is constantly filled with gladness.
11. You listen constantly for the voice of God.
12. Your mouth is filled with endless praise to God.
13. God's word flows within you as it consume the very essence of your being.
14. You discover life and health in His word.
15. You learn to use your tongue wisely in life, by rightly dividing His word of truth.
16. God reveals to you, the majestic power of healing.
17. You die to sin and live for righteousness.
18. The Lord's stripes become your perpetual source of healing.
19. Your scars and scar tissues disappear both physically and psychologically.
20. You receive a perfect body in the afterlife, for even though your body dies and decays within the earth it is interred, yet with a wholesome body, perfect and fit in all Godliness will you meet your maker.
21. The Lord's sacrifice on the cross of calvary propels and satisfies your healing needs, as you are blessed with a status of divine manifestation, complimented through divine eradication, rejuvenation, reconstruction, and total restoration of all that ails you within and those lost without.

Scriptural texts of healing to read, memorize, and to write on the tablet of your heart.

Luke chapter 6:17-19
Matthew chapter 4: 23
Acts chapter 10: 36-38
Revelation chapter 22: 1-2
Psalm 103: 2-3
Psalm 147: 3
Isaiah chapter 30: 26
Isaiah chapter 61: 1

Exodus 15: 24-26 9KJV) "And the people murmured against Moses, saying, what shall we drink? And he cried unto the Lord; and the Lord shewed him a tree, which when he had cast into the waters, the waters were made sweet: there he God) made for them a statute and an ordinance, and there he proved them, And he (God) said, if thou wilt diligently hearken to the voice of the Lord thy God, and wilt do that which is right in his sight, and wilt give ear to his commandments, and keep all his statutes, I will put none of these diseases upon thee, which I have brought upon the Egyptians: FOR I AM THE LORD THAT HEALETH THEE." Amen. (God synonymously establishes himself by characteristically installing and instilling His divine capability by function and purpose as; Jehovah-Repheka 'The lord is healer'.

Proverbs 4: 20 - 22, (18: 21 (NKJ) "My son give attention to my words incline your ears to my sayings:; do not let them depart from your eyes, keep them in the midst of your heart. For they are LIFE to those who find them and HEALTH to all their flesh." "Death and life are in the power of the tongue and those who love it will eat its fruit."

Jeremiah 17: 14 (NIV) "HEAL me o Lord, and I will be healed; save me and I will be saved, for you are the one I praise."

Jeremiah 30: 17a (NKJ) "I will restore HEALTH to you and HEAL your wounds, saith the Lord."

2 Chronicles 7:14 (KJV) "If my people which are called by my name will humble themselves, and pray, and seek my face, and turn from their wicked ways; then will I hear from heaven, and will forgive their sin, and will HEAL their land."

Hosea 6: 1(KJV) "Come let us return unto the Lord: for He hath torn, and He will HEAL us; He hath smitten and HE WILL BIND US UP."

Isaiah 53: 4 to 5 (KJV) "Surely He hath borne our griefs, and carried our sorrows: yet we did esteem Him stricken, smitten of God, and afflicted. But He was wounded for our transgressions, He was bruised for our iniquities: the chastisement of our peace was upon Him; and WITH HIS STRIPES WE ARE HEALED." A-men.

Malachi 4: 2 (KJV) " But unto you that fear my name shall the Sun of

Righteousness arise with HEALING IN HIS WINGS: and ye shall go forth, and grow up calves of the stall. Amen and a-men.:))))) Hallelujah!

" To live as a Victorious Christian, is to be able to scripturally attain spiritual capabilities grounded firm and deep within faith that demonstrates your mastery over adversities, by utilizing the divine formula of balancing the ratios and proportions, which constitute their overall density, in order to curb, deter and subsequently halt the frequency with which they recur, while calling on God and the Holy Angels for divine intervention to aid and assist you, by totally obliterating the source from which said adversities are incubated and spawned." (ANQ)

Chapter ten:

The self-instructing trip to victory over the circumstances that outweighs you.

Victory in the life of the child of God, is a sure thing guaranteed by the Father above, without question. Yet it may elude you, or slip through your fingers if you fail to adopt the 'right Christian attitude' (RCA), or forget to observe the required 'divine protocol' (DP) during its acquisition process. Thus failure to live a well balanced christian life eventually renders you 'spiritually malnourished' (SM). As children of God, we often attribute our difficulties and encounters of extreme hardship perpetuated by those excruciating stumbling blocks that often tend to hinder the divine manifestation and physical realization of our victories and conquests as christians journeying across the tempestuous winding river that leads to 'victorious manifestations' (VM), on the adversary, which is partially justified. But you and I know fully well that, these stumbling blocks, though installed by the adversary, may have been nursed, propagated, as well as cultivated by us overtime through disobedience to the word of truth, in terms of ill-considered decisions and choices, and constant lack of judgement. There is also the possibility of inadvertently breeding as well as clinging selfishly and arrogantly to bad habits and divers fetishes. An attitude that may have kindled an obsessive dependency on those vices which in turn may set ablaze a self-destructive inferno, persistently fueled by our lack of a meaningful and effective prayer life set within the safe confines of studious fellowship in the word of truth; these vices being strong enough, often take us hostage within the fiery state of continuous physical as well as psychological bondage, leaving us dangling by inches on its edge, as we cling in frailty to the delicate remnants of our slackened spiritual lives, which by then is fully displayed and negatively represented for all to see as that condition which I term; 'weakened christian status' (WCS). A conscious self-driven status acquired by means of bad habits such as lack of self-discipline, total dependency and building confidence in people around us, instead of totally relying and trusting in God while believing in our very own 'God endowed abilities' (GEA).

Such self propelled negativities are what I term, weights of indiscretion and retrogression; the most deterrent of factors that tend to prevent believers from reaching their 'God set goals' (GSG) in life. It is therefore very crucial for a child of God to periodically as a form of spiritual routine, to rightly observe divine protocol by means of investing in a prayerful time of self-inquisition, and spiritual rehabilitation, to cleanse and purify themselves as well as unburden themselves of those weights of adversities; together with those of spirit dampening imperfections of the flesh, in order to adequately prepare themselves for a float-worthy or buoyant swim in the 'divine waters' of progressive manifestations, ultimate divine conquests, and those of eminent victories.

At this juncture, I will like to clarify the fact that these waters have been made eternally accessible to those who carry weights of self-driven negativities, as well as to those without; a category which is very few amongst us; thus rendering the overall percentage of Christians who are able to keep afloat in the prosperous and rejuvenating waters of said divine rivers, totally dependent on the average weight of adversities they carry. These weights are then proportionately quantified by their degree of speculated buoyancy, and multiplied by the ratio of its negativity induced density, based on specifications denoting the type of adversity, its massiveness, plus the intensity of weighted burden it exudes, with which the gross decline in spiritual elevation of said believer is detected, within their 'weakened spiritual status'. This may seem like balderdash to the math genius, but due to my personal experience in the arena of (WCS), I came to the realization that, I had invented a spiritual theory which spells out the realistic fact upon self-observance that, believers practically living victoriously in trying times and even under dire circumstances, and those barely thriving as they are encapsulated within the lean and mean environs of intense adversity, are to be found in the same divine waters. The latter category of which I not so long ago was a part of, wrong choices made outside the will of God, through spiritual disobedience, are revealed as kicking hard, but helplessly against the wild currents and billows propelled by the aggregate weight of their various weaknesses, which in turn, determines their hopeless status, as sinkable candidates or those liable to do so. But all is not lost for the transgressor, or the disobedient child of God; oh no! For he or she too, can come into blessings by turning their negative circumstances around through the faithful act achieved only by doing the absolute; which is acquiring the hope laden ability to keep afloat while shedding the weights of adversities, through the sound christian gesture of fishing for a chance to mend their broken relationship with the Father above. Then and only then can one lose the heavy burdens of adversities, by tossing them on the river banks of the pure in spirit and heart, where acceptance of transgression is transformed into washed out debris of true and contrite confession, set inside the mould of regret, remorse, and genuine repentance, before diving back into said river, to safely swim in all buoyancy, pursuant laps in quest for divine victory, armed with the gracious ability to accomplish the good as well as conquer the vice. For at such a time, the tide always turns to favor the repentant child of God. Dear reader in Christ, in what swim category are you? Is it one propelled by 'spiritual buoyancy' (SB) or that which is weighed down by spiritual imbalance? You tell me, for like you, I have transgressed time and time again; but have always found forgiveness in the Lord God Almighty, whose loving arms are stretched out still, for a sinner such as I am, who falls down more than enough but gets up and dares as well as ventures to live Christ-like, to the glory of God and God alone, and to the strengthening of His Holy Church; hence this literary work, set humbly to ascribe greatness to God, my rock and salvation, in Jesus' name, Amen.

As our journey draws closer to its end, let us take time to thank the Lord for blessing us with the understanding, and wisdom, to apprehend our shortcomings and to comprehend His word of truth within the divine intellectual walls of utter retention. Shall we thank Him also for His goodness, grace and mercy, that endures forever, in Christ Jesus' Amen? Brothers, sisters and elders in the Lord, this is once again your ministering flight attendant reminding you to fasten your seat belts, for in a few minutes, we shall be touching down directly onto the 'vote of conviction' runway at the 'Healingshire airport'. Please be sure to leave your carry-on luggage containing your trials, tribulations, transgressions, and uncertainties, intact in the overhead compartment. It is very important to heed these instructions by not being tempted out of doubt and wavering faith to take anything out of your carry-on luggage at all, as this will spiritually discredit your acquired prayer status, contaminating the effective acceleration and sure deliverance of your journey's goal of procuring eminent divine victory through grace and healing. Please do not worry or even cast a thought in mind upon these baggage anymore; for they will be appropriately disposed off; cast into the billowing 'sea of forgetfulness' (which we will be traversing shortly) by qualified divine personnel. You are therefore cautioned to make mention or speak of them no more. Amen? Thank you and God bless you all; "over to you Captain Grace."

"Dear passengers in Christ, this is your Pilot Captain Grace once more wishing you all, complete victory in Christ, it is half past noon in the 'land of conquest'. The average temperature is comfortable and cozy with minions of Ministering Angels, going about their duties functionally and purposely for God's children in their throngs and bands. There is absolutely no humidity to excite your discomfort here, but rather a light feathery breeze emanating from the purity exuded by the countless mass of Angelic aura encompassing this beautiful land. All is absolutely well under God's mighty hand that offers safety and security for His own. Please remain seated until the 'fellow ship' has fully landed, before releasing your seat belts. One again, it has been a very spiritually, as well as scripturally enriching journey and I am glad to have experienced the goodness and benefits of God's healing word of truth with you. Your ministering flight attendant will continue waiting on you after the flight, until you board your shuttle to Victoryville; from then on, you will physically be on your own; yet, by faith and by the divine surety of God's promises in His word of Truth concerning you His children, you will be spiritually covered in his loving omnipresence as (Jehovah- Shamah); it is well with your soul and body; be blessed in the Lord. This is 'Captain Gee' signing off."

Dear reader, I hope you are experiencing a change in circumstances as we make get closer to Victoryville; it is normal to feel the sudden temptation to look back towards 'the sea of forgetfulness' but you must resist this act in order to preserve your faith from any tarnish by entertaining that spirit of unbelief, uncertainty and doubt. I stress on this at this time in our journey because, after all is said and done, we are mortals who need constant encouragement during times like these when the flesh once tainted with adverse weakness, wrestles with that of the spirit of to adequately receive from God; but we will prevail Amen? Please shall we follow the Guardian

Angels to the shuttle terminal marked 'Victoryville', and wait patiently for further instructions from your resident spiritual attendan. Also remember that, your regular checked-in luggage's retrieval need not be a worry to you, since they are presently undergoing purification by fire administered by the Angelic Thrones of Light*. They will be delivered to you precipitously upon completion, free of all adverse spiritual contaminants that stimulate as well as propagate the stagnation of your continuous spiritual growth and scriptural advancement. Please excuse me for a moment while I attend to this call. Uh oh! I just received express information from God the Father, through a Messenger Angel that the Angelic Dominions of light* have detected a hidden uncertainty within one of you, which must be spiritually nipped in the bud, by way of scriptural teaching, revision, and excavation in the specific criteria of the weakness detected, so as to utterly shatter that uncertainty which though hidden in your heart, was openly and effortlessly revealed to God who longs and desires victorious Christian lives for all who love Him and are called in utmost devotion according to His divine purposes. Please open your Bibles to 2 Samuel 22:3(NIV) as I assume my ministering attendant role.

"My God is my rock in whom I take refuge. My shield and the horn of my salvation, He is my stronghold, my refuge and my savior from violent men you save me." Beloved in the Lord Jesus Christ, this scripture dually depicts God's divine protection for us, which is revealed through His everlasting role and title as 'The Great I Am' the heavenly and Fatherly embodiment of the Holy Trinity, which also reveals His divine rank as the most potent and 'Highest Spiritual Authority', (HSA) exalted far above all gods, in the entire universe. It also portrays trials in a Christian's life as a test of 'spiritual fortitude' (SF); which in the long term, benefits our lives by awakening our channels of scriptural alertness towards the accurate performance of our relevant spiritual duties, that need to be tended to, updated, and revised to uncover our disguised blessings, in order to facilitate their full manifestation to the glory of God, and to accelerate the majestic elevation of His 'Universal Divine Authority' (UDA) as Lord of all, while thwarting the adversary's negative devices. Let us then analyze the previous scriptural text, by tackling the word 'rock'. A noun by grammatical definition, which geologically describes a physical relief feature made up of soil components, which have fused and bonded overtime due to weathering and other natural phenomenon. It may also be characterized as a nugget-like, massive, or even colossal structure, partially buried beneath the earth's crust, or one that is stably or unstably situated atop it, formed overtime by solidified compositions of molten earthly substances usually induced by forces of nature, as in volcanic activities, or one that comprises of solidified portions of soil components and debris held together to form a stable structure, which may be transported from place to place due to the activities of humans, animals, as well as that of other living organisms, thus altering its appearance and size respectively as, rugged or smooth; pebble-like or huge in nature. Thus in a nutshell, "A rock is a hardened relief structure formed overtime by varying elements made up of simple as well as complex soil components, compressed, compacted, and fused overtime by the process of weathering, after divers natural occurrences." (ADA) why do I bother writing the above since you know what a rock is? Because I want to establish and accord merit to it's nature literarily by extracting as well as defining its components to the last speck, as an object likened unto my God. For my own definition of it, gave me the chance to ascribe greatness unto God, while at the same time, doing my literary work.

Now shall we continue our lesson please; we are all well aware of the fact that a rock is usually impermeable no matter its size. We also know that depending on size, when the need for breaking up a rock is relevant, mechanical force is applied by the systematic and sometimes strategic utilization of explosive mechanisms or heavy machinery appropriate for the task at hand. During medieval times, rocks were considered as the most vital as well as indispensable structures of fortification. They were used in their natural state as the rugged and shapeless impermeable massive or small structures forged overtime by natural causes, to build castles and fortresses with strong battlements for espionage and protection. They were also hewn and forged with primitive prehistoric tools usually made from them during the stone age, to form hollow dwelling places, shelters or habitats to protect people from the harsh elements and wild animals. Some were also carved during that age into shields and other forms of battling as well as hunting equipage. They were also piled systematically, one atop the other horizontally to build walls for the purpose of regional demarcation, to enforce property boundaries, for the purpose of protection in times past, against arrows and spears thrown by warring tribal factions during battles and other disputes. They have also been very useful in ancient as well as modern times for the prevention of land-shifts and erosion in areas where the gradient of the land is severely uneven and unparalleled; and also serves as the vital material for the effective construction of levees for areas under sea level, as well as used for the restoration of landscapes after natural disasters. It is as such, an invaluable material that most vitally compliments the hard work of expert, modern day soil conservationists and land preservationists, as well as landscape architects, to secure and stabilize for the long term, geographical and vegetative features. These therefore are the fortifying and reliable characteristics, functions and purposes of the noun that by way of a simile, is accorded to the likeness of God. So you see dear reader, it is not only characteristically appropriate, but also very synonymously accurate to the letter. A rock; a structure that exudes stability, fortitude and strength; yes! Such is the security God's name projects, instills and installs within us His children.

"...my shield and the horn of my salvation, my refuge from violent men you save me..." This part of the scriptural text depicts a battle scene, or any form of unrest, with God functioning as the embodiment and subsequent source of all security, reconnaissance, protection, as well as the ultimate fortification needed in said battle to ensure its eminent victorious outcome. I will define the 'shield' as; "Any independent or stationary object or structure that serves as a barrier of protection for its bearer or user, by keeping them from coming to divers harm, or suffering injuries and fatalities, as a result of negative acts or actions projected, as well as inflicted by an outside source or force." (ADA). That is what our God is to us; a barrier of protection and of defense for our sure protection and security. Whereas a 'stronghold' is by my definition a: "A steady and secure structure or enclosure designed to serve as an impenetrable and indestructible abode when aggressively, dangerously, or brutally attacked, violated and held under siege." A clear example for movie lovers if you are one dear reader, is to be found in Tolkien's Lord of the rings; 'The two towers' in which the famous defeat of Saruman and his evil army at 'Helm's Deep' took place. That was clearly a great example of a fortress. But to continue our lesson, may we now reestablish in our hearts through these teachings, how good our God is for securing for us, such blessings of confidence through His divinely inspired vote of living words of truth, which portrays Him as a God of incomparable strength and protection, through which the greatness of His majestic prowess is displayed, within the extensive vastness of His magnificence.

This is therefore the most justifiable reason why we ought to adapt the spiritual attitude of total reliance on God, in all things; not only for reasons of guidance and encouragement, but as an avenue of transition, as we cast our cares on Him who cares for us more than anyone else ever would. This above act must be carried out in shiftless faith as we throw ourselves willingly, not reluctantly or lukewarmly at His majestic feet for the purpose of deliverance, rehabilitation, recovery, reestablishment and restoration. We must always perform this gesture without pride, or self-righteousness, while acknowledging Him as the divine counsel and true director of our lives. Let us further dig deep into God's divine generosity and His power to decree eminent victory into our thirsty situations, by reading 1Corinthians (10: 13) retreat to (1: 8) "No temptation has seized you, except what is common to man, God is faithful. He will not let you be tempted beyond what you can bear, but when you are tempted, He will also provide a way out so that you can stand up under it." "He will keep you strong to the end, so that you may be blameless on the day of our Lord Jesus Christ."

To me, this scripture holds the best offer of divine assurance for the child of God facing adversities and uncertainties. Where else in this life can one freely receive love possessing such combined degrees and variations, underlying faithfulness of such magnitude and extensive vastness. Love that is so rich and true, simply bursting into divine fragrances of expressly conveyed realizations, accomplishments, as well as the definite fruition of its gifts. But there is a catch dear readers, but not the type that accompanies and entangles worldly promises too good to be true, but that which requires from you fervent faith in God, dipped into the palatable condiments of the ardent and unshakable belief in His son Jesus Christ, the only Mediator who points you towards the sole direction where the 'illustrious divine benefits' (IDB) allotted to you and I by the Father, can be retrieved and beneficially utilized. Beloved reader, Jesus Christ is the sacred instrument with which the girth of the threshold of your spiritual life is measured. Therefore always keep that in mind, in order to hold your spiritual life in check and in balance. God is surely walking the variant paths of these lessons with everyone who reads this book; for His words of truth rightly divided, within and without these pages renounces, as well as drowns, the works of adversities, incubated and hatched by the desolate one and his demonic cohorts, while His divine direction for our lives is victoriously pronounced in boldness, as they are elevated and exalted, by our devout spiritual ability to comprehend and absorb the productive core of His teachings, as inspirationally portrayed by the power that expressly drives them scripturally, while typically describing and characterizing, His directive role as the caring divine shepherd, Jehovah-Raah.

As a victorious Christian, your experience in God will take effect on others around you, and spread globally from your very home, into communities, districts, counties, and so on; through a system I term 'divine osmosis' (DO); during which the scriptural tactics you utilized and the visible results displayed in your life will be spiritually, as well as physically, transported within a divine solvent state into the dampened lives of other believers who are cast down and utterly distressed; a condition which renders them less vibrant and weak. Yet, nonetheless spiritually ready to receive of and partake of your breakthrough. Why would I say that and how could that be? You may think. Is this Author in contradiction against herself? Oh no dear reader, this Author is right on the level that divides the word of truth; so why would you not just you read on. If you have followed our lessons from the beginning, you would remember that I stressed on the fact that, scripture teaches us about how, God's power is made perfect in our weakened states; therefore when we are most weakened, then are we more than likely assured to receive strength. Hence my scientific swing in the scriptural direction. I must confess that, this scripture has always been my favorite; Amen? My classmates must remember me as very funny, immature, and very childish in school. And they are right to remember me thus; for then, I was a child and spake and acted as a child; but now I am a woman and have rid myself of all childishness. Alright shall we proceeds with our lesson? Thanks for being patient with me:) Apart from all the above, I remember being taught in biology that, osmosis, which is the passage of solvent material through a partially permeable membrane or in our case and by my literary adaptation a human; is proven scientifically to be able to take place only from a region of higher concentration to that of a lower one. So what do you say to my scriptural adaptation and application of this scientific process, to the spiritual lives of Christians both living victoriously and vice versa or as we have earlier discussed; 'in different spiritual swim categories' huh? I am talking about taking a theory so entirely scientific, and adapting it so perfectly that when scripturally applied to the process of divine intervention, it fits to the socket like a perfect joint.

The lower concentrate vessel being the distressed child of God and the higher one the Child of God who has experienced the complete reversal of atrocities and diversities brimming with victorious divine essence of the boundless blessings of God; affecting the downcast believer spiritually, as well as physically, by the sharing and hearing of his or her verbal testimony, and the virtual display of blessings in the life of the victorious believer that, his or her very uplifted state, causes a supernatural revival in the downcast believer's life. Thus, spiritual osmotic transference of goodness as well as joy, is seeped divinely by the weakened believer from the victorious one, through the divine membrane of reassurance, faith and belief by way of testimonies absorbed and evidence of breakthrough witnessed, establishing within said downcast child of God the evident truth that, what God has done for others, He will also, for him or her. Amen?

Such generosity coupled with other forms of help given in the physical capacity and beyond, should never fall short of the child of God living victoriously for their continuos blessing as well as for the strengthening of the church which is the evident body if Christ. When we as Believers pass on our victories and conquests even outside the Church, we win souls as well as keep the Body of Christ within spiritual balance, and as such reveal our worthiness of the title 'spiritually elevated role models' (SERM). This spiritual generosity exhibited by way of sharing your breakthroughs with others less fortunate, and by the mode and attitude by which your life's testimony is disseminated to people at large, may serve as the greatest source of physically evident encouragement to other believers, as well as non-believers, struggling at the crossroads of indecision, difficulty and confusion on their way to the very destination that you have reached, by solely depending on His grace and mercy. Your personal victory thus shared, not only verbally and physically, but practically with others also grants you a double portion of spiritual stamina that will in turn furnish as well as replenish your overall 'Christian Vitality' (CV), and bless you with immeasurable peace as you live victoriously in Jesus Christ. Do not be deceived, by false philosophies of men that spin threads divisive theories on the looms of sound religion, for the Lord God is still in business like in the days of yore; perfecting discord and unrest, until it rests on peaceful foundations laid down and rightly divided within His word of truth. Beloved reader, remember this scriptural text from Proverbs 11: 10 and Micah 5:9, as we sing together this chorus of victory. Lift up your hands in triumphant victory to God over all the vices, you have encountered and overcome by His grace through the divine hope, encouragement, and healing derived from His word of truth Amen.

Shouts of joy
When the righteous prosper, the city rejoices
when the wicked perish there are shouts of joy.
when the righteous prosper, the city rejoices
when the wicked perish there are shouts of joy.
shouts of joy, there are shouts of joy

shouts of joy
shouts of joy, there are shouts of joy.
when the wicked perish
there are shouts of joy.

Let us conclude with this hymn

All hail the power of Jesus' name
Let Angels prostrate fall
Let Angels prostrate fall
bring forth the royal diadem
And crown Him
Crown Him
Crown Him, crown Him, Crown Him, Crown Him, Crown Him.
And Crown Him Lord of all. A-men.

Your shuttle has at last arrived, passengers in the Lord; as you get on board, please keep your mind focused on what the Lord has promised you through His word of truth and immerse your new life of victorious Christian living in Him; for " in Him we live and move and have our being." (you may research this scriptural text and record it in the subsidiary pages of your copy allocated for 'notes' thank you. Remember that the former things have passed away with the presence of the truthful evidence which testifies that your souls have been renewed, as well as your minds and bodies; for your joys have been restored. There is also renewal and reversal of circumstances, and adverse situations which are upcoming as future trials because you have been girded with belief, and equipped with full confidence, as a divine bonus from the great provider, knowing full well by faith that, your future is secured in victory to the glory and honor of His mighty name. Deuteronomy 32: 4 (KJV) proclaims God's strong hand of justice and utter perfection as follows; "He is the rock His work is perfect all His ways are judgement, a God of truth and without iniquity, just and right is He." In Exodus 14:14 He promises to fight for you and hold your peace. You must therefore, keep believing and trusting in His word as you approach your victorious destination, and thank the Lord for granting you divine wisdom and the enlightenment to comprehend as well as absorb the teachings concerning His mighty power, as revealed by Godly inspiration, within the pages of this guide to effective prayer.

Bless the Lord for the unlimited source of His living word, which is life and truth in all actuality. Which also by His divine power and authority, is projected as a weapon of great spiritual notoriety and potency. Yes it is a weapon quick enough to cut asunder the foe within the fray that keeps hounding you and I; that adversary, the old serpent and his cohorts of darkness who refuses to be vanquished; yet is soon to be brought under submission to divine authority as we God's children continue to dwell within the world that he has held within his scaly grasp; a world of which we are not a part of even though we dwell within it's walls; "but thanks be to God who always leads us in triumphal procession in Christ; who through us spreads everywhere, the fragrance of the knowledge of Him, for we are to God the very aroma of Christ among those who are being saved and those who are perishing." 2 Corinthians 2: 14 to 15 (NIV). Therefore brothers and sisters in Christ, go ye therefore into the world and proclaim ceaselessly God's greatness as you journey towards your ultimate victorious goals; Ascribe unto Him paramount majesty, by stating this affirmation; " Who is this king of glory? The Lord strong and mighty, the Lord mighty in battle." Psalms 24: 8 (KJV) oh yes! The Son of man is the captain of the host; if you do not know, then I am pleased to make it known to you:) Recite in newness of heart and mind, drenched in the divine waters of pure dedication to the cause of redemption through Christ, Psalms 27: 1 (KJV) "The Lord is my light and my salvation; whom shall I fear, the Lord is the strength of my life of whom shall I be afraid." Once again we have come across the strength of God in scripture; Beloved reader and child of God, I will like you to keep this in your thoughts as well as within your spirit even after you have finished reading this book, which I believe will never happen due to the spiritual potency and anointing poured into its effectuation by the grace of God. Please do remember that, "your threshold to divine victory is built upon the impenetrable nature of the spiritually built architectural structuring of your scriptural stronghold." (ANQ) Therefore seeing that, the embodiment of your stronghold comprises of substances impermeable, likened unto that of a rock, the adversary will flee from you taking with him, his devices of darkness and destruction, thus freeing you at the crossroads of confusion and indecision onto the highway of accomplishments in order to embrace your eminent victory. Now, as you prepare to enter the city of Victoryville, (situated in the land of Conquests), which is your one and only sure destination as a Christian living in God's will; a destination that affects you both in life and also in death, as one who sleeps in Christ in the latter, you must never entertain doubts about God's constant presence because, as long as you have pledged steady acquaintance with him, so also will He deliver you all the way into perfect peace at the end of your mortal life; hence the ever popular blessing for the dead; "Rest in peace" ; plus other sayings of the Master as well as texts from the Bible;- "I leave you peace my peace I give unto you..."; "may the peace that passeth all understanding keep your hearts and mind through Christ Jesus our Lord." and many others. Please remember to collect your newly purified and sanctified checked-in luggage now arrived from Healingshire Airport and transformed from their former status of adverse contamination, into brightness and purity for your blessed future, loaded with great expectations, at the 'victorious baggage claim counter', before checking into the 'abundant life suites', where you will be lodging in serenity. My thoughts and prayers go with you as you get closer to the final pages of this book. I therefore pronounce upon your life a dramatic transformation of prayer performance, which will indefinitely yield response from God (Jehovah-Jireh) the great wellspring of sure providence.

May your spiritual intellect and scriptural credentials exceed the required maximum, as your mind expands in the things of God, and soars higher in degrees, and altitudes of spirituality soundly embedded within the rightly divided word of scripture, than it was before you read this book. And may the faith that compelled you to endeavor to purchase this book, also propel your spirit into the anticipated blessings derived from a victorious Christian life, guided by the hand of the Lord most high, from glory unto glory, into more glory. And finally, beloved reader, may any unsettling regards that you have nursed towards prayer, be totally eradicated, and restored into Godly boldness and righteousness, Amen."

Also, do keep in mind that prayer is the only communicative channel that spiritually links your innermost and earnest desires to God; If you would only learn to talk to God as Father, friend, and confidant, as David did, as a lowly shepherd, and later as an anointed King, to attain his victorious life in God. To take this spiritual route in prayer, is to avoid the possibility of finding oneself time and again in the useless circumstances of being plunged and trapped continuously within the murky waters of a redundant prayer life, which is a pitiful situation indeed; Dear reader just grab a dictionary and read the full meaning of redundancy even if you have an idea what it means, (for I believe you do) and I know you will thereafter make sure that you or your fellow sheepfold members in Christ never suffer that atrocity. At this juncture I will like to stress again the meaning of prayer in my own words as; " The sole spiritual prerequisite that secures and ensures one's intimacy with God, through spiritually induced and faith compelled verbal outpourings of one's needs and desires, driven by hope laced in blessed anticipations." (ADA) But dear reader, always remember to utilize the essential spiritual ingredients that makes one uniquely qualified to be 'heard of God' amidst the throng of other praying Christians, which is the spiritual ability to rightly divide the word of truth concerning one's particular situation at hand, by the expert scriptural utilization of the synonyms of God in their entirety by way of consolidating His specific performance power and divine function, to your specific need at the time of prayer, while applying appropriate and timely Angelic Ministry, and you will be expressly attended to by God, as the 'most vivacious Christian' (MVC) praying on the blazing fields of the gloriously converted in Christ.

Prayer is not a difficult spiritual habit to cultivate. Neither is it a far-fetched divine notion when you own a Bible, a concordance, and a copy of this book. As Christians, of this particular high tech era of divers scientific experiments, disputes, and grand discoveries, that at times or most times discredits our doctrine and our faith, while posing as distractions of the flesh, taking abundant precedence over the things of the spirit. We must vigilantly strike scripturally as these vices are vividly and boldly set on display worldwide and spread by global proportions, glorifying as well as commercializing tempting shortcuts to achieving success and swift worldly recognition, which are geared to hasten and enhance one's social status; as they are vigorously fueled by their constant parading through the global media, which in turn have placed us in positions, where we have no choice, but to boldly take up spiritual arms, bound by loyalty to our faith in God, to push as well as thrust beneficial resources and sources of moral well being, self motivation, and success, within the tireless inducement of true religion, backed by the church of the divine trinity we honor and serve worldwide, to obliterate this cacophony of adversities, as the Church of Christ is speedily driven further and further away into the impractical archives of obsolete spiritual ideals. I therefore implore you to persist in Godly steadfastness, your Christ-like ideals, avoiding all distractions of the flesh, in this choice you have made to walk in the light of Godly direction. Before I bid you Godspeed; leaving you with the knowledge you have acquired herein, to enhance your new spiritual life, I pray that you depart from your old self into the celebration of your new found prayer life, while you walk into the blissful realms of complete victory in in the Holy Trinity.

"May you move mountains of adversities, as you grow in prayer; putting on the identity of your faith, by holding on to its hope laden reigns, with hands forged from firm grips of unflinching commitment. May you be unmovable, unshakable, always abounding in the paramount love of God, Amen." "Now salvation and strength, and the kingdom of our God and the power of His Christ has come. For the accuser of our brethren, who accused before our God day and night has been cast down. And they overcame him by the blood of the lamb, and by the word of their testimony, and they did not love their lives to the death." Yes! they overcame him by the blood of the lamb hallelujah! Please refer to Revelations 12: 10 - 11 (NKJ).

The life of a Christian is not totally a fun and free ride linked to professing Christ in the heart, while living without dedication and commitment to God's Word of truth. But if you would only commit yourself wholeheartedly to Christ, then will you discover the joys that accompany the salvation package. Beloved reader, I can assure you that, everything you touch and every area of your life will ultimately and positively be affected. If you take the narrow path of commitment, that is only easily navigated smoothly through the fervent acquisition, and the continuous nourishing sustenance solidified through the unification of its divine components namely; hope, encouragement, peace, knowledge, and strength, derived from the word of God. My personal life's experience as a Christian, and a practical one at that, taught as well as walked me back to the stumbling blocks that I overlooked during my life's walk with the Lord, and others that I simply ignored, and postponed, to tackle later without thinking that they were going to recur in time, in the form of adversities that will come to invade, haunt, and massively upset my entire being to the point that they could not be ignored or overlooked but must ultimately be wrestled into total submission, and looked squarely in the face while tallying their total adverse weight, spiritually on the righteous scales of chastisement and reprimand, before being cast into the cleansing furnace of the refining fires of God's word of truth. I must admit I did take a period of divine lashing because, I needed it to ensure my full emergence from the soldering cauldron as a tried and true vessel of God.

So you see dear reader in Christ, when you set your heart, mind and entire being into the definitive mould of 'Spiritual Discipline' (SD) through obedience to God, you will discover that, the Christian faith is not at all difficult to live out as some term it to be. The closer and more intimate you get with God, the greater your desires to totally live dedicated to His precepts. Thus collectively, you are indubitably awarded the 'Divine Trophy' (DT) forged and sculptured from elements consisting of the most resistant spiritual constituents while living within His grace to testify to the world at large, as the firsthand witness to the victorious transformations of impenetrable standards that cannot be contended with by vices and adversities of the perpetrator. You must also realize that, a divine status as earlier described, does not denote exemption, or immunity to temptations trials and adversities upon its awarding, but rather assures you and I of a safe and sure survival as well as a definite triumph over subsequent negativities in the offing. The word of God makes this clear in the book of Psalm 46:1-2 KJV; "God is our refuge and strength, a very present help in trouble. Therefore will not we fear, though the earth be removed, and though the mountains be carried into the midst of the sea." This scripture projects a message of definite assurance that, even though we exist in the world, our sure source of power as well as the magnitude with which our call for help is spiritually conveyed is not by carnal might but strengthened by an omnipotent God who is able to lift the most enormous burdens and erase the worst calamities, by obliterating our shortcomings, with powers beyond human transcending. God's ways are unsearchable and His paths are past finding out; nothing is too difficult or complicated for Him; Yet, He needs that long term commitment of complete and utter loyal servitude drawn from faith and belief from you and I, in order to relay and convey His loving affability, and divine solicitude readily into your life.

Please do not misconstrue this to mean we are saddled with an existence that is not readily covered by His unfailing love if we do not deliver these spiritual prerequisites; for His love is boundless and has ever been availed onto all and sundry, for we are His creation; But the difference in the essence embedded in the love projected is found in its gradient and measured by the yardstick that separates the believer from the unbeliever; this dear reader is what separates the wheat from the chaff, as God's divine protection is made manifest. The fact is that you cannot rely on someone you barely know for long term protection, and so will that person not in turn respond to your call for assistance as promptly as you would have it since they have no knowledge of your troubles and needs due to the absence of a relationship history, or one of close acquaintance for that matter. These sorts of relationships are built on lasting commitment and utter trust; for when you have known and acquainted yourself with Him like I have over the decades, through thick but especially boney thin, and have held on to your faith nonetheless, in order to glean the fields of hardship for shreds of faith and hope laden grains of aspiration, while building confidence for the sake of harnessing the most appropriate spiritual credentials, by faith testing feats forged from the wicked mind of the desolate one, then will you attach great value to the indispensability of cultivating within spiritual discipline, the life prolonging habit of scripture memorization, as you call to mind verse 10 of Psalm 46. "Be still and know that I am God: I will be exalted in the earth." (KJV) Then and there, this very affirmation of faith that is set within the performance laden mould of God's word of truth, radiates as the only power source conducive and forceful enough to arm you with the strength and courage needed at that material moment, to gather those crumbled pieces of your losses, failures, and disappointments, only to moisturize them with hope, and to successfully re-set them as reversed circumstances in that performance powered mould, together with your other victorious testimonies in Christ Jesus, to the glory and honor of God The father.

Please refrain from utterly focusing on victory without exercising the discipline to learn to fight the hard way when despair pays you a visit; for with the quest for a victorious Christian life, is one on whose highways are strewn with obstacles. That is why you as a Christian must be instructed within the fellowship, on how to resist those vices in a manner that leaves you not sinking into its whirlpool of ultimate destruction, but rather device scripturally laden spiritual strategies and lay them out in a fashion whereby, it is liable to sever the rearing aggressive head of said adversity and destruction, and thereafter plunging it into the dismal abyss from whence it emerged. However, if you find yourself getting depressed, suffering spiritual weakness due to its adverse weight of negativities, Quickly snap out of that state by calling on a fellow Christian, for 'immediate spiritual uplifting' (ISU). Yes, I said call a fellow believer not a Pastor; why? Because the Pastor pastures the church at large and has many responsibilities, but this matter must go through the restorative channels within the body of Believers as a divine rule to test the spiritual alertness to responsive care and scriptural discipline of, and within members of the fellowship. And to reveal the gradient to which the timelessly fed word of truth into those vessels are being processed and manufactured into the practical Christian lives of the body of Believers. Do not try to feign bravery at this time, call for spiritual backup from fellow believers whom you know to have overcome impossible faith testing trials by referring to the visible extent and magnitude of the adversities they once encountered and overcame, as well as the level of Christ-like attitude exhibited by those individuals or individual during said tribulation, and weigh them against the practical long term evidence maintained and sustained within that conquest in relation to their present Christian lives.

Call on Believers endowed with such 'practical spiritual credentials' (PSC) by way of not only their experience, but also their Christlike comportment exhibited without pride or shame regardless of their christian age; for God Himself has planted them within the fellowship of Believers as 'divine therapeutic vessels' (DTV) spiritually equipped to serve healing waters, drawn from the conquest laden wells that once contained their painful experiences, for the spiritual renovation, revitalization, renovation, reconstruction and maintenance of the body of Believers. Such decisions must be made while your life force is not totally weakened, but thriving within the confines of the word of truth; do not wait until you are excessively down trodden to fight scripturally as well as spiritually. This must not take place while your 'spiritual thinking cap' (STC) sits sloppily in faithlessness, unstarched and unpressed, upon your head. You must realize that such adverse situations teaches you how to exercise 'preventive spiritual measures' (PSM) by instigating within you the humble and 'right Christian attitude' to reach outside yourself, while helping you to curb the recurrence of similar subsequent shock waves of adversities before they materialize.

You may also use this preventive spiritual measure tactic, by marrying it to your advanced ability to project your very own spiritual intellect, while at the same time managing to arrest the adverse situation at hand, through the study of God's word; If you physically possess that level of spiritual might during a crisis, on a consistent basis. This formula we are discussing at present, has the divine ability to mature into what I term, an "adversity survival kit' (ASK), which should always be readily accessible, revised, and constantly updated. Soldiers of Christ like you and I, must never be caught unawares or taken in ambush by the adversary. Never! We must always be outfitted ready to do battle, attired in the armor of God, which comprises of the helmet of hope, breastplate of righteousness, shield of faith, shoes soled with the foundation of scriptural prowess and a sword of truth forged and soldered to cut asunder all vices and negativities of the desolate one. But brave as I presently am and as stronger in spirit as I have grown to be, once upon a time, not too long ago, I too was taken unawares because I lost my spiritual alertness, a state that diminished by leaps and bounds my scriptural acumen during a fierce domestically induced spiritual battle of rigorous proportions; Yet in the midst of all that 'spiritual combat' (SC), just as the adversary was reloading his weapon of adversities, I was awakened from my invalid state and spiritually thrust into a convalescing state, by the help of scriptural tools and a readily available divine therapeutic vessels; a husband and a wife, who propped me up into a better Christian posture while I on the other hand, begun a vigorous assignment by excavating and applying the appropriate memorized scripture, from the archives of my mind as the Holy Spirit was quickened within me. I fired scripturally at the adversary's mind which is always the focal point of weakness, when the heart is morally contaminated, or discarded within the throes of sin. I shot into his camp bullets forged from metals of aggressive scriptural proclamations of courage, recovery and conquest, laced with hope substantiated faith, from the only true God within whose mind dwells the most potent stream of all wisdom and knowledge. Those scriptures proceeded from my lips with meaning, in spiritually balanced appropriation for the situation at hand, shattering the negativities and vices I was confronted with into nothingness simply because they were rightly divided from the word of truth. I won, but not by floating lazily and idly in the lukewarm waters with a 'half baked Christian attitude' HBCA). I fought the darkness with divine fury derived expressly from the word of God. Yes I had set out to win, not to enhance my social status, but to prove to Believers and non- believers alike that God, the Chief 'commander in chief' is still on active duty, backed by faith clad armies of people who still believe in His divine capability to attain conquests, through the evident testimonies of His loyal servants, of which I too am a devotee.

The word of God as I have stressed throughout this book, by various means is the main tool you need to reach your destination when rightly divided with the appropriate secondary teaching tools that should of course be rightly divided to support and amplify its power to perform. As a christian always remember that, it is more precious than gold, and sweeter than honey, and the honey comb; as David the Psalmist clarifies in Psalm 19: 7 - 10 KJV. " The law of the Lord is perfect, converting the soul, the testimony of the Lord is sure, making wise the simple. The statutes of the Lord are right, rejoicing the heart: the commandment of the Lord is clean, enduring for ever: the judgements of the Lord are true and righteous altogether. More to be desired are they than gold, yea, than much fine gold: sweeter also than the honey and the honeycomb." Yes I can testify to that effect that really, "God's word is to those who find it in earnest, a priceless treasure to attain; and a sure sweetener, that divinely re-activates and re-stimulates the taste buds on the distorted and bland palates of all who have swallowed the bitter pill of atrocities." (ANQ) It is the centerpiece on your table of righteousness, and the crown moulding on your walls of faith and hope. It spiritually and physically encapsulates you in life by making you an outstanding figure in your household, community, city, country, district, State, region, continent, village, town and hamlet, as well as the world at large, to the glory of God, as He shines through you, for all to bear witness, and to willingly acknowledge Him as The Great I Am; the one who is, and was, and evermore shall be. Whose greatness extends from generation to generation, enthroned in faithfulness that reaches to the clouds.

"Now unto Him who is able to keep you from falling, and unto Him who allows you into His presence, by His faithful mercies, blameless and filled with joy. To the only God our Father and to Jesus Christ His only begotten Son; be the glory, and the majesty, the wisdom and the prophesy, both now and ever Amen," To the same God who has called me to share His goodness and providence in my life with you as an heir of the Father, and joint heir, with His Son my Lord, Master and Savior, Jesus the Christ, who has also appointed me, even me, a forgiven transgressor, who even now continues to fall and get up into His everlasting arms of love which are constantly stretched out to receive me, who though bearing no acclaimed theological status in this world, or highly celebrated within the global Christian media, like other Authors of most Christian books whose fame projects their books into the literary markets for ratings, but has nonetheless blessed me me with the impeccable gift of salvation which surpasses all of the above, to evangelize his Word of Truth through writing; a medium He my creator deemed most suited due to the girth of the gift He endowed me, as His unique creation. To this end do I fervently believe He intends to use me, yea to propagate a succession of literary works inspirational, as His divinely inspired and approved Author, anointed by His Angelic Dominiums, to record scripturally fortified commentaries, laden with the truthful experiences and teachings, that compliment His word of truth, that I experienced while abiding in His steadfast grip of pure security, as I continuously write with hands blessed by the Master, while compiling His worthy words and works of spiritual instruction, and testimonies of the greatness of His power to be published, so that all who are seeking to know Him, will drink deep from this literary wellspring of life, together with those who delight as well as desire His gift of salvation. May all who partake of this divine work, get spiritually infected with the fervent realization of knowing why I have never ceased to magnify God's name, while they in turn rejoice with me, in Him for all time." On my humble knees do I pray to God as follows:

"O Lord God Almighty, I offer unto you the proclamation of thanksgiving. Father, for years I waited patiently for you to show up as I cried Abba Father! Clutching unfailingly to your hand of deliverance and providence, and you have inclined your ear unto me, hearkening to your Child. Thus, have thou rescued me from the grasp of the gravest adversities, setting my feet upon the solid foundation of your word of truth, and re-establishing my footing in you forever. For thou o Lord, has put a new song into my mouth; surely endless praises fill my heart and ascend thine throne from my mouth filled with gratitude to you o Lord, my strength and my redeemer. Many are they who shall bear witness to these testimonies, by reading and divinely absorbing the anointed contents of this work and fear thy name. Let those who tread this earth lopsidedly draped in faded cloaks of Christianity and wavering faith, attain spiritual alertness, as they are transformed into upright well attired starched and pressed Christians, postured on feet of righteousness and strength, rooted in your word of truth. May those who have at one time doubted your very existence, authenticity and power be converted and transformed into witness bearers, on account of this great written testimony. Yes Lord! May they testify willingly and shamelessly about your magnificence, while ascribing unto you all the glory, laud and honor. Tirelessly will they proclaim your works, as I, even I tread this earth in evident existence of your profound ability to deliver your creation from dire straits; establishing within them the hope that does not disappoint which promises them greater blessings than you have given me, as yo in turn lead them from victory unto victory; bathing them in your glorious glories. For numerous o Lord are the wonderful works that thou has wrought on my behalf; they are countless, unutterable, and incomparably laden with thy kindness. Therefore on bended knees, stricken by awe and wonder, call I upon you who are worthy of all praise, to open my lips, and cause my mouth to profess your praises, in endless adoration. Amen." (Portions of Author's prayer is personalized from (Psalm 40:1- 5)

Beloved reader, I leave you not as one who is scripturally celebrated in the pulpit, but one who has been assigned by His Majestic Holiness, The Lord God Almighty to disseminate His word of truth, concocted within a formula based on principles woven from the fabric of 'higher spiritual standards' (HSS), that strictly demand its right scriptural division, in order to ensure as well as assure the proper propagation and cultivation of His word, for the subsequent preparation of a bountiful harvest, in the fields of glorious Christian victories. Receive this final proclamation on your life dear reader, by the power vested in me as God's messenger in print; "May the Lord answer you when you are in distress. May the name of the God of jacob protect you. May he send you help in the sanctuary and grant you support in Zion and may He give you the desires of your heart, and make all your plans succeed. We (the children of the Most High) will shout for joy, when you are victorious (for your joy is ours to celebrate by right of fellowship) and we will lift up our banners in the name of our God. May God grant all your requests." Amen. (Psalm 20:1,2,4,&5a) NIV. "And may your comprehension, absorption and retention of God's word of truth be manifested in your life as 'illustrious divine benefits' (IDB) from the Father of providence; Jehovah -Jireh. So let it be recorded in heaven by the Angelic Dominions. And let the appropriate spiritual summoning of Ministering Angels incorporated within the scripturally effective projection and utterance of your humble supplications to God the Father, through His Son Jesus Christ our Lord and Master, be brought into full manifestation here on earth, to His majestic glory as you are released into 'victorious christian living' (VCL)." Amen.

Bible study on God's grace

Romans (1: 5) (5: 20) (6: 14 -15)
Ephesians 2:8
Colossians 3: 16
2corinthians (6: 1- 2) (9: 8) (12: 9) (13: 14)
1Timothy 1: 1-2
James 4: 6b, 10.
1John 1: 6 -9.
Revelation 22:21

Scripture references of victory

Exodus 14: 13-14
2Samuel 22 (please read the entire chapter:)
Numbers 6: 24 to 27

1Chronicles 16: 7-12
Psalm 20 & 24 (please read entire chapters) (31: 21-24)
Proverbs 11: 10-11
Micah 5: 9
1Corinthians (1: 4-9) (10: 13)
2corinthians 2: 14 to 17
Revelations 12: 7 to 11.

Doxology
Praise God from whom all blessings flow
Praise Him all creatures here below
Praise Him above ye heavenly host
Praise Father, Son and Holy Ghost.

Glory be unto the Father, and to the Son and to the Holy Ghost
As it was in the beginning
Is now and ever shalt be
World without end. A-men, A-men.

Benediction

"Grace to you and peace from God the Father, and the Lord Jesus Christ.

Blessed be the Father of our Lord Jesus Christ, and the Holy Spirit that instructs us unto all righteousness to live and move and have our being within the anointed confines of the Holy Trinity;

Who has also blessed us with every spiritual blessing
in the heavenly places in Christ.
The Lord bless you and keep you.
May His face shine upon you and be gracious to you;
and may He accord you the peace that surpasses all understanding, so that you may grow in Him and glow with His light. Amen."

Scriptural instruction.
"Study to show thyself approved unto God,
a workman that need not be ashamed,
Rightly Dividing The Word of Truth.
But shun profane and vain babbling;
for they will increase unto more ungodliness."

2Timothy 2: 15 and 16 KJV

My gratitude
"Thanks be to God for sending His son Jesus Christ, who purchased us with great sacrifice, that facilitated the birth of the redemption story which in turn has multiplied globally in truth and in deed, and has won me a place in the congregation of believers through Its continual overturning of all aspects of social segregation by the recipe of its origins embedded in the very source which birthed the equality of all men; the great institutor of goodness and peace; the creator of all things visible and invisible, The Lord God Almighty; under whose wings of providence this fellowship of unity and love exists.

All thanks be to God for endowing me with the superb wisdom, to make this divine dream a reality for all the seekers of the true word, to be partakers of, while using me as a professing vessel to spread His aroma to all who are willing and able to spiritually inhale its divine fragrance. My gratitude ascends His throne for granting me the strength, health and tolerance, that surely but steadily, has propelled me toward this expected end, to the glory and honor of His mighty name, Amen."

EPILOGUE

Anchor in the storm of life

"Will your anchor hold in the storm of life
when the clouds unfold their winds of strife;
when the strong tide leaps
and the cables rip,
will your anchor grip and there remain?

Do you have an anchor that keeps the soul?
Is it steadfast and sure to withstand the rolling billows?
Is it fastened to a rock which cannot be moved;
grounded firm and deep in the Savior's blood?"
(Words adapted from a popular hymn)

As you journey spiritually in Christ, on the turbulent seas of earthly adversities, there is only one to protect your families and loved ones; and that is by anchoring your life with God through the power, truthfulness, and potency of His word, through Christ Jesus. As you endeavor to do this, I pray that, your spiritual status will ripen and age, scripturally as you walk in His statutes. Your blessings are awaiting; go forth and claim them in The name of the Father and of the Son and of The Holy Spirit, Amen.

Abbreviations (listed as they originally occur and are used within the text)

FSF 'fast spiritual fixings'
SID 'spiritual idleness and dormancy'
ESE 'effective scriptural eloquence'
SC 'spiritual credentials'
SA 'spiritual acceleration'
SI 'spiritual intellect'
SST 'strategic spiritual tactics'
SSK 'spiritual survival kit'
SSC 'spiritual crisis coverage'
CLC 'Christ life coverage'
SD 'spiritual discipline'
ADW 'authentic divine warranty'
ESA 'expedited divine warranty'
SC 'scriptural credentials'
DW 'divine wisdom'
ISN 'immediate spiritual nourishment'
AESI 'advanced and expedited spiritual intervention'
ESI 'expedited spiritual intervention'
UF 'unshakable faith'
SW 'spiritual weakness'
PCS 'practical christian status'
SKA 'spiritual know-how and ability'
SR 'spiritual responsibilities'

IBS 'intensive Bible study'
IDA 'immediate divine acquisition'
GSBI 'Godly spiritual backup and intervention'
PC 'prayer concentrate'
EDM 'expedited divine manifestation'
DP 'divine performance'
SD 'spiritual detour'
SF 'spiritual focus'
WAS 'wrongfully applied spirituality'
DA 'divine accuracy'
SFA 'spiritual ferocity and aggression'
CA 'christian asset'
SGSC 'spiritual grounding and scriptural credentials'
STC 'spiritual thinking cap'
SP 'spiritual pomposity'
VSE 'vital spiritual essence'
SZB 'spiritual zest and boost'
PDS 'pure divine psychotherapy'
UDF 'ultimate divine fuel'
DE 'divine expertise'
ISI 'immediate divine intervention'
DT 'divine transformation'
GE 'Godly expectation'
GLDP 'Godly light of divine perception'
TFA 'The Father above'

SW 'spiritual warranty
DA 'divine authority'
DR 'divine revelation'
AP 'aggressive proclamation'
DSS 'divine security and surveillance'
DI ' divine intervention'
SSDI 'systematic and strategic divine itinerary'
DPSE 'divine psychological scar erasure'
DH 'divine healing'
SSE 'spiritually sterile enclosure'
ASHC 'adverse spiritual hindrances and contaminants'

SSP 'spiritual surgical procedure'

SSBT 'spiritual surgical backup team'

DSHR 'divine system of healing and remission'

IOG 'instruments of God'

PHR 'pure healing and restoration'

SDPP 'standard divine precaution and protocol'

DPD 'divine precautionary duty'

SA 'spiritual antennae'

GCS 'good christian sense'

DA 'divine accuracy'

DR 'divine revelation'

IIPS 'intensive individual prayer session'

ESR 'extensive spiritual research'

ESS 'expert spiritual sight'

IDB 'immediate divine backup'

UDP 'utmost divine power'

AAA 'Angelic aid and assistance'

DE 'divine espionage'

EEE 'extreme emotional exhaustion'

HSE 'heightened spiritual exuberance'

DP 'divine protocol'

DC 'divine canopy'

RDE 'realistic divine expectation'

HESS 'heightened and elevated spiritual status

CDC 'canvas of divine conquest'

SCRD 'spiritual combat ring of defeat'

DFJ 'divinely refined justice'

SA 'spiritual aggression'

SL 'spiritual lucidity'

SD 'spiritual discipline'

PSY 'potential spiritual yield'

DSSR 'divine stillness and spiritual reflection'

SO 'spiritual or scriptural obligation'

SF 'spiritual focus'

SE 'spiritual elevation'

ISI 'intensive spiritual intervention'

GSA 'gigantic spiritual air'

SW 'spiritual wisdom'

EDA 'expert divine acumen'

IVSI 'intensive verbal spiritual intervention'
SH 'spiritual habit'
SS 'spiritual sight'
CSR 'constant spiritual rebellion'
ESD 'extreme spiritual discipline'
SDSP 'spiritually driven self preservation'
DI 'divine immunity'
GSH 'good spiritual habit'
DT 'divine transit'
SG 'spiritual guidance'
ISM 'immediate spiritual maneuver'
TGR 'total Godly reliance'
ST 'spiritual therapy'
SE 'spiritual excavation'
SR 'spiritual recovery'
SERM 'spiritually elevated role model'
SC 'spiritual combat'
TMHG 'the Most High God'
PDR 'pure divine rectification'
SS 'spiritual snack'
SN 'spiritual nourishment'
VC 'victorious Christians'
ASA 'appropriate spiritual absorption'
VCB 'victorious christian benefits'
ISGT 'indispensable spiritual groundbreaking tool'
WCS 'weak or christian status'
RCA 'right christian attitude'
DP 'divine protocol'
SM 'spiritually malnourished'
VM 'victorious manifestation'
WCS 'weakened christian status'
GEA 'God endowed abilities'
GSG 'God set goals'
SB 'spiritual buoyancy'
HSA 'highest spiritual authority'
SF 'spiritual fortitude'
UDA 'universal divine authority'
DO 'divine osmosis'
CV 'christian vitality'

MVC 'most vivacious christian'
SD 'spiritual discipline'
DT 'divine trophy'
ISU ' immediate spiritual uplifting'
PSC 'practical spiritual credentials'
DTV 'divine therapeutic vessel (s)'
PSM 'preventive spiritual measures'
ASK 'adversity survival kit'
SC 'spiritual combat'
HBCA 'half baked christian attitude'
HSS 'higher spiritual standards'
IDB 'illustrious divine benefits'
VCL 'victorious christian living'

* * * * * * * * * * *

KJV King James Version
NKJ New King James version
NIV New International Version
NSV New Standardized Version
NAS New American Standard version

* * * * * * * * * * *

Abbreviations following certain special quotations

ADA 'As Defined by Author'
ANQ 'Author's Notable Quote'
AOP 'Author's Original prayer'

NOTES

NOTES

NOTES

NOTES